WOMEN IN HIGHER EDUCATION

EMPOWERING CHANGE

EDITED BY JoANN DiGEORGIO-LUTZ

Westport, Connecticut
London

Library of Congress Cataloging-in-Publication Data

Women in higher education : empowering change / edited by JoAnn DiGeorgio-Lutz.
    p. cm.
  Includes bibliographical references and index.
  ISBN 0–89789–887–7 (alk. paper)
  1. Women in higher education. 2. Feminism and higher education.
  I. DiGeorgio-Lutz, JoAnn.
  LC1567.W649 2002
  378'.0082—dc21   2002067945

British Library Cataloguing in Publication Data is available.

Library of Congress Catalog Card Number: 2002067945
ISBN: 0–89789–887–7

First published in 2002

Praeger Publishers, 88 Post Road West, Westport, CT 06881
An imprint of Greenwood Publishing Group, Inc.
www.praeger.com

Printed in the United States of America

∞™

The paper used in this book complies with the
Permanent Paper Standard issued by the National
Information Standards Organization (Z39.48–1984).

10 9 8 7 6 5 4 3 2 1

For Marissa

Contents

Contents

Acknowledgments

There are many individuals whom I would like to thank for their support throughout this entire project. First, I would like to thank the contributors to this book for their conscientiousness in delivering their chapters in a timely manner and for their willingness to share their experiences. I am also indebted to Lynn Taylor at Greenwood Publishing Group, who never failed to reassure me throughout key critical moments in the preparation of this book. I also want to thank Suma Vattikonda, who helped me by preparing the tables and figures presented in the text. I am also grateful for the abundance of support that my department head and colleagues in political science always provide. I am truly fortunate to work with individuals such as Paul Lenchner, Charles Embry, Ayo Ogundele, and even our resident curmudgeon, Charles Elliott. I must also thank Joe Davis and Patrick Migliore, who patiently understood my need to delay our other research endeavors as the final form of this manuscript began to take shape. I also want to thank Larry Goldberg whose professionalism and patience played a major role in the final stages of this project. Lastly, I want to thank my young grandchildren, whose extended visit forced me into seclusion to complete the final editing of this book.

Introduction

JoAnn DiGeorgio-Lutz

Women in higher education have made significant progress over the years in our quest to achieve gender equality. More women are receiving advanced degrees, more women are ascending to the ranks of deans, provosts, and presidents, and ostensibly, institutions of higher learning are increasingly promoting gender and women's studies programs. Regardless of whether we struggle to pursue that quest for equality as undergraduate and graduate students, faculty, or administrators, the struggle to advance the notion of gender and empower women in higher education is borne by all of us. Our ability to create change within higher education should be equally enhanced by the diversity of our academic backgrounds. Even though women have a greater presence in the humanities, education, and social sciences, we are not alien to the disciplines of math and the natural sciences. Despite our gains in advancing gender equality, however, our efforts at true empowerment are still met with significant resistance by the walls that house an academic culture that often remains resistant to gendered voices for change. Despite the fact that women constitute the majority in a numerical sense, women in higher education still remain a relatively unheard minority population when it comes to defining the values, goals, and ever-evolving mission statements of colleges and universities as our institutions attempt to adapt to an increasingly technological world in the delivery of higher education. Even though institutions of higher learning are becoming more responsive to their external environment, they are impaired when it comes to responding to voices of change from within. The declining elite comprised of males of European descent still manage to dominate the university's agenda from both within and without.

The idea for this book grew out of my belief that women are making substantial inroads at empowerment in higher education. Within my own institution women have ascended to the ranks of assistant dean, director of the honors program, president of the faculty senate, department heads, and even vice president and provost. Additionally, the women undergraduate students in my classes have set their sights on such post-graduate endeavors as law school and graduate programs in areas still somewhat dominated by men. Also, more women faculty are being tenured and fewer seem to be fleeing. My pedagogy is met with little resistance by my colleagues, and the women in my survey courses are increasingly taking an active and vocal role in their learning, much to the chagrin of their male counterparts. Despite my optimal beliefs about our progress, the struggle is far from over, but the goal is not insurmountable as the chapters in this work attest.

The chapters that follow represent the thoughts, experiences, and insights of eleven women and one man who are brought together in this book because of their commitment to promoting the issue of gender and their dedication to empowering women in higher education. Our approach in this book is both theoretical and applied. On one level it evaluates pedagogy from the perspective of what we teach, how we teach, and curriculum development that enables and empowers women. On the other level it examines the institutional barriers that continue to thwart the educational development of women, while also examining the areas in which institutional support does promote our efforts toward change.

In Chapter 1, Margaret Snooks describes the unprecedented opportunity she had to apply a woman-centered perspective to the area of health and fitness in developing a course on women's health and fitness. She explains the ongoing process of the course and reveals for us the many hurdles and hidden topics that are prominent in this field, along with the students' difficulties with much of the course's contents. She describes the course's evolution over the past five years and her unique experiences teaching this course every spring semester.

Cindy Simon Rosenthal illustrates for us how experiential learning is a strategy for exposing the blindness of gender issues that permeate much of political science and other disciplines in Chapter 2. She incorporates insights from her work with empowering students and making education more meaningful with diverse pedagogy, such as having her students participate in the Model United Nations and other empowering projects.

In Chapter 3, we are afforded a global perspective by Annica Kronsell who provides us with some insights into higher education in Sweden. She recounts for us her days as a graduate student and the strategy of homesteading that she and a few committed others employed as a means of empowerment. She underscores the importance of mentors and describes the workings of the graduate seminar room as well as the organizational norms prevalent within the university in Sweden that are not unlike our own.

In Chapter 4, Sharlene Hess-Biber describes the relationship between feminism and interdisciplinarity. She explains that feminism is not restricted to a single discipline, but the attempt to forge interdisciplinarity in place of multidisciplinarity has not been without challenge. She reviews the progress toward this endeavor and suggests ways in which interdisciplinarity can be achieved.

Susan Isaacs, in Chapter 5, discusses the social revolution of art in which the development of art courses about women, either as subjects or creators of art, has raised a number of important questions. Some of the issues she explores include the format of such a course. One of the approaches that she describes centers on the issue of paradigm shifts and of looking closely at the ways in which women have been visualized and how these images affect visual culture.

Chapter 6 affords us a description of Peggy Douglas's transformation and development of radical pedagogy within a feminist construct. She details her experiences along with her definition and understanding of radical pedagogy. She also provides us with an overview of the mentors who influenced her transformation and the ways in which radical feminist pedagogy can empower our students.

Justyna Kostkowska describes for us in Chapter 7 her experiences in teaching gender and sexuality issues using Virginia Woolf and Jeanette Winterson. She allows us into her classroom to witness how these texts challenge the traditional views of gender and sexuality and how in teaching these texts one must be aware of the existing gender and sexual stereotypes in order to precipitate change. We are present in the classroom discussion as they explore issues surrounding Winterson's text that is narrated by a persona whose gender is never revealed and how Justyna engages classroom discussion toward a statement against gender as a defining characteristic of an individual.

In Chapter 8, Kenneth and Susan Miller provide us with a model that delineates factors that administrators and faculty can use to evaluate university policies, programs, and practices for evidence of both gender equity and inequity. They build on their theme of the ways in which universities have been known to discriminate against women.

Margaret Madden takes us into the world of higher education administration in Chapter 9 as she discusses what shapes her beliefs about leadership in her role as an academic dean. She thoroughly details how feminist values can clarify and expand existing attributes of good administration by providing us with six feminist principles gleaned from psychology that constitute a framework for effective administration that supports feminist values.

In Chapter 10, Sue Rosser shares the results of survey data collected from women scientists and engineers who were to benefit from the National Science Foundation's POWRE awards. Her chapter reveals the barriers that academic women scientists and engineers find the most challenging in their careers. Even though the respondents express their concerns through the lens of science and engineering, the issues they raise are easily identifiable by women across all disciplines within the university.

Lastly, in Chapter 11, Bonnie Morris shares her experiences confronting the backlash against women's studies. She describes the continued lack of awareness among the administration and students alike of what women's studies courses aim to achieve. Her experiences remind us that we still have a long way to go, but her efforts serve to inspire.

1

Expanding the Academic Knowledge Base: Helping Students to Cross Gender's Great Divide

Margaret Konz Snooks

Many faculty members are teaching man-centered courses but do not know it. The corollary is that many students are involuntarily enrolled in man-centered courses and have little or no understanding of how their course work is limited in scope. These two outcomes are partly a consequence of academic traditions, but may also reflect the current knowledge base of many disciplines.

This chapter discusses the development of a course in which women are central to scholarly inquiry. The issues and processes that are outlined here can be beneficially applied to both woman-centered and gender-balanced courses. One assumption of this chapter is that course development and design are scholarly acts that merit analysis and discussion. A second assumption is that gender is an appropriate perspective that can be beneficially applied to any discipline. Many faculty members are not cognizant of their own gender bias and its impact on their teaching. It is hoped that this discussion will help expand diversity and inclusion in college teaching, thereby empowering women.

The chapter is based on actual experiences in designing, implementing, and evaluating a course on women's health. The approach discussed here may serve as a model for other disciplines and for faculty members interested in broadening the scope of existing course content. Such a revision would make excellent material for any faculty member's annual report. This chapter may also help others avoid common pitfalls experienced in the progressive effort to offer gender-balanced or woman-centered courses. My own experience suggests that there may be a rich knowledge base in many disciplines that is yet to be recognized and tapped because of gender bias in traditions associated with course content and implementation.

COURSE BACKGROUND

My doctorate is in sociology, and I teach in a program titled "Fitness and Human Performance" in the School of Human Sciences and Humanities at the University of Houston-Clear Lake (UHCL). Master's and bachelor's degrees are offered to students interested in the *human* science of health and fitness. As is true of many fields this one has been man-centered rather than gender-balanced or woman-centered. For the most part, men have studied the health and fitness of men. Most of the knowledge base in specific content areas such as the physiology of exercise, biomechanics, and sports medicine is based on studies of men. Many of the famous longitudinal studies of health and fitness of "everyone" included only subjects who were men. Paffenbarger's studies of 15,000 Harvard graduates or of San Francisco longshoremen are examples that come readily to mind (Paffenbarger Jr. et al., 1986). This discipline is also heavily allied to sports science. With some exceptions, coaches are men and are primarily interested in developing elite male athletes. Several journals are dedicated to studying and improving the performance of athletic males, whether they are preschoolers, school-aged, teens, or adults.

Very gradually the discipline is changing to give more attention to women's health and fitness, but it could not yet be identified as gender-balanced. Some recent studies have included women, although never to the extent that men are included (Blair et al., 1989). The famous Framingham studies collected some data on "wives," but men were clearly more important than women (Dawber 1980). Recent woman-centered studies of fitness and health include the Boston Nurses Health Study (Fuchs et al., 1995), which is revealing previously unknown and newsworthy information about the health of women. The ongoing National Institutes of Health (NIH) Women's Health Initiative will tell us even more about older women, but data will not be available for several years.

On this campus since 1975 there has been a women's studies program that encourages gender-balanced courses. For a course to be designated a women's studies (WS) course at least a third of its content must be about women. As the WS flyer points out, "Women's studies is a point of view as well as an academic discipline, and it complements the established academic disciplines." Students complete a "concentration" consisting of at least three courses or nine hours of women's studies courses. Upon graduation students receive certificates in women's studies and may list this concentration on their resumes. Courses taught under the WS rubric are so listed in the catalog and schedules. The courses are also listed under the discipline or origin such as anthropology, history, literature, psychology, etc.

There is a campus group known as the "Women's Studies Faculty" made up of about seventeen faculty members teaching a total of twenty-six graduate and undergraduate courses with the women's studies designation. A smaller number of faculty members meet monthly to talk about ways to promote and broaden the WS concentration and how to administer the scholarships given by the women's studies program. Directly encouraged by discussions in this group and aware of the expanding knowledge base on women's health and fitness, I proposed to colleagues and administrators that I develop and teach a course about women's health.

Of course there are many regulations pertaining to new courses, and in Texas final approval must be obtained from the coordinating board. A less arduous route would be for faculty members to individually broaden the focus of scholarship in their existing courses and expressly include women. To be allowed to develop any new course at UHCL, a faculty member must demonstrate to that school's curriculum committee that the course would have scholarly merit. There must be sufficient research to support such an offering. Academically sound articles and books must be readily available for student edification. In this case, the course also had to be recommended by the program chairs in both fitness and human performance and woman's studies.

COURSE DESIGN

Once course approval was given, I proceeded to write the course and offered it for the first time in 1996. Here was an unprecedented opportunity to apply a woman-centered perspective to the substantive area of health and fitness. Here was a chance to expand students' thoughts and ideas about the interrelationships between gender and various aspects of health. The women's health course is roughly 90 percent about women, so it easily exceeds the WS requirement that at least one-third of the course content include women. An important discovery was that the perspective taken in this course and the knowledge and skills offered in this course are new to almost all students. Since that first semester, women's health has successfully been offered at both the graduate and undergraduate levels each spring. Enrollment and interest in the course continue to grow and, yes, men do take the course.

The general purpose of the course is to study health and fitness issues from a woman-centered perspective. This means an overview of relevant topics and many of the issues in women's health fall into three general categories. There is an array of fitness/health issues unique to women, such as premenstrual syndrome (PMS), Cesarean delivery, ovarian cancer, and the sad "athletic triad" characteristic of some young women that includes anorexia nervosa, amenorrhea, and the risk of bone damage. There are also health/fitness issues that disproportionately affect women. Among these are thyroid disease, adult-onset diabetes, and osteoporosis. Finally, and perhaps most importantly, there are life-threatening myths about women's health that are perpetuated in our society by physicians, emergency room personnel, men, and even women themselves. One example is heart attacks. It is widely believed that gender is a risk factor for heart disease and only men experience heart attacks. Students are often surprised to learn that the leading killer of women in the United States is cardiovascular disease. Another myth is that women are unlikely to develop lung cancer. In reality, lung cancer is the major cause of cancer death among both women and men.

Theoretical Framework

The initial decisions made in designing a course involve finding an appropriate theoretical framework. Almost all courses taught in the fitness and human performance program mirror the dominant approach to health in the world. This approach is known as the biomedical model of health. Every illness and injury is reduced to basic biochemical or physiological processes. Under this fairly narrow theoretical perspective, the understanding, prevention, and treatment of disease and injury focus on physical or physiological aspects. Those who embrace the biomedical model tend to ignore the sociocultural context in which all humans exist, as well as the psychological, intellectual, spiritual, and emotional responses to illness or injury.

To write a woman-centered course and to adequately address women's health issues in any society, it is necessary to take a much broader view of health and illness. I discarded the reductionism of the biomedical model and adopted what is known as a "systems approach" to health and fitness (von Bertalanffy 1968). This woman-centered health course would go beyond the purely physical and include the sociocultural and the psychosocial aspects of health. A basic tenet of systems theory is the principle of hierarchical organization. Changes in one level of a phenomenon affect all other levels both exterior to and internal to that phenomenon. The phenomenon being studied is women's health, so a woman may be viewed as a system that is also a part of many other systems. The human body can be reduced to the level of subatomic particles, but there is more to be gained by moving in the other direction to demonstrate that the body is only one aspect of any human being. Health is affected by larger systems, such as relationships, the family, community, the culture, and society as a whole.

This woman-centered health course was designed and based on a type of systems theory known as the biopsychosocial model of health (Schwartz 1982). This theoretical perspective broadens the health/fitness discipline by going beyond the physical or biomedical aspects of illness and injury. Using this perspective, the psychological and sociocultural aspects of health can be recognized and their impact evaluated. Prevention, diagnosis, and treatment of illness or injury can include the sociocultural context in which each person exists. The focus of any course using the biopsychosocial perspective can include each person's unique psychological makeup that may influence prevention, treatment, and recovery. The human body, whether female or male, lives in a social and cultural context that both affects and is affected by that person's physical health and emotional state.

By using a systems approach I was able to counterbalance the biological emphasis and give import to understanding health, disease, and injury in terms of psychological and sociocultural aspects. This theoretical approach markedly facilitates the use of a woman-centered perspective. The biopsychosocial model of health and fitness is used to advantage looking at the health of any person, including men, but this theoretically broader approach is particularly helpful in a woman-centered course. It legitimizes issues that particularly affect women, but are ordinarily out of range in traditional courses. Using this model the standard physical interactions of different levels within the human body are important, but the interactions between the body and the mind are also recognized and "reckoned with." The mind plays an important role in both prevention and recovery from disease and injury. In addition, the social and cultural context in which an individual exists and in which illness and injury occur becomes important for this broader and more thorough scholarly study. The health of all people is better understood if viewed within its sociocultural context.

Recovery from illness or injury is usefully analyzed from a biopsychosocial systems perspective. For example, a woman's/man's emotional state impacts her/his physical health. The reverse is also true whereby a woman's or man's physical health affects her/his emotional health. (Think about things like lower back pain or migraine headaches impacting everything one does.) Relationships with family members, friends, and co-workers affect and are affected by the physical and the emotional reaction to the health condition. From this vantage, students begin to understand that lifestyle choices and even relationships can make a woman "sick" or injured. Students begin to see that all sickness and injury have physical, mental, and relational components.

Systems theory and the biopsychosocial model are particularly useful in getting at the "hidden" health issues of women. These include alcoholism, the abuse of drugs other than alcohol, sexual harassment and sexual discrimination, rape, battering, depression, sexually transmitted disease (including AIDS), and unintended pregnancy. In contemporary U.S. society women live longer than men, but during their lives women experience more illness than men do. In addition, the last ten years of a woman's life is often very poor in quality. By using a systems theory approach and the biopsychosocial perspective, it is possible to broaden the range of topics and bring a woman-centered viewpoint to the subject matter of health and fitness.

Here are three cogent examples of the advantages of applying a woman-centered perspective to health and fitness issues. Most of the research on cardiovascular disease is based on studies of men. There is considerable evidence that anger, hostility, and the expression of these emotions contributes to heart disease. When discussing this important health issue, a case can be made that the hostility and anger of women may have different origins and therapies than the anger of men. For many women, anger and hostility may be a response to their experiencing less control in their lives than men have. The control issues become an important causative factor in the onset, treatment, and recovery of women from heart attacks and strokes.

A second example rests with the roles women traditionally play in our culture. Women's roles often require health-damaging self-sacrifice. Women may literally harm or destroy their physical and/or emotional health to help and support their husbands, children, and aging parents. Responsibility for others can drain the strength and energy of women, resulting in their own illness. One example may suffice. Caring for aging parents is a role that falls disproportionately on daughters rather than on sons. Studies show that the caregivers of Alzheimer patients experience enormous amounts of stress (Kiecolt-Glaser et al., 1988) that damages health by compromising or lowering the effectiveness of the immune system. The result is that women are more likely to get sick as a consequence of the care-giving role.

Women often view their health as less important than that of their spouse and children. Women do the vast majority of family health care, but women are more vigilant about the health of others than their own. For example, women are less likely than men to get surgical relief for arthritis even though their pain and disability are comparable to that of men. Women with angina get fewer referrals for cardiac procedures than men (Maynard et al., 1996). These are just a few examples of the greater breadth that a woman-centered perspective brings to the study of health and illness.

ISSUES OF DIVERSITY, INCLUSION, AND RELEVANCY

At UHCL the majority of students are women; this is also true at many other colleges and universities. Because diversity and relevancy are now thought to be meaningful for college course design, it is important to discover issues and class content to which women can relate. In addition, new topics and issues in any course are better understood if presented to students in a framework to which they can relate their own experiences. While a woman-centered approach broadens the course content of health and fitness, it is a more difficult perspective for many students. Most students, both women and men, are better versed in a traditional, man-centered approach. There are some decisions in course design and implementation that may ease the difficulty of student adjustment to a new perspective.

Sequence in Course Design

One significant component in course planning is the sequence in which new ideas, theories, concepts, and information are offered. Sequence can influence students' ability to grasp issues and can also facilitate their willingness to consider new and different ways of looking at things. That first semester my students could readily understand and apply systems theory to health and fitness. They most easily understood the logic of the human body being a system reducible to genetic or subatomic particles. The next intellectual step required students to broaden their thinking toward a more "holistic" approach to health. Most students already believed that when they are under a lot of stress (final exams) they feel tired and are more likely to "catch" a cold. Students eventually recognized that the mind and body are interconnected, one influencing the other. For example, the mind is especially dominant in human perception of stressors or threats. Students grasped the idea that they experience *feelings* of stress when they are only *thinking* about taking a final exam. They experience the feeling of being threatened when they only *imagine* their lover romantically involved with another person. After some discussion students can accept the idea that what goes on in their minds can set off neurochemical reactions in the body that, in turn, compromise or weaken their immune systems.

The next step in the sequence of this course was more difficult. Students had to develop the intellectual vision necessary to understand that a relationship exists between the body, the mind, *and* the sociocultural context. In addition, they had to understand that this complex relationship is bi-directional. Students already believed that air and water pollution put their health at risk, but it was a huge "stretch" for them to comprehend that the *social* environment can also put their health at risk. Once that was understood, then they began to realize that health risks are different for women and men, even within the same society or culture.

For example, the alcohol-related motor vehicle accident often results in injuries that change or end a person's life. While it is possible that a woman is driving, in most cases it is a man who is "driving under the influence of alcohol." In a traditional situation, the driver is a man and the date or partner is a woman who may be afraid or reluctant to question his driving capability. In our society women are *not supposed to* challenge the "macho" male's ability to "hold his liquor." It is somewhat troublesome for a man to take car keys away from another man, but it is even more difficult for a woman to do it. One outcome of these very powerful societal norms can be injury or even death for the woman passenger.

Deduction versus Induction and Textbook Selection

In designing a woman-centered or gender-balanced course, it is important to give considerable thought to sequencing in relation to variations among students as to the extent of their preparation and readiness to accept new ways of looking at old issues. As is true of many faculty members, I tend to sequence courses from the general to the specific, from the abstract to the concrete, from the complex to the simple. This may be a serious tactical error in designing woman-centered courses. Originally I planned to first discuss the sociocultural context in which women grow up and live. I hoped this would lead to lively, thoughtful, and telling discussions about the ways gender expectations and socialization in the family, the schools, and the mass media lay the groundwork for future problems for woman's health and fitness. Next would come specific and concrete topics such as exercise, nutrition, disease prevention, and health risk reduction for women. In the design of gender-neutral or woman-centered courses, a better approach may be a reversal of this sequence. It may be easier for students to proceed from the simple, concrete, and specific to the complex, abstract, and general.

The choice of textbooks certainly affects the sequence of the course. The first time I taught the course, I chose a feminist and admittedly provocative book, *Women's Health: A Relational Perspective* (Lewis and Bernstein 1995), which I believed would enhance the intellectual level of the course. The text opens with the statement, "Throughout history, the most salient factor affecting the health of women has been their position in society." The authors explain that earliest human cultures may have been partnerships with women and men assigned roles that were equally respected and valued. As humankind became less nomadic and property was acquired, hierarchical warrior cultures developed. Women and children came to be viewed as the property of men. Women were subjugated to men, relegated to the productive role, and no longer valued for their knowledge and skills. A lower value being placed on women relative to men still exists in contemporary U.S. society and negatively affects the health of women, including their access to health care and the quality of that health care.

Students, both women and men, reacted strongly and negatively to the book's opening statement. They vociferously denied that this was true, and many were prepared to walk out of the classroom at that point. Most of our students are older and more settled in traditional lifestyles than is true of other campuses. Students majoring in fitness and human performance are particularly accustomed to a man-centered biomedical approach to health. Most students are more comfortable with concentrating only on the physiological aspects of (men's) health and being very specific and concrete.

I believe I transgressed the learning paradigm of most students in the class that first semester. It was intellectually easier on the students to begin with the specific and move to the general. In retrospect, I should have anticipated their discomfort with having to make the intellectual leap that I expected. After giving the matter some thought I revised the sequence of the course and began with concrete, specific, familiar, and more acceptable health topics. Over the fifteen weeks of that first semester the students moved very gradually toward larger conceptual and theoretical issues. The revised sequence was more palatable to students, and by the end of the course they were more knowledgeable, open, and comfortable with the intricate and pervasive links between society, gender, and health.

AGE-BASED APPROACHES IN WOMAN-CENTERED COURSES

One way to initiate students into new ways of thinking is to begin with the familiar. Taking an age-based or stages-of-life approach to a subject often offers contrasting gender-based societal experiences that students remember from their own lives and can readily understand. For example, childhood is different for girls and boys. Students recognize that these differences may begin with clothing, room décor, books, toys, and playmates. Studies show that socialization at home and education in school is often gender-based. Boys may be shamed and not allowed to cry. The same expectation is not applied to girls. Boys may be conditioned to ignore pain and injury; as adults, men may continue to pay little attention to illness or symptoms such as pain. One consequence of this is that their illness or injury may become more serious and less amenable to treatment. Not being allowed to cry has other possible health-related outcomes including the inability to feel and express emotions such as sadness as a way of coping with grief or loss.

In other ways gender-based socialization may benefit boys' health and fitness. Boys are more likely than girls to run, climb trees, play roughly, sweat, and learn ball-handling skills. One outcome is that girls have significantly less upper body strength than boys. Girls are less likely to "exercise" vigorously and are often less well-coordinated in many sports than boys. Girls are not as likely to be chosen early when teams are formed, which may affect self-esteem and the further development of physical skills connected to life-long health.

Much of what goes on in the schools is gender-based. Boys are encouraged more than girls in math, science, and technology (AAUW 1992). Better pay is linked to engineering and computer programming jobs that continue to be dominated by males. Good health is often related to the ability to pay for it. Single parent families headed by women are in the lowest socioeconomic category and are the least likely to receive good health care.

Continuing with a stages-of-life approach leads to a discussion of adolescence that is also a significant period in the lives of girls and boys. Changes during puberty for girls, such as menarche, involve physical health-related issues, but personal and societal reactions to those changes are often even more significant for future health. The research indicates that girls who experience early breast growth are reacted to differently than those who do not (Danza 1983). This differential reaction may affect the girl's health, her psychosocial development, self-esteem, success in school, and life chances. Dysmenorrhea, the abdominal cramping or pain associated with menstruation, is hormonal in origin but its experience by girls is affected by sociocultural learning and expectations (Logan, Calder, and Cohen 1980).

Most adolescents strive for independence from their parents. At this stage of life parents may become more protective of daughters than of sons. This familial attitude is often viewed as "over protection" by the daughters who may rebel against parental control via a psychological illness such as anorexia nervosa or health risk behavior such as smoking, excessive alcohol use, and/or promiscuous sexual behavior. Discussion of the initiation of smoking behavior can be followed by a discussion of gender-based advertising. "You've come a long way, baby" advertising campaigns reinforce the idea that smoking is "liberated" adult behavior. The cigarette-smoking billboard woman models are slim, stylish, sexy, fun, and appear to be happy and healthy.

In adulthood, there are also differing gender-based health-related experiences. Discussions of the woman-centered health aspects of sexual intercourse, pregnancy, and childbirth also include more traditional topics such as nutrition, fetal development, infertility, contraception, and abortion. Psychosocial facets of childbirth include consideration of the partner's responses to pregnancy and birth, changes in the family structure, stressors for the new mother, postnatal depression, and the "medicalization" of pregnancy and childbirth. Breast feeding has social and psychological aspects, as well as physical outcomes for mother, child, father, and even grandmothers. Premenstrual syndrome (PMS), which is probably hormonally based, also has important political and economical implications. If PMS is defined as a psychiatric disorder with an objective reality, then it can be used to justify discrimination against hiring women in sensitive positions or even electing a woman to be president of the country. This is why some feminist writers refer to PMS as a "double-edged sword."

Menopause, the cessation of menstrual periods, entails biological health issues, but also has many sociocultural and psychological components. For a woman, ageism may be worse than for men who are just reaching their "peak" economic value. For women, there are negative stereotypes about menopause that may affect self-esteem, their boss' perceptions of job performance and, subsequently, income. Women may be devalued by society for their loss of reproductive capacity. "Hot flashes" are a cause for embarrassment, secrecy, and mean jokes.

Older women are more likely than older men to be affected by bone frailty or osteoporosis. Many women in their youth avoided dairy products due to the mistaken perception that dairy foods are "fattening" and only contribute to weight gain. Being overweight must be avoided at all costs by women in our society. Possible consequences of osteoporosis are bone frailty, hip fractures, institutionalization, and death, usually from pneumonia. The use of stages-of-life or a life-span perspective for gender-based analysis helped students apply the biopsychosocial model of health and better discern the relationship of women's (and men's) health to psychological and sociocultural factors.

COURSE DELIVERY AND THE BENEFITS OF OUTSIDE SPEAKERS

Course delivery models vary among faculty members. Many combine lectures, reading assignments, and class discussions about key topics. In less traditional, gender-balanced, or woman-centered courses students may appreciate hearing new ways of thinking about issues from professionals outside of academia. Women professionals from medicine, psychiatry, and health research helped to open student's eyes and minds to a woman-centered perspective. Having outside speakers added variety to the course, but it also served to legitimize the woman-centered course design. A woman who is a gynecologist spoke to the students. She discussed such issues as what age women should begin breast self-examination, how to ensure accurate Pap smears, the timing of mammograms, causes of "honeymoon" cystitis, ways to prevent urinary incontinence in old age, and the danger that self-treated "yeast infections" may actually be the more serious STD, gonorrhea.

The second speaker, a psychiatrist who is a woman, advised students about ways to deal with stress. She suggested that both women and men should acknowledge the power of stress and the fact that it is very damaging to health. Students should know their limits and recognize that even positive changes are stressful. She stated that a woman's low self-esteem sometimes interferes with good medical care because women are more likely than men to omit important symptom information saying that they "don't want to bother the doctor." The psychiatrist had worked with men who batter their partners. She explained that the *first* time battering occurs, men feel helpless and hate themselves. It is important to get these men into therapy at once because, later on, men tend to disconnect their actions from their feelings and blame their practice of battering on the woman. To the amusement of the class, the psychiatrist also reported that male mood cycles are briefer than females' and may fluctuate seven times a day. Finally she noted that male physicians are more likely to attribute a woman's symptoms to emotional origins; consequently they are more likely to prescribe antidepressants to women than to men.

The third speaker is a lead investigator in research on women's health. That NIH initiative is the largest national research project ever undertaken on women's health. The researcher established that most of what we know about health and the prevention of illness is based on samples of men. She emphasized the importance of including women in clinical drug trials because women react differently than men to medications. There are ways to include women in clinical trials without endangering their health or putting a fetus at risk.

All three speakers gave vivid, true-to-life emphasis to issues previously considered in class discussions. This reinforced the validity of the woman-centered perspective and the biopsychosocial approach. Course evaluations by students indicated that this was a favorite course component for both women and men. It was clear to students that the three speakers believed in the importance of women's health issues and a woman-centered perspective. Students said that the guest lecturers were excellent sources of information and opinion.

Writing Assignments

A third valuable way to design courses to make them gender-neutral or woman-centered lies in the subject matter required for student papers. In this course the writing assignment was envisioned as the capstone experience and designed to link class discussions, textbook readings, lectures, and presentations by the outside speakers. Each student designed and conducted a semi-structured interview of one woman. They wrote narrative reports of the interview, analyzed the information, and reflected on what was said in relation to the course's content. The papers could focus on a woman's experience as a patient or as a health care professional.

Students were provided with basic information about the interview process, about important ethical considerations such as protection of confidentiality, and a list of possible questions. The student papers on the results of their interviews were truly wondrous. There were common themes from the women interviewed as patients. Many of the women reported humiliation and anger after inept gynecological examinations and talked about condescending male physicians who were poor listeners. The women regretted their lack of assertiveness in dealing with physicians. Many believed they were given inadequate information about side effects of treatments, including surgery. One woman told about a clamp being lost in her body during tubal ligation surgery. She had to be reopened when an infection developed. Her surgeon would not believe that she was in pain and delayed the second surgery for a long time. Another woman patient had not been told that following a hysterectomy she would be more vulnerable to bladder infections that she now has on a regular basis. There was an emotionally moving interview of a thirty-six-year old woman whose mother had taken diethylstilbestrol (DES) during pregnancy in 1960. The woman had a copy of an advertisement from 1957 touting the benefits of DES to produce bigger and stronger babies. Because of the damage done to infants by taking that drug during pregnancy, more than five million women are at risk of developing vaginal cancer.

In evaluating the interview process, one student wrote that she would like to do multiple interviews about women's encounters with the health care system because the interview was such a "mind-blowing" experience. This writing project clearly had the powerful effect of further broadening the perspective of students in this woman-centered course about health and fitness issues.

Assessing Student Expectations for Course Design

Assessing student expectations on the first day of a course can be an effective way to increase student learning. Once the learning goals of students are known, then the faculty member can tailor the course to meet student expectations. At the beginning of this woman-centered course, students had no expectations outside of the standard biomedical model. Some students wrote that they were interested in learning about breast cancer. A few were also interested in heart disease, thyroid disease, lung cancer, birth control, pregnancy, and menopause (so they could help their own mothers). They were confused about contradictory information published in newspapers about research findings on health and fitness.

It was obvious that students' level of sophistication with health issues grew over the fifteen-week semester. In end-of-class evaluations students wrote that they wished we had spent more time than we did on topics such as sexual harassment, rape, assertiveness training, effective parenting styles, communication with physicians, side-effects of drugs prescribed for women, nutritional needs and exercise during pregnancy, fetal alcohol syndrome, and sudden infant death syndrome (SIDS). Many students wrote that the most valuable part of the course was class discussion. One student thought that the course should be required for all men.

By the end of the course students could apply the biopsychosocial model of health to an enormous variety of illnesses and injuries that affect women. They could talk and write about how recovery or failure to recover can be influenced by emotional states and levels of social support. Students could discuss the fact that avoiding injuries and illnesses is affected by psychological, relational, and cultural factors, as well as by physical factors. Students understood the basis of the statement, "Throughout history the most salient factor affecting the health of women is their position in society."

One fortuitous event occurring late in that first semester gives evidence of the students' expanded perspective. A newspaper story appeared explaining the results of a six-year study of deaths due to automobile air bags. The students were enraged to learn that airbags were originally designed to deploy and protect the chest of the *average adult male*. No design consideration had been given to the effect when the airbag deployed in the face of women or children. Deaths had occurred. Today airbags have been modified, and there are warning signs about this in all newer models of cars. Excluding women from simulated airbag trials had resulted in unnecessary injury and death. The students recognized the sexism implied by the study and brought the newspaper clipping and issue to class.

Other Issues of Diversity and Inclusion

Changing the approach of a course by teaching from a gender-neutral or woman-centered perspective meets some of the criteria of making courses more diverse. In the literature there are often man-centered research reports that subtly purport to produce information that can be universally applied. The class discussions, guest lecturers, and writing assignment made it very clear that what is true of men's health and fitness may not be true for women's. We also discussed the fact that, even in the field of women's health, the few studies focused on white, middle-class women. Only recently have research initiatives practiced fuller inclusion. The health and fitness of women of color is different from that of European-American women. This may reflect genetic differences, but it also reflects differences in education, discrimination, income, and health care. For example, the incidence of breast cancer is highest for European-American women, but African-American and Mexican-American women have higher death rates from breast cancer. Research indicates that lesbians may shun routine medical screening to avoid questions about their sexual life (Stevens 1992). Medical diagnoses of older women continue to be impaired by their physicians' inability to distinguish pathological conditions from physical and mental changes that are simplistically believed to be part of aging. The moral of these discussions is that in designing courses to be more woman-centered, faculty members must also be aware of age, ethnic, income, and educational subgroups among women and men.

In some countries in the world today, women die at much younger ages than in the United States. In other countries, women live longer than women do in the United States. These particulars should generate important questions to ask and explore. Why is there such a disparity in life expectancy? What physical, cultural, and psychological aspects of society explain the variations in health and life expectancy?

Course Outcomes

By the end of the course that first semester, students acknowledged that even today women and men continue have a different position or status in contemporary U.S. society, and that difference impacts peoples' health and fitness in both positive and negative ways. They understood that because of differential treatment in society, women have health and fitness needs that are different from the needs of men. Students could think in terms of and apply the broader and more inclusive biopsychosocial systems approach to health and fitness. We further agreed that any research study claiming to be able to generalize its results to the health or fitness of everyone should include both genders and a representative sample that includes variation in ethnicity, income, and education. Finally, students could laugh at the following quote: "Higher education for women produces monstrous brains and puny bodies, abnormally active cerebration and abnormally weak digestion, flowing thought and constipated bowels" (Clarke 1873).

SUMMARY AND CONCLUSIONS

This new woman-centered course on women's health presented an ideal opportunity to explore interrelationships between gender, physiology, psychology, and sociology. An inferential teaching approach allowed students to understand that the most salient factor affecting the health of women is their position in society. Using the biopsychosocial model of health behavior analysis is an appropriate theoretical perspective. A broad definition of health makes it possible to examine a wider range of topics. Macro topics that provoked student thought and discussion included the medicalization of women's natural processes and the "double-edged sword" of defining premenstrual syndrome as a psychological illness. Macro topics included the idea that the political and economic context of women's health shed light on the fact that women's mortality and morbidity may reflect discrimination in education, occupation, and resultant poverty. Micro topics include preparation for Pap smears to assure accuracy, eating disorders, and autonomy in patient-provider communication.

Women guest lecturers enriched discussions. A research psychologist spoke on the importance of inclusion of women in clinical trials. A psychiatrist discussed differential treatment of women in clinical practice, men who batter, and both pharmaceutical and behavioral amelioration for depression. A gynecologist presented data on components of complete medical examinations, avoidance of AIDS, and side effects associated with contraceptives and estrogen replacement therapy. For a research project, students interviewed women about their medical experiences and gained further insight into women's health issues. Student evaluations indicated "eye-opening" satisfaction with the course.

In short, taking a woman-centered perspective elevates the academic level of any course. Students are empowered both professionally and personally in understanding their own health and the health of other people everywhere.

2

Teaching about Gender through Experience: A Pedagogy of Engagement

Cindy Simon Rosenthal

Political science and other social science disciplines have grappled with the challenge of "mainstreaming" race and gender into the curriculum—often with mixed success. The most common strategy—the "add and stir" approach that adds to a course a few readings and lectures on women and minorities—often sends the message that the study of subordinate groups is separate and distinct from the ways that dominant groups contribute to the dynamics of social inequality (Silverberg 1994). At the same time, using gender as a theoretical and analytic lens in a course presents its own pedagogical challenges, including the problem of initial student disconnect that this chapter addresses.

In this chapter, I briefly review the source of student disconnect, outline the value of experiential learning as a strategy to engage students, describe and critique efforts at introducing experiential learning into the classroom, and then conclude with key lessons learned. I draw from three attempts between 1997 and 2000 to introduce an experiential learning component and field research project into my course entitled "Gender, Power, and Leadership." As a means of transforming students' gender understandings from abstractions into concrete lessons, each version of the course was based on a pedagogy that engaged undergraduate students in research from development of hypotheses through the interpretation of data.

THE PROBLEM OF DISCONNECT

Every fall semester someone invariably circulates a list of historical notes reminding college instructors of the range of first-hand experiences in the typical lifetime of new incoming freshmen. Most were born after Geraldine Ferraro's historic vice-presidential candidacy; none ever read newspaper job ads organized in neat columns for men or women only; to most the women's movement is ancient history; and the students are unlikely to know that their grandparents were committing a crime in some states if they practiced birth control. While enjoying the rewards of feminism, many of today's twenty-something undergraduates resist any association with things "feminist"(Fox-Genovese 1996) and consider gender as a largely irrelevant construct in their lives. Perhaps this should not be surprising given the fact that today's traditional undergraduate student grew up in an era of conservatism in which the very word "feminist" has been demonized and socially constructed with negative connotations such as "feminazi." In the face of such frustrations, bell hooks (2000) wrote the slim volume aptly named, *Feminism Is for Everybody,* to engage anew young men and women with a set of beliefs that have been made foreign and alien to their experiences. For the instructor who teaches courses about gender, similar frustrations challenge pedagogical creativity. If many students resist the notion that gender shapes life opportunities and experiences in profoundly different ways for men and women, and if students reject the language of feminism and question its usefulness for describing what they experience in their own lives, then how does an instructor teach about gender? Three problems reinforce student disconnect. First, in political science (and I suspect in other disciplines), the presence of masculinity as an ideology informing politics goes mostly without remark, and its influence remains largely unexamined. Because mainstream texts and many instructors neglect to discuss issues related to women, we should not be surprised to find students unexposed to gender as a conceptually powerful tool for studying politics. As Duerst-Lahti and Kelly conclude, "gender's invisibility in the realm of leadership and governance lies in masculine assumptions" (Duerst-Lahti and Kelly 1995, 26).

Second, because most enterprises and institution are gendered, women and men experience organizations differently (Kenney 1996, 456). Those who do not "experience" the institutions directly often find it easy to reject the argument that gender shapes the processes, procedures, and cultures of organizations. Both the popular and scholarly literature on the implications of gender in politics and the public sector, in the work place, or in a host of social relationships, speak most directly to students who have some direct experience with issues of work place discrimination or differential treatment. In my classes about gender and politics, the students typically divide between traditional undergraduates (i.e. unmarried young men and women) whose faith in the equality of political life is undaunted and older women whose work, marital, and social experiences (i.e., "been there and done that") instill them with a pragmatism and awareness of how gender shapes the interactions of women and men.

Third, as academics are wont to do, the focus on gender as an intellectual issue poses additional problems. As sociologist Karin Widerberg notes:

gender is primarily considered an intellectual issue and not also as a personal and political one. The fault is of course not theirs [the students'], but is embedded in the discipline . . . in the way it is researched and taught. The students learn about society from a ruler's perspective. Class and gender are, accordingly, things others "have." If asked about their own class and gender experiences, the first reaction is usually total blankness. (Widerberg 1998, 194–95)

Widerberg cautions instructors to resist the temptation to correct this deficiency in students by simply lecturing about gender in abstract terms:

it is of little use to just step in and "straighten things out," that is, telling them how wrong they are about gender and what gender is all about. Of course, they *might* (emphasis added) learn about my understandings of gender but they will not learn about their own and neither will I. (Widerberg 1998, 195)

How then can blankness and disconnect be overcome? One strategy is to transform the teaching of gender into a rich experience of discovery in which the students participate as active learners.

EXPERIENTIAL LEARNING AS PEDAGOGY

Experiential learning offers a successful strategy for promoting more thoughtful education and, consequently, is a useful curriculum strategy for dealing with student disconnect. Experiential learning has been promoted as a key to making education more relevant to diverse student populations and as a strategy for matching different student learning styles to complex subject matters (Kolb 1984). Kolb defines experiential learning as a "holistic integrative perspective on learning that combines experience, perception, cognition, and behavior" (Kolb 1984, 21), and he identifies four essential stages in the cycle: concrete experience, reflective observation, abstract conceptualization, and active experimentation. Kolb argues that learning represents a "continuous process grounded in experience," during which knowledge grows as new information and experiences are assimilated. His work also recognizes that varied classroom activities help to reach different types of students. Fox and Ronkowski found political science students evenly distributed among the four learning styles that Kolb associated with his model and urged variation in instructional strategies to reach students who would otherwise find the discipline "dull, difficult, and uninteresting were it presented through only one method" (Fox and Ronkowski 1997, 736).

Kolb's conceptualization of experiential learning has been modified to incorporate many different classroom activities. For example, Svinicki and Dixon (1987) noted that laboratories, observations, simulations, fieldwork, films, problem sets, and reading texts are all forms of concrete experience. Student logs and journals and certain forms of small-group discussion foster reflective observation. Listening to lectures, writing papers, building models, and constructing analogies draw upon abstract conceptualization skills, while simulations, case studies, fieldwork, projects, and homework require students to engage in active experimentation. The various activities associated with Kolb's model are shown in Figure 2.1.

Instructors who use experiential learning strategies report favorable results (LaPorte and Hadwiger 1991; Taylor 1994; Miller 1996; Kathlene and Choate 1998). Most authors cite the benefits of active learning to energize and engage students, to "bridge the gap between theory and practice," and to develop higher order thinking skills (Bonswell and Eison 1991, 53). Kathlene and Choate conclude that in a simulation students "readily engage in this intensive learning experience, generating enthusiasm and high productivity" (Kathlene and Choate 1998, 74). Widerberg (1998) reports both positive student reaction and her own professional satisfaction in the use of "experience stories," where in-class writing assignments about personal sit-

FIGURE 2.1   Kolb's Experimental Learning Cycle and Classroom Activities

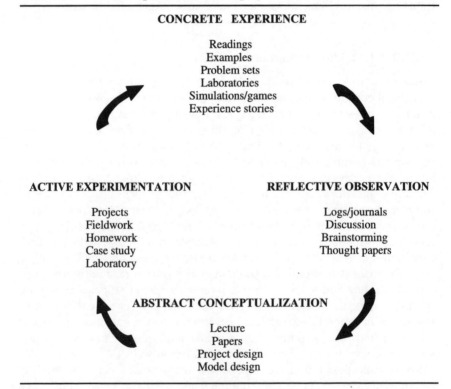

CONCRETE EXPERIENCE

Readings
Examples
Problem sets
Laboratories
Simulations/games
Experience stories

ACTIVE EXPERIMENTATION

Projects
Fieldwork
Homework
Case study
Laboratory

REFLECTIVE OBSERVATION

Logs/journals
Discussion
Brainstorming
Thought papers

ABSTRACT CONCEPTUALIZATION

Lecture
Papers
Project design
Model design

Source: Adapted from Swinicki and Dixon (1987).

uations help students connect abstract concepts with concrete experience and then promote class discussion, analysis, and reflection.

In addition to expanding the repertoire of pedagogical activities aimed at reaching students with diverse learning styles, experiential learning has the added value of promoting what Fink (1998) describes as "higher level learning." Fink argues that most undergraduate teaching focuses on learning as knowing (i.e., understanding and remembering content information), learning as thinking (i.e., applying, analyzing, or creating with information and facts), or learning how to learn (i.e., developing the skills needed to tackle other subjects). Less common are courses that incorporate higher level learning strategies, courses that challenge students to size up the significance of what has been learned (i.e., connecting different realms of knowledge), and to make psychosocial changes through reflection on one's self and relations with others (i.e., metacognition).

The absence of higher-level learning coincides precisely with the shortcoming identified by Silverberg when she criticized the "add and stir" approach to incorporating gender and race in political science curricula. The "add and stir" approach simply treats gender and race as new content areas for students to know about or to think about analytically. Because teachers fail to encourage students to engage in self-reflection, metacognition, and psychosocial discourse, Silverberg points out they should not be surprised when only African-American students read assigned material on race, only women read the material on gender, and white males read only the material that "[does] not include the words 'race' and 'sex' in the title" (Silverberg 1994, 718).

TEACHING GENDER THROUGH A FIELD RESEARCH EXPERIENCE

Between 1997 and 2000, I designed three different class projects in the upper-division undergraduate course, "Gender, Power, and Leadership," based on an experiential learning pedagogy. The course description emphasizes the exploration of the gendered nature of leadership with a special focus on the experiences of women in leadership positions in governance. Specifically, the syllabus identifies the following three questions: (1) is leadership a culturally "gendered" concept that marginalizes women within political structures; (2) are there fundamental social, psychological, and structural dilemmas that confront women in leadership roles; and (3) is there empirical evidence to suggest that women leaders behave in different ways than men in similar roles? In addition to the usual readings, lectures, and written assignments, the course included a field research project designed to encourage students to learn more about the gender dimensions of leadership.

The goals of each project were not only to make gender more visible to students and make connections between theory and experience, but also to acquaint students to how rigorous social science research produces gender insights through real data and analysis. Projects were selected in part based on their potential to produce empirical data that would lead to theoretically rich and potentially publishable results. As a consequence, the three projects were quite varied in their content and purpose. The three projects included an interview project (1997) focusing on the public and private sphere dilemmas and rewards and differences that men and women in elected or high-level appointed office face when making career decisions (Rosenthal 1998). It also included an observation project focusing on the gendered nature of participation and discourse in an event of political socialization, Model United Nations of the Southwest, and a content analysis project focusing on the theoretical concepts of autonomy and heteronomy as seen in the media coverage of Elizabeth H. Dole and George W. Bush during the early presidential primary campaign period for the election of 2000.

In each project, a set of classroom activities was designed to follow Kolb's experiential learning cycle. The sequence and type of experiences are illustrated in Figure 2.2. In each project, the students first completed a reading, a "concrete experience," that acquainted them to the theoretical issue underlying the project. Students then engaged in in-class discussions designed to foster "reflective observation." For example, with the interview project and the content analysis, the students discussed the specific issues women and men faced when trying to balance their public and private lives, the meaning attached to significant social relations of family and marriage, and the power of institutions such as the media in constructing and reinforcing gender roles.

In addition, the students critiqued the research methods used to generate the findings or conclusions drawn in the reading. The critique of methods allowed students to move to the stage of "abstract conceptualization," which included a lecture on different epistemological approaches in the social sciences and the relative advantages of different methodological research strategies. Finally, in an activity designed to encourage "active experimentation," the students worked in small groups to develop alternative empirical research strategies, to formulate research hypotheses, and to write items for the survey instrument. In the end, because of the need to have the project well-planned and prepared in advance, the choice of methodology was imposed by the instructor, and the rationale for the particular research design was explained after students had an opportunity to discuss various alternatives.

Each project concluded with a second round of experiential learning activities. Students received training in the specific data collection techniques,

FIGURE 2.2   Kolb's Experimental Learning Cycle in an Undergraduate Course

CONCRETE EXPERIENCE

1. Students introduced to concepts through reading assignments.

6. Students participate in training to prepare for data collection.

7. Students collect data outside the classroom.

ACTIVE EXPERIMENTATION

4. Students form hypotheses based on topics addressed by book and in lecture.

5. Students participate in small group discussions focused on question development.

10. Students discuss the data and offer interpretations.

REFLECTIVE OBSERVATION

2. Students discuss topics addressed by the book and critique the authors methodology and findings.

8. Students write reaction papers reflecting their feelings and incorporating their findings.

ABSTRACT CONCEPTUALIZATION

3. Instructor lectures on different epistemological approaches and research design.

9. Instructor lectures on analysis and preliminary findings.

practiced the method either through role-playing interviews and coding of sample articles or videotaped parliamentary debates (all concrete experience). Rigorous training was an essential, not only to insure consistency and reliability in the data collection effort, but also to ease student anxiety about the projects. For example, in the interview project, the students used Q methodology combined with open-ended questions about the personal rewards and drawbacks of public service, and thus they needed to be comfortable with the particulars of Q methodology. In the Model UN observation, students were instructed in how to code turn-taking, types of turns taken by delegates, and other information about the committee setting they were observing. Because many of the students had never participated in a similar kind of event, the training also acquainted them with what to expect in terms of parliamentary procedure, norms of debate, and jargon.

At the conclusion of their data collection, students were required to write a paper about their experiences guided by thought questions (reflective observation). For example, the interview project asked students to write about the following:

- In what ways did your interviews confirm or refute the ideas presented in either Divided Lives or Beyond the Double Bind?
- Which of the "double binds" seemed to be most important to understanding your interview subjects' political careers?
- Divided Lives used a case study approach to understanding the tension between public and private demands; contrast that approach to the more empirical approach used in our interviews.
- What advantages or disadvantages do you see in each approach?
- What did you like and dislike about the interview project?
- What particular insights do you most value from the experience?

In the case of the Model UN observation, the students were asked to identify and describe leading delegates whom they observed; to describe informal interactions, nonverbal behaviors and dress among the delegates; and to critique the strengths and weaknesses of the research strategy. For the content analysis, students wrote papers describing the conclusions they drew from their ten-article subset of the sample of more than 300 articles and offering their reactions to the project. Finally, once the preliminary data were compiled, the instructor reported the results in class and students spent time discussing the data and offering alternative interpretations (abstract conceptualization and active experimentation). Each project led to a fruitful discussion of the strength and limitations of empirical social science methods for understanding gender dynamics.

STUDENT RESPONSE

Student reaction to the projects was ascertained by three methods: (1) comparison of courses with and without the projects using the standard university evaluation instrument; (2) content analysis of student papers on the three projects; and (3) student feedback through both in-class discussions and follow-up interviews. The standardized evaluations provide some insight into how students valued the course with and without the research experience; the content analysis provides greater nuance into the reasons students valued the field research experiences and the most important pedagogical aspects of the projects. The follow-up interviews by a research assistant, not the instructor, were designed to ascertain the longer-term impact of the projects after the course was completed. While the reaction papers differed somewhat in terms of their content, the reaction papers were content analyzed in an attempt to aggregate and compare the reasons student gave for assessing the projects favorably. These comparisons are reported in Table 2.1.

Standardized Course Evaluations

Gauged by their responses on the standard university evaluations, student reactions to the projects were extremely positive. Table 2.1 compares mean ratings for the course as it was taught without a field project and the three courses that included projects. In two of the three courses with projects, the students' overall evaluation of instructional effectiveness suggests that the projects added significant value to the course. The more the project took the student beyond normal classroom experience, the more positive the evaluation. The media

TABLE 2.1 Student Feedback of Gender Projects Using Different Methods

Student indicator	Course without project (1996)	Elite interviews (1997)	Model UN observation (1999)	Media analysis (2000)
Course evaluation questions				
Overall instructional effectiveness**	4.3 (72)	4.6 (92)	4.6 (92)	4.3 (70)
Stimulated continuing interest in subject**	3.9 (52)	4.2 (79)	4.4 (87)	4.0 (63)
Reaction papers				
% giving positive evaluations of overall project	NA	88.6	94.7	67.9
% giving reasons*				
• "Doing" was more fun than reading, lectures		39.1	89.4	15.4
• Theory was connected to real life actions		62.8	36.8	61.5
• Gained increased awareness of gender		54.5	63.2	69.2
• Appreciated the rigors of research process		NA	42.1	NA
	N = 40	N = 35	N = 39	N = 35

Notes: NA—assignment not applicable or did not solicit relevant information; *Other reasons were given but only the most frequent responses are reported here; **Percentile rank with courses of comparable size in the College of Arts and Sciences is shown in parentheses.

content analysis was most like a traditional course activity—reading and writing—which may explain why student ratings were quite similar to the course without a field research project. Indeed, since the media content analysis never took students physically outside of the classroom, it was not an experience with the same impact as the elite interviews or the Model UN observation.

Content Analysis of Student Reaction Papers

Students reacted favorably to all of the projects, but there were important differences. The most consistent benefit, from the perspective of the students, was the gain in awareness of gender's impact on political life. As Table 2.1 illustrates, in more than half of the reaction papers and irrespective of the project, students consistently rated the gain in gender awareness as a reason they valued the project. Of the interview project, students wrote that the interviews heightened their awareness of problems that women, in particular, face in leadership roles in politics and public administration. In the media analysis, students reported being surprised at the extent of the inequality in the amount and content of coverage given to Elizabeth Dole's campaign. Of the Model UN project, students noted the recognition of distinctive gendered behaviors among the delegates.

Students also cited as a reason for their positive evaluations the connection made between theory and real life actions. Table 2.1 shows that in the elite interviews and the media analysis projects two-thirds of the students valued the opportunity to make important theoretical connections through the projects. Perhaps because the Model UN observation involves a simulation rather than a real-life event, only one-third of the students cited the theoretical connections as important.

Finally, it should be noted that student reactions varied considerably in terms of seeing the projects as more fun than traditional classroom activities. In particular, the students did not see the "doing" of the elite interview and media analysis projects as containing as much "fun" as the observation project did. In retrospect, the results in Table 2.1 should not be surprising. The requirement that the each student interview two elected and appointed officials increased anxiety about the task. Even though the interview subjects were selected by a sampling procedure and contacted in advance by the instructor to solicit their participation, many students were reluctant and uncomfortable about interviewing public officials. Because students had to schedule their own interviews, some encountered difficulty coordinating their schedules with the public officials. The media analysis project, by contrast, was the most similar to a traditional classroom assignment of reading and analysis. Because the media project provided less of a contrast with traditional course assignments, it seemed to generate less enthusiasm overall. While the project was evaluated by the students as providing important connections to theory and revealing gender differences in political coverage, few students were effusive in their praise of the actual task. The media analysis also was conducted as a fairly solitary activity,[1] and thus did not evoke the same degree of camaraderie or group experience.

The student reaction papers on the Model UN project were the most detailed and yielded the most complete exposition of the benefits, thus it seems most appropriate to consider the students' own words and comments. Highlighting the value of increased awareness of gender, one female senior political science major wrote:

I loved this observation project. It really reinforced many issues we talked about in class, for example: the gendered behavior and different characteristics between a male leader and a female leader. Although our readings are significant to the class, I believe in my afternoon of observing this Model United Nations I have learned quite a bit. I saw with my own eyes how girls are taught so early in their lives how they are 'supposed to act.'

A male junior political science major similarly wrote:

I am thankful for the knowledge I gained. I was able to observe the differences in the delegates' behavior. I was able to see the differences gender makes in behavior. The differences in the ways men and women approach their roles were made obvious to me, and I was able to distinguish styles of leadership and weigh their effectiveness.

Another young man, a junior public administration and affairs major, added:

Male and female interactions are a constant in everyday life, however, they are also greatly misunderstood. As our readings have shown, many of the scholars are in disagreement as to the causes, solutions, and future implications involved with the differences in these interactions. The Model United Nations provided an arena for observations to be applied to our readings . . . As an observer I was afforded the opportunity to place solid connections to what I have been struggling with in the texts.

Highlighting the opportunity to connect theoretical concepts to everyday life, a female political science major noted:

As for the project itself, I thoroughly enjoyed the experience. It was exciting to see theories and hypotheses come to life through a project. As an undergraduate student, most classes simply cover reading and library researching. With this field research, I acquired a first-hand experience on topics covered in books and lectures. After reading Kathlene's work on gender behavior in the Colorado State House, I became fascinated about how speaking patterns reveal so much insight. My interest intensified while collecting similar data on gender behavior amongst perhaps future politicians. The point of this project could not have impacted me if [the professor] simply lectured about it. Seeing the experience in person placed me in the role of an actual political scientist.

Confirming this point, a senior women's studies major commented:

I think overall the project added a concrete example to back up our readings from class. It was disappointing to discover that girls really are participating less and are less knowledgeable about politics than boys their age. Only by documenting this behavior can we begin to recognize reasons why less women are involved in politics as adults. I thought that it was refreshing to participate in a hands-on learning experience when so much of work in this area is spent in the classroom reading theory. Theory is a very valuable tool but until it is applied, it does little to actually change the status quo. It is my hope that projects like this will lead to a restructuring of structures so as to bring down the barriers that keep women out of this important process.

Students in the Model UN also were prompted to write about the perspectives they gained on the rigors and methods of empirical social science research. Particularly in the area of feminist scholarship, where skeptics often question the rigor and biases of the research, students learned that gender insights are indeed the product of carefully conducted research. A female junior political science major wrote:

By participating in this survey, I was allowed the opportunity to examine the hypotheses we discussed in class through a researcher's eyes, and I was able to discover for myself the veracity of these ideas. By conducting this research I gained a more complete understanding of the concerns we addressed in class about male and female behavior in certain activities. Had we simply stayed in the classroom and read about research like ours in a book, I would not have gained as much of an understanding.

Adding to this point, a female women's studies major agreed:

Learning in class the proper ways to collect data can be tedious. Putting this information to use, however, speeds up the learning process while at the same time making it very obvious that collecting data can be a difficult and time consuming project. While reading the studies in our textbook, I will now have a better understanding of how the researchers collected the data. I believe that the hands on experience our class received will solidify the reading material about gender because we were watching the committee members interact, important connections with the readings were present. Watching the Model UN conference provided necessary proof that gender power exists in real political situations.

For some students, the projects provided significant break-through experiences. In the interview project, a male student, who had resisted the idea that women in leadership positions faced different and tangible constraints as a result of private sphere demands, confessed to having his mind totally changed by the interview he conducted with a high-level female appointee in the Department of Corrections. For two female African-American students, the Model UN observation provoked disappointment and anger over the absence of minority participants. One sophomore public administration and affairs major wrote:

The other thing I disliked about this event was the lack of minority faces. I could probably count on one hand the number of minority faces I noticed. This probably occurred because of inner city schools not having these types of programs available to their students. But there is also a stereotype going around about inner city students only being interested in music and rap, and maybe their school boards have gotten a whiff of this insult to many of these students. I fear that the lack of involvement from minority children will carry on into adulthood and will continue to add to the ongoing struggle of minorities in politics.

Finally, students commented that the project provided them with an important shared experience that led to a productive dialogue. Indeed, in-class discussions throughout the projects were lively, challenging, and engaging. In follow-up interviews conducted with the students in the first project (the interviews with political elites), students reported that the interviews they did made the class discussions more meaningful personally and collectively.

The interviews also revealed an important secondary benefit of the interview project in particular. Many students, but particularly the female students, saw their interviews as valuable mentoring. Students described the experience as "positive" and "unique" and valued the opportunity to speak candidly with state leaders in informal or more personal settings. As one student wrote in her reaction paper:

The value of this experience is indescribable. Speaking with public servants and leaders makes them seem more real and human. When they become real people with real struggles, we begin to have more compassion and appreciate them even more.

Several female students noted that they had had limited personal contact with female role models in politics and public service. Because the interviews focused on making career decisions and the dilemmas of balancing public and private life, the interviews naturally led into discussions of the students' own aspirations. One female student who interviewed an Oklahoma Supreme Court justice reported:

My conversation with my female interview subject was a very positive experience. We had a great conversation about life, work, and family. I have never really given much thought to "mentoring" as a concept, but I certainly learned a lot in talking with her. Not to sound cliched, it was refreshing and inspiring to get advice from someone who has some of the same basic ideas as I do. She encouraged me to trust myself and my own decisions and to not be driven by the ideas that having money and a "five-year plan" are everything.

Follow-up Interviews

The follow-up interviews generally confirmed the benefits identified by students in their papers. Informal contact with students after the class also underscored the initial positive reactions of students. In encounters with students from the classes in subsequent semesters, they ask about the progress of the research and about publications that have come from the projects.

LESSONS LEARNED: THE PEDAGOGICAL AND THE PRACTICAL

The differences among the project are important to note because they illustrate the pedagogical tradeoffs that must be confronted in designing an effective field research experience. Clearly the nature of each project influenced student reactions. The more the project represented a break from a traditional classroom experience, the more likely it was to be highly valued and seen as fun. Second, the projects that more closely connected theory to the practice of real politics, the stronger those connections were for the students. All of the projects helped students gain gender awareness.

While a positive experience, field research of this type presents major challenges to an instructor, and not every teacher will have the resources or time to lay the groundwork for such a project. In each project, I was aided in the planning, coordination, and administrative tasks by undergraduate research assistants of the Carl Albert Congressional Research and Studies Center who helped develop the research strategy, prepare all of the necessary materials, made advance arrangements, helped to conduct training for the students, did data entry, and handled other administrative details of the project.[2] Where available, a graduate teaching assistant could handle many of these tasks with the added incentive of co-authoring research papers that come from the analyses.

The administrative details also force tradeoffs that may limit the opportunities for experiential learning to occur. In both the elite interview project and the Model UN observation, many students felt that more interviews and longer, more varied observation periods would have enhanced their experience. In this case, the balance between the pedagogical goal of structuring the ideal student learning experience and the practicalities of size and scope of the projects tipped more to pragmatic considerations of administration.

Timing is also critical. In order for the experience to complete Kolb's learning cycle, a narrow window of opportunity exists to lay the necessary theoretical groundwork, involve students in discussions of research design, execute the data collection, and do some preliminary analysis so that the students can see, discuss, and evaluate the results of their research within the constraints of a semester. While the obstacles may seem overwhelming and resources scant, some elements of field research can be adapted to other settings. I have used field research effectively in capstone courses where fewer students are enrolled and thus the administrative burdens considerably lessened. Short research assignments can also engage students directly with data that exposes important theoretical insights about gender. For example, students can be asked to administer a short opinion survey about feminist values to five or six friends and then analyze what they find. Alternatively, students can be asked to systematically analyze gender cues and biases transmitted in outlets of popular culture (i.e. magazine, television, popular music.) In follow-up writing assignments, students typically begin to see and to understand how feminism and gender have become socially constructed. While these examples are not methodologically rigorous, the act of "doing" the task temporarily suspends the student judgment and then makes more visible the nexus between theory and gender in practice.

CONCLUSION

To help students see how deeply gender is embedded in the processes, procedures, and cultures of political and governing institutions, it is often first essential to put them into a new experience that will help them set aside, at least momentarily, their unconscious (or conscious) resistance to the material. Scholars and teachers must confront the reality that feminist theory and scholarly research will reach and resonate with only a limited number of undergraduates. One strategy to overcome these obstacles is to craft field research experiences that expose the dimensions of masculinism and the marginalization of feminist values.

The projects described here represent a systematic pedagogy that employs Kolb's experiential learning cycle to teach about gender and politics. To the extent that classroom and learning activities cause students to "experience" more directly the gendered nature of the world around them, they become better equipped to understand that gender is not merely an abstraction but rather real systems that directly impact their lives. A shared field experience also creates a basis for classroom dialogue that overcomes the oppositional nature of many contemporary political conversations on gender.

In attempting to suggest strategies to improve science education for women, Lundeberg and Moch note that researchers have shifted their attention from "what's wrong with women that they don't like science" or "what's wrong with science that women don't like it" to "what's wrong with the teaching of science that women don't like it"? In this chapter, I have similarly attempted to shift from asking why students resist courses on gender to considering how we might improve teaching to reach students more effectively. As Lundeberg and Moch conclude, a part of the answer lies in finding strategies that provided "connected learning," where students place abstractions into real life contexts and relate the concepts to their own experiences (Lundeberg and Moch 1995, 327). When the classroom helps students make those connections, the learning is rich and rewarding.

NOTES

1. In anticipation of the lack of a group experience, a coding "party" was held, but only about one-fourth of the students opted to participate.

2. The author wishes to acknowledge the invaluable assistance and contributions of several students who helped with the administration of the field projects described in this chapter. They include Jocelyn Jones, M. Lynsey Morris, E. Barrett Ristroph, Deneka Turney, Jodi Velasco, Jana Vogt, and Alisha Jones.

3

Homeless in Academia: Homesteading as a Strategy for Change in a World of Hegemonic Masculinity

Annica Kronsell

While conducting interviews for a project on women in the Swedish military, my colleague and I were often struck by the similarities in the way military women described their realities and the way we interpreted our own lived experiences as women in the university. I was further enticed to make that comparison after having come across Mary Katzenstein's comparative work on feminist protest inside the church and military (1998). She skillfully draws attention to and explores the move of social protest and mobilization inside institutions. This is the focus in this chapter. Over the years, social movement research has studied grassroots activism and mobilization around women's issues and environmental concerns. Major attention has been paid to protest and articulation of critical and alternative politics outside institutions. As the public increasingly adopts the values carried by such social movements and puts them on institutional agendas where they become legislative concerns, there is an imminent need to more precisely study such phenomena. To simply conclude that the development reflects a process of institutional co-optation or alternatively, a paradigmatic shift, does not, I argue, pay sufficient attention to the complexities of institutions and social change. Focusing on Sweden for example, we note both a high political representation and an extensive participation of women in the workforce. Such observations could lead one to assume that ideas associated with the feminist or women's movement have been successful and, furthermore, institutionalized in Sweden, however this seems only to be partially the case. If we turn to the military or academia, the figures look bleaker because 97 percent of officers and soldiers are men, and 85 percent of the full professors are men.

In an attempt to try to understand institutional change, I focus on the changes that have come regarding gender and feminist issues in one important state institution—the university. I do this by drawing attention to a particularly important location of the university—the seminar room—and to processes of "homesteading" within the university. I point to a number of processes that have been important for the inclusion or exclusion of feminist ideas into one particular institution. The major conclusion from this study is that the changes had much to do with the rapidly increasing number of women entering the department over a short period of time. Despite sensations of "homelessness" these women had ambitions to create a space for themselves within the department and did so through "homesteading" practices. Somewhat surprisingly, perhaps, the study shows that their relative unawareness of oppressive institutional structures facilitated their efforts. Furthermore, it is suggested that aspects in the opportunity structure worked beneficially to support women's homesteading strategies and bring about institutional change.

While this chapter studies the specifics of one particular academic setting, it will draw on studies in other fields in order to reflect on and more broadly contextualize the processes at hand. The focus is on the academic environment, but it can have broader relevance as I argue that the university institutions can very well be compared with the military and the church—the institutions Mary Katzenstein compares in her work. A particular ceremony, important in the academic setting of Lund, can demonstrate the connection between such institutions. It is the remarkable tradition of the Ph.D. commencement exercises of long tradition and high standing at the Lund University, one of the oldest universities in the country. The connection between the church, the military and the academy is succinctly expressed in this ceremony.

The commencement parade starts at the main University building. The participants are all dressed in black, women in long black dresses and men in tuxedos; there are no exceptions allowed. The parade includes various flag bearers representing different faculties and functions. The head of the University goes first, alongside the bishop (incidentally both were female the time I watched, which was also the first time in history), together with the governor of southern Sweden (landshövding). The procession is not long, but proceeds very slowly. It passes through Lundagård ancient grove of trees in the center of Lund, to its destination, the magnificent, gothic cathedral built in the twelfth century. The parade is watched and followed by a crowd of relatives and curious onlookers. When all have been seated in the cathedral, the ceremony starts. The tedious, three-hour ceremony is conducted in Latin. In the ceremony all the new doctors are called up to the center of the cathedral to receive a ring and a top hat or, alternatively, a laurel wreath, depending on the faculty to which they belong. Lastly, they are saluted faculty-wise by several canon shoots. As a result, on this Friday afternoon in late May, all of Lund echoes of canon shots.

The ceremony is an impressive event with much symbolic content. Through the act of receiving the ring, the new doctor is married to academia. It indicates where the doctor is to direct his/her main attention and loyal servitude. This marriage is blessed by the church. We may also note the exclusionary practice in the use of Latin, historically the language of the learned. Hence, it is not the church of the common people, but the church of the elite who blesses the new doctor in his/her marriage to academia. The whole ceremony is sealed by the sounds of canons. All is watched, awed, and admired by the crowd. The military seal connects the academic ceremony not only with the military institution, but also, albeit implicitly, with the project of nation-state building, affirming what interest the new doctors are to serve.

Although the importance attached to this ceremony might seem negligible in view of overall academic politics, focus on such a ceremony can give us important clues about the norms and values that constitute institutions. Mats Alvesson (1993) suggests that ceremonies can point to what he refers to as "culture" of institutions and argues that such cultures are important to study if we are to understand institutional processes. One of the important connections between the three institutions comprised of the church, the military, and the academy is that they, of tradition, have been exclusively male. Institutions largely governed by men have upheld and recreated norms associated with masculinity and heterosexuality. Unquestionably, such institutions presume the male as the norm. Thus, when someone mentions the professions associated with those institutions, such as an officer, a soldier, a priest, a professor, a researcher, to date, most people are likely to envision a male. A woman occupying such a professional role is instead considered deviant. Although the gendered practices of these institutions have taken slightly different forms, they have basically excluded women from their central activities. Nevertheless, women have been involved in auxiliary functions by serving these institutions in different ways, most notably in the roles of secretaries or cleaning personnel in the university.

Having said this, what difference can a minority of women possibly make within these institutions? One answer would be that they make little difference because a much larger number of women are required to produce change. Some feminist work points to the need for a critical mass of around one-third women to make an impact. In the absence of such a critical mass of women, the inclusion of women remains symbolic, and prospects for institutional change are meager (Kanter 1977). A different answer may be that the inclusion of even a small percentage of women makes all the difference in the world. This is because it can completely alter the way institutions are perceived and understood. It is only when women step into the jobs, functions, and roles traditionally associated with masculinity that institutionally-embedded norms become apparent and visible (Kronsell 2001; Kronsell and Svedberg 2001).

In order to arrive at a fuller understanding of how gender politics are played out in an institutional setting such as a Swedish university,[1] I want to focus on micro-politics. According to Patricia Mann (1994, 31) a micropolitical analysis has several purposes. First, it points to the serious political implications of everyday life and decisions of individuals. Second, it can provide ground for understanding how political organizing and struggle takes form because it focuses on how individuals negotiate in the complexity of institutionalized relations of domination. In order to understand how feminist resistance is shaped within such institutions, this approach can be valuable. The narratives offered here are self-biographical, generated from the experience I have had in making a profession for myself in a university institution with a long tradition of male researchers, teachers, and professors.[2]

HOMELESS IN THE SEMINAR ROOM

Although the male-as-norm is an abstract notion, it becomes real when everyday practices are carried out in different sites within institutions. One important location in the academic setting is the seminar room. In many ways the seminar room resembles the corporate boardroom or other familiar salons of power previously inaccessible to women. Women entering the territory of traditionally male institutions are repeatedly faced with the fact that they are different. A sensation of awkwardness or displacement may be associated with a woman's experience in previously exclusively male territory. The sensation can be described as *homelessness* as suggested by Christine Sylvester (1994).[3] Homelessness can describe the sensation felt by the female researchers in the seminar room. The narrative below describes such a seminar.[4]

The graduate students and professors met weekly around the large rectangular table, typically, to first listen to a presentation by a researcher or graduate student followed by a discussion. Certain fixed yet, informal seating arrangements were always observed. They were almost strictly hierarchical in order of seniority and academic status. The discussions more often than not were nothing like what I understood as discussions, i.e. an open exchange of thoughts and feelings on the topic at hand. Instead, it often resembled a challenging session, where the presenter was repeatedly challenged and everyone taking turns to position himself on the subject in focus. Sometimes jokingly we called it cock-fighting and at times, that was the best description, critical, sarcastic comments delivered in a snappy but yet abstract language. Surprising to me, it seemed a highly esteemed, and also an acceptable way of being in the seminar room. (Kronsell 1990–1997)

Alvesson and Billing try to understand the complexities of gender and organizations and write that "in organizations, meetings often function as rituals" (1997, 109). They suggest that it is in meetings that norms and values of the organization are transmitted and to be learned by those new to the organization, as well as confirmed and reproduced by those with a longer institutional affiliation. In Swedish social science, the seminar is one of the most important events or occasions when such norms can be transmitted in the organization. In this space the culture of the organization can be reinforced and reproduced to newcomers. It is not surprising then, that the seminar felt like home to some who seem to fit right in and feel at ease, yet, to others felt more uncomfortable and even hostile.

In the space of the seminar room, my sense of being lost was acute. I felt a knot in my stomach and a panicky feeling, and with desperation thought: I will never be able to say things like that, i.e., talk about matters in such confident terms. The result was that I remained mute with a decreasing sense of security, rather than what would be assumed, a sense of security growing as I became more familiar with the setting. I noted that the few other women present also were quiet and stayed silent. (Kronsell 1990–1997)

The description refers to my initial experiences as a graduate student. What was striking to me in my observation of this seminar setting over some time was that women remained silent for a long period of time. Their insecurity seemed to be accentuated in the seminar setting while many of the young men[5] on the other hand, seemed to rather quickly grow and gain confidence. At every new seminar they seemed to grow into their role as researchers. They got better at taking up space, asking long elaborate questions, and positioning themselves in relationship to the others. They did not seem afraid and even had the confidence to be openly critical a times. It was notable that they seemed to develop these skills quickly, and it did not take long before they were engaging in long monologues of complexities. They could often sit with their legs spread wide apart, arms crossed behind their heads, even rocking back and forth on the chair, as if trying to fill more and more of that space of the seminar room.

It is interesting to note the resemblance between this description of the men in the seminar room and some of the narratives in Blackmore's work on women in educational leadership. In organizations, Blackmore argues that the body itself is a site of domination as well as a site of resistance. She continues with an example: ". . . women generally do not sit in meetings with legs splayed widely and hands clasped behind head, arms openly outstretched to embrace the world" (Blackmore 1999, 173). She explains that this is because women's bodies are subject to the male gaze, institutionalized into a set of repressive practices. This, then, disciplines the female body in certain acceptable ways of moving, sitting, and acting. While the categories *male* and *researcher* or *professor* collapse and becomes one and the same, the disciplinary institutional practices that affect male bodies also discipline the body of the researcher or professor. For researchers with women's bodies, such disciplinary acts work differently. They are first and foremost women and only secondly researchers.[6] This is demonstrated by the fact that in the seminar room their bodily movements are subjected to disciplinary practices[7] related to their female bodies.

Women's silence in the seminar should not come as a surprise if we put it into a larger perspective. Rather, it is what we would expect by looking at studies of girls and women in the classroom. From early years through college education women take up much less space, listen, and are silent to a greater extent than boys and men are (Martin 2000, 85–90). It is likely that the women in the seminar room had been subject to similar experiences before and probably fell into a pattern of ordinary behavior under such circumstances. Nor does the experience seem limited to this particular university. Morley (1999, 83), in her study of feminist academics in three countries found that many women experienced a sense of insecurity in their organizational environment. They struggled with how to appropriately and effectively express themselves. There seems to be something more general about these experiences as noted when comparing the similarities in experience in the seminar room with that of women in management positions, whom Sue Maddock (1999) has interviewed. She says that:

The most quoted complaint was that in meetings women managers were bypassed or just ignored. The overwhelming majority of middle managers complained that their managers did not listen to their comments about their work. The impact of such daily negative and denying reactions left them feeling undermined, marginalized and underconfident. The consensus was that this occurred because men thought that women had little to say or wondered what on earth they were talking about. (Maddock 1999, 167)

In a traditionally male organization the way women act and talk can appear ambiguous to the long-established group of men and, hence, be difficult for them to read and understand. This may set women apart unfavorably (Alvesson and Billing 1997, 108). Difficulties in communication between men and women may contribute to the way they perform and feel about engaging in the activities of the seminar. However, misunderstandings do not fully account for the power asymmetries of the gender relations played out there. When we are dealing with traditionally all-male or dominantly male institutions, as women engage in the organization they also trespass male boundaries (Gherardi 1995). In doing so, they compete with men over resources like jobs and research grants which, in the previous absence of women, were in practice reserved exclusively for men. The seminar room is an important place for academia and as we have seen, a place where women and men feel differently at ease.

Christine Sylvester's concept 'homeless' was extremely helpful and became a useful metaphor to describe the sensation we had in the seminar room. The concept 'homeless' made us aware that the feeling we had as individuals, described something more than our personal fears and insecurities. (Kronsell 1990–1997)

In thinking about homelessness, the gender dynamics of the seminar room became clearer. Many women and a few men did not feel that they belonged, and therefore could not function well in a place that by tradition is infused with norms of hegemonic masculinity.[8] The recognition of homelessness placed personal, individual insecurities and disappointment in an institutional context of gender relations. It was partly triggered by the increase in the number of female graduate students in the department during the 1990s, which seemed to have caused an unexpected institutional chock and exposed various forms of gender biases embedded in the institution. This development was crucial and the background for the "homesteading" process that began to take shape.

HOMESTEADING AS AN ACT OF RESISTANCE

We gathered over coffee in our offices to talk about our impressions. We had lunches, and organized some just for the women in the department—graduate students and staff. We got together a lot, just to talk. We started talking to each other about the way we felt in the seminar room and as women working in the department. This was important because we came to understand over time, that the feeling was not only our own, but felt among other women as well. Although we had different interests, experiences and personalities, this understanding helped us build confidence and a sense of security. We became more and more convinced that there was nothing wrong with us, but the reason was elsewhere, somewhere in the walls of the department, traded down through practices in the seminar room and other spaces. (Kronsell 1990–1997)

The narrative gives weight to Kanter's (1977) argument that a critical mass is needed in order to bring about organizational change because the possibility to engage with other women (and some men) who felt like strangers in the organization was essential. The process of lifting the personal to conceive it as political was facilitated by the turn to feminist literature. However, it needs to be pointed out that "female cannot be unilaterally equated with feminism, nor are all feminists reflexive about their location in organizational power relations" (Morley 1999, 75). As the homesteading process took form and progressed, the engagement with feminism also became uncomfortable to some. In a way, and particularly over time, it tended to divide women from feminists. Due mainly to the stigmatization often associated with feminism, some graduate students seemed to have felt forced into an inopportune position. They had to make a choice of whether they wanted to be feminists (and perceived as hostile to men) or women researchers (i.e. not create trouble around current gender relations).

Christine Sylvester's writings (1994) seem to suggest that the only cure for homelessness is to find a home. Thus, homesteading is the strategy we employed. It meant making and shaping a political space for ourselves in order to go beyond and surpass the life of contradictions and anxieties of homelessness. In practice, homesteading was about trying to intervene in the dominant discourse. Homesteading aimed to change the dominant discourses on the role of the researcher, on methodology, teaching, learning, and on the proper subject of political science. Homesteading became something similar to what Katzenstein has described as change through discursive politics. Discursive politics is "the politics of meaning making" and is about "the efforts to reinterpret, reformulate, rethink and rewrite the norms and practices of society and the state" (Katzenstein 1998, 17). Our ambitions were limited to try to rethink and reformulate the norms and practices of the seminar room. That, we felt was a difficult enough task.

Our initial approach was to try to influence the seminar agenda by suggesting subjects and books that we thought interesting. This way we hoped to guide the seminar discussions in the direction of issues we cared about. One of the very first such seminars discussed Rebecca Grant's and Kathleen Newland's anthology: Feminism and International Relations. Two graduate students, male and female, took responsibility for the presentation and discussion. It turned into a lively and extremely engaging debate which gradually grew more hostile and personal than anticipated. Faces turned brightly red of excitement and some took, it seemed, personal offense to suggestions made in the book that international relations researchers and their theories had gender biases. Some were eager to dismiss such accusation by calling them ridiculous or unfair yet, others questioned whether gender had anything at all to do with political science. (Kronsell 1990–1997)

We can note that while the first institutional shock came with the acceptance of an increasing number of female graduate students in the department, the second shock came with the introduction of gender on the seminar agenda. By introducing gender as a subject, the gendered norms of political science research were challenged. There was a clear hostility as some researchers, exhibiting irrational gut reactions, attempted to police the borders of international relations and political science from feminist interventions. Perplexed, we took part in this exciting event, joyous at the attention that indicated interest in the topic, yet at the same time shocked by these emotional outbursts in this otherwise very disciplined seminar space.

Surprisingly, we found ourselves in the position of defending and explaining feminist theory, although most of us were novices. As researchers in women's bodies we were somehow assumed to represent and speak for feminist authors. We quickly realized that this was both an unfair expectation and a very difficult task. Although we praised the success of the seminar because it was very engaging and moved far from the usual proceedings, we were not satisfied because we did not think we had successfully defended the contributions of feminism and international relations. We were afraid that our performance had only led to an easy dismissal of the subject for political science at our own department and took the responsibility for this upon ourselves.

The experience taught us two important lessons. First, the reactions and the discussions in the seminar exposed and made the gendered nature of both our subject and some of the institutional practices much more clearly visible. Although we had a notion of this before, it was now beyond doubt that the research field and the daily practices of the department were infused with male-biased norms. Second, we came to realize that homesteading meant so much more than just introducing a few new issues on the seminar agenda. Homesteading seemed to require much more work and dedication on our part, more than some of us were perhaps willing to invest.

RADICALIZATION AND SUCCESSFUL HOMESTEADING

Although some of the women researchers were and had been involved in the women's movement and were clearly feminists, from the start I was not. I have always been a critical thinker questioning discrimination and injustices in general, but had not been a feminist. I even had shunned the word before, as I was afraid to be associated with a stigmatized feminist label. (Kronsell 1990–1997)

As a result of these experiences, many of the graduate students in the department became radicalized. While they had not earlier been particularly concerned about gender or feminist issues, they were now seeing things in a different light. Katzenstein makes a similar observation as she argues that women in the military were radicalized when confronted with the practices of the institutions. She states: "activists in the military came to their feminism from within the institution and were not co-opted from the outside. . . . most activists in the military environment developed their views of gender issues in the institution itself" (Katzenstein 1998, 70). In other words, by living the gendered relations of the everyday practices of, in this case the military, gender relations become visible. The female officer takes those insights seriously and tries to understand them. Radicalization does not imply that we can expect radical or paradigmatic change within institutions, it only connotes the process that the individual woman is faced with. According to Katzenstein, whose definition I follow, radicalization within institutions does not mean that radical politics are adopted. Rather, it names the process whereby the individual in her work becomes aware of the gendered norms that infuse the institution and takes action according to this insight. If it will make an impact on the institution depends on whether a more permanent political space for feminist politics is created as a result of it. Obviously, it is possible for the radicalized individual to leave the institution and to decide to have nothing to do with it.

The option of exit (Hirschman 1970) has certainly been the choice of many women in the military and is also frequent in the academic setting.

However, our concern here is processes of institutional change, so we will turn to look at homesteading practices and give some examples of its success.

After the experience of the seminar room we began to realize that real homesteading would require more of us than simply applying feminist theory as an extracurricular activity, in the after hours when 'real' work was completed. We felt the need to probe deeper, to read, discuss and learn. One graduate student, well read in feminist literature, organized a reading course which was outside our curriculum. We read literature that we then later hoped to include in our dissertation work. (Kronsell 1990–1997)

Homesteading is about making a home, finding a place of refuge, tranquility and security. After the first seminar on gender issues we came to realize that we needed a space of our own where we could meet and discuss topics of interest, a space free from the practices of the seminar room. The various women scholars in Morley's study also accentuated the importance of space both in terms of having a proper office and a particular space for women (1999, 94). It seems to be necessary at least in two ways: the recognition of agency associated with having "a room of one's own" as Virginia Woolf puts it, and as a sanctuary, an alternative space to freely develop thoughts and try new ideas in a comfortable ambience.

The women academics from Greece, Sweden, and Great Britain discussed in Morley's study were overwhelmed by the burden of having to be bi-textual, i.e., they were required to know the mainstream texts well and on top of that be well-versed in critical feminist thought. This was necessary for women acdemics, while mainstream academics could proceed successfully in their careers without ever having read, referenced, or acknowledged feminist scholarship (Morley 1999, 162). In many ways this was also true in our case. We were expected to defend feminist theory in some logical, simple, way— making very complex issues simple enough to grasp for those who had never acquainted themselves with women's studies or feminist theory. At the same time it was assumed that we were familiar with most mainstream work.[9] While this was certainly burdensome, it was also very engaging.

Through critical feminist thought, political science and IR suddenly became much more interesting. Personally, for the first time I got really excited and could not let go of reading the literature, thinking about it and discussing its contents. (Kronsell 1990–1997)

The women in Morley's study also felt exhilaration when they worked with feminist studies, but Morley is doubtful whether this excitement turns into energy that can lead to social change (1999, 164). While assessing social change is an extremely difficult task it is also questionable whether one can introduce new meanings, practices, and thinking in a traditional organizational context without a great deal of work. I would consider the development in our case as something more than individual satisfaction, but I would have more difficulty in assessing how it has contributed to great institutional change. Some change was put in force, and I would not hesitate to claim that. It opened up and, in some ways, secured a space for feminist research and teaching in ways that were not possible ten years earlier. The first Ph.D. completed by a woman in the department came in 1987. The second Ph.D. came six years later. It is only after 1993 that women in the department started getting Ph.D. degrees regularly. It is thus a considerable feat that out of the total number of dissertations since 1987, women wrote fifteen of them and men wrote thirty-three of them.

Because the seminar room had been such a traumatic experience for many of us, we developed an explicit strategy from the very beginning. Initially, it consisted of a kind of support group for all the women at the department. Later, the strategy developed into ways to gain knowledge and confidence through readings and discussions in a smaller setting. The ambition was to bring this into the larger seminar and engage the discussion there. The idea was that this would supercede silence, since we would be more prepared to speak among familiar faces. The atmosphere would be more supportive due to our previous experience that could then somehow spill over into the larger seminar.

Subsequently, we organized the course on feminist theory that gave us the tools and concepts to understand more clearly both our feelings of homelessness and suggest homesteading strategies. As a follow up, we arranged a number of monthly seminars discussing various issues of concern, such as representation, power, science, and teaching. All was discussed from a feminist or women's studies perspective. We took responsibility for the seminars in turns and advertised across the whole university because we wanted to engage with people outside our department as well. These seminars were successful, and many interesting people attended. In this stage we began to connect with feminist thinkers outside the academic setting, and we also met and got to know some of the women working with women's studies at various other departments of the University.

Looking back, it seems as if this strategy was rather successful, but it also depended on what constellation of people were present. Thus, we made this effort to change the seminar room atmosphere more befitting to our interests and needs. Indeed, our own seminars were strengthening and encouraging because we placed our own concerns and interests firmly into political science. We managed to articulate a political science discourse including feminist theories and methods, rather than dismissing them to the after-hours or margins.

Initially, I argued that the organizational culture of the department was infused with male norms due to its historic tradition of being an all-male profession. It was also the gendered character of the institution that made the resistance politics (homesteading, carried out by women and feminists to expand the discourse on political science) both necessary and possible. Although I would be inclined to attribute the success to those who actively participated in the process, there were certain factors that may have enhanced and facilitated the process that I refer to as the opportunity structure.

THE OPPORTUNITY STRUCTURE

In this section I outline factors in the broader societal and institutional setting that I believe influenced the development on gender and feminist issues and the shape it took in this specific department of the University. These are the gender equity norms in society, the particular governance structure of the department, the role of mentors, and outside support.

Equity Norms in Society

The Swedish academic setting of the early and mid 1990s was subject to broader societal norms, while at the time highly concerned with gender issues and the unequal distribution of men and women in different careers and positions. Katzenstein (1998) stresses the importance of having a legislative framework to lean back on for the women that she studies to survive in and change the discourse of the military and church institutions somewhat in their favor. Similarly, in the Swedish context, laws of equal opportunity and laws against sexual harassment have been important to guarantee women the right to a fair and safe working environment. In addition, particular policies and programs aiming at encouraging women's careers in the University have been launched. While the strategy of creating thirty special professors' chairs for gender studies related to different academic disciplines stirred up a controversy, other "affirmative action" policies are accepted without much criticism. Examples of such activities are prioritizing a women applicant for a position in an academic environment dominated by men or special research grants and scholarships awarded exclusively to women. The political support for gender equality in general, I surmise, has also played a significant role for the feminists' homesteading in the department. This is because general equity norms in the broader societal context are momentous to the possibility of changing gender relations within institutions where women are a minority and also late-comers. Without such gender equity norms, change would most likely be much slower.

Governance Structures of the Department

Men in male-dominated organizations have an interest in supporting the status quo because it is advantageous for them to do so. By keeping women out they also eliminate 50 percent of a possible competition over jobs and resources. Although these are undeniably some of the material factors making gendered practices within an organization enduring, it is a macropolitical approach that can not sufficiently account for the mechanics in institutional practice that seem to perpetuate a gendered order. To understand this it may be more useful to focus on processes of homosocial reproduction as ways in which gendered organizations are reproduced. These are subtle processes and are advanced, for example, by Alvesson and Billing in their work on gender in organizations, arguing that in male-dominated power structures there is a tendency to homosocial reproduction, which means that men seek, enjoy, and prefer the company of their own sex. Accordingly, disadvantages for women in the institutional setting are reproduced because those in central positions will "advance attitudes and values which make it easier for the people holding them to move upwards in the hierarchy" (Alvesson and Billing 1997, 71). In male-dominated institutions these values and attitudes reflect the male-as-norm. This reproduction of values contributes to the gendered division of labor. So while men might not consciously or overtly exclude women, they may have a tendency to favor connections with other men in work, research, and leisure time, hence reproducing the homosocial environment in which they are a part and making it difficult for women to engage in it. Furthermore, it may be one explanation why men's wages in the Lund University remain higher than women despite them being in identical jobs. At least that is what the President of the University Faculty Union, Karin Warfvinge, argued in a recent study on wages and gender differences: "I think men choose other men for positions because they understand each other more easily" (quoted in SDS July 9, 2001 my translation). Thus, the need for various broader societal measures to encourage women to pursue a research career may be essential in order to break such homosocial patterns. Such homosocial relations, I will argue, fit well with an organizational model that would consider governance structures in the organization as modeled on paternal family relations.

Individuals new to organizations normally try to figure out how the institution works and what are the informal rules and unwritten norms. In the case of the department, it was difficult to do. In one way it seemed very loose and open and, indeed, there was a lot of talk about tolerance and pluralism. Yet, there seemed to be an authoritative element to it as well. In one way, the "not seeing" how the governance structure worked meant you were oblivious to it. This, then, seemed to leave openings and opportunities that we took advantage of as female graduate students. Much later, when I came across Sattler's study, I found it striking that one of the informants in the study, Sheila, "sees the larger university as a hierarchy based on a father model." She is quoted as saying: "I think the whole university is set up in a patriarchal fashion with daddy at the top, and you know and on down" (Sattler 1997, 117). Such a paternalistic model may very well also explain the governance structure of our specific academic department and the norms according to which it was run. I came to realize a bit later, as I had familiarized myself with the work place and the space of the seminar room, that it resembled a traditional paternal family. Relationships modeled on those between fathers and sons, i.e., a homosocial pattern, seem to have historically formed the organization.

In his well-known work, *Images of Organization,* Gareth Morgan (1986) argues the relevance of the paternal model to the corporate world.

In viewing organizations as unconscious extensions of family relations we thus have a powerful means of understanding key features of the corporate world. We are also given a clue as to how organizations are likely to change along with contemporary changes in family structure and parenting relations. And we see the major role that women and gender-related values can play in transforming the corporate world. (Morgan 1986, 212)

Although Morgan discusses the corporate world, the paternal organizational model can be relevant for organizations more broadly. According to this paternal model, in organizations "one person defers to the authority of another exactly as the child defers to parental rule" (Morgan 1986, 211). It can be expected, then, that in the department the model sons are picked, groomed, and raised by the fathers. Starting from such a view of the organization we may explore the role of the daughters.

The paternal authority structure was at first completely invisible; hence, we may conjecture that the daughters were either oblivious to it or, alternatively, they sensed it as paternal. What appeared most salient was that while there was a relationship between fathers and sons, the daughters fit into a different role. The role we can ascribe to them is as the "rambunctious daughters." Following this line of analysis, somewhat to the envy of the sons, the rambunctious daughter often gets what she asks for. So did we. For example, we would not hesitate to suggest a topic for discussion, invite a guest speaker of our choice, and ask to have some refreshments after a seminar. We learned later that this was a novel way of doing things. Although we liked to attribute it to our own cleverness and the way we convincingly argued the value and importance of our requests, perhaps it reflected the relationship between fathers and their daughters. The daughters often are, at least in the eyes of the fathers, charming, clever, and perhaps a little manipulative. Consequently, the fathers spoil their daughters and give them everything they ask for. Yet, all the while they know that the daughter will marry and be gone soon enough. In the end, it is the son who follows the father's footsteps, takes over, and honors his legacy.

Being largely based on relational psychology, this model is difficult to verify but serves as a heuristic tool to help us understand institutional dynamics. One indication that may nevertheless empirically support it is the fact that it is exclusively young male researchers who are participating as research fellows in projects initiated by the tenured senior academics in the department. All the women who have stayed with the department after their Ph.D. have either been financed though university grants through teaching and/or by generating their own individual projects. It should be noted that getting external funding on one's own in an extremely competitive environment is no easy task.[10] Being a young woman with only limited publications but favored by gender equity norms may not be as beneficial for research funding as being under the wing of an established senior male scholar.

If we continue for a moment to expand on the paternal family as an institutional model, we might consider the mothers. Where there not any mothers who could perhaps support or mentor these daughters? Feminist work has often pointed to the need for role models to set examples to mobilize women. In the early 1990s there were certainly some mother figures in the department. One particular woman had worked there for over thirty-five years and she was, no doubt, very motherly in her duties. She was the head administrative secretary and as such performed tasks associated with work that women traditionally have been expected to do, work of service and support. While the mothers were certainly supportive of the daughters, the relationship was somewhat tenuous. The mother may be simultaneously proud, yet envious of the fact that the daughter ventured further than she ever did or dreamed of doing. The daughters, too, had an ambivalent relationship towards the mothers. They needed to distance and differentiate themselves from being associated with typical female roles and needed to affirm that they were researchers and not secretaries.

The Importance of Mentors

In Sattler's study the university teachers talk in detail about how they mentor younger students and make them aware of gender structures in the classroom and in the college environment. Sattler concludes that "these women's mentoring activity functions both to assist junior faculty in subverting the system and to perpetuate the structure of the university" (1997, 125). In our case there was no feminist or female professor in the department, and it was obvious that the "mothers" described above could not fulfill that function. However, one senior female lecturer was generally supportive and did much to encourage gender issues on the teaching curriculum and include textbooks authored by women. Somewhat controversially, I suggest that the lack of a mentor who could set the agenda for feminist issues may have been, in this case, actually beneficial. Due to this lack, we had to find our own way. There was no one telling us about the structure of the department or how bad things were. As a result, we were particularly ignorant about hierarchies in the paternal organization and felt as graduate students we had the right, the knowledge, and the energy to challenge some of these gendered practices. Mentors may be very important in raising feminist consciousness and providing general support. This notwithstanding, it can also be discouraging to have it all told to you, i.e., that you are a victim of oppressing gender relations. In teaching I have experienced these drawbacks right in the classroom. When confronted with feminist ideas, theories, and literature, young women can be fiercely critical—reaching almost a point of denial. It is possible that the process of becoming aware of gender structures puts a damper on their dreams of future possibilities. There is, therefore, a risky moment of victimizing in becoming acquainted with feminist literature. Because much feminist work points to the structural components of gender systems for the individual woman, it may portray women more as victims than as agents actively in charge of their lives.

Opportunities also arose somewhat paradoxically out of the combination of formal, often articulated, pluralism of the academic environment and the very informal nature of the paternal organizational structure. The freedom for graduate students to pursue their own subjects of interest when writing a dissertation and their freedom of choice of theoretical frameworks is something that was repeatedly evoked within the department and by its leadership. The praise of pluralism and freedom of choice as the key to building a strong academic discipline, and a good institution was one of the norms of the department articulated in the seminar room. It did not particularly state that feminism was desirable, but with such a strong pluralist norm it would be difficult to exclude it openly. Sattler's 1997 study of feminists and feminist teaching is a qualitative study that compares teachers in the public schools with teachers in the universities. One of the most striking differences between the two groups of teachers is the freedom that university teachers have to influence their own curriculum and pedagogy, as well as their choice of topics. It seems, then, that in the university setting there is academic freedom and more tolerance relative to other societal institutions. This also means tolerance and openness to feminist concerns. This freedom was crucial for our possibilities to influence the department's agenda. For example, there were no strict guidelines about required readings. Although some of the classic political science texts were considered mandatory, there was some room to exchange and add texts to the reading list, and it became a way to introduce, for example, feminist theory. Furthermore, because the norm was that the choice of dissertation topics, methods, and theoretical frameworks were entirely up to the graduate student, it opened up the use of feminist theory in our dissertations as well.

From the experiences drawn on in this chapter, one can conclude that it is not always necessary to have a mentor and that the lack of one may even open up possibilities. However, what seems to have been crucial in this case was the fact that there were a sufficient number of women sharing an experience and being interested in making some changes. Out of this, a small group pushing for gender awareness was created. Being part of a group in an otherwise individualistic environment gave the necessary strength to our cause. At the same time, the creation of this visible group of mainly women was obviously perceived as threatening. We received hate mail, and tension arose in sporadic conflict, mainly as a result of the perception of a feminist fraction within the department. Finally, seeking support from the outside compensated for the lack of feminist mentors and scholars within the department.

Networks for Inspiration and Support

I attended my first International Studies Association conference in Washington D.C. in 1994. There were many panels and many papers on thousands of topics. Since it was my first time there and I wanted to be an ambitious graduate student, I attended panel after panel. I listened to good paper presentations and worse ones. The panels that got me really excited were the ones within the section on feminist theory and gender studies (FTGS). I found myself going to more of their panels every day and it was both refreshing and inspiring. I liked the subject, the researchers and the way they presented their material. In the evenings we went to dinner and socialized. I was so full of new ideas and energy when I came home. (Kronsell 1990–1997)

I went back to these panels year-after-year for inspiration and so did some of the other women at the department. They also had similar experiences in other conferences and workshops, often outside Sweden. These conferences played a significant role for our further achievements at home because they provided examples for what could possibly be done within the field. Furthermore, it provided inspiration and guidance encouraging us to go on with our ambitions; hence, in a way it substituted for a mentor inside the department. If we ever had any doubts whether feminism and international relations was a field with research relevance, the FTGS eliminated any such doubts. We were convinced that this was not only an exciting field full of research opportunities, but it was highly relevant and in desperate need to be investigated.

Although not actually involving themselves with our daily struggles, various feminists outside our department contributed support and inspiration to carry on with our work. As part of our effort to change the experience in the seminar room, we invited different scholars to hold lectures in seminar form—always with the support of the department. After the formal lecture we would arrange an informal gathering. Through such encounters we were able to gain insight into our own situation as we compared our experience to stories lived in other institutional settings. As the invited scholars conveyed their stories to us, we gained knowledge about the broader university and research context. Sometimes we would even get advice regarding strategies. Susan Gibson, then at Oxford University, came up with the idea to organize a conference. She said that a conference would make a long lasting impact, both inside and outside our department, and thereby place our efforts on the academic map.

We decided to organize a conference and called it "A World in Transition: Feminist Perspectives on International Relations." It was a broader initiative, but in the end five graduate students carefully and meticulously planned it and searched for funding. We spent much effort in creating a good proposal and, to our great surprise, managed to secure funding for the entire project. It was a large conference, and we financed participants from Russia and Eastern Europe, as well as graduate students and lecturers. The first day was open to the public and hosted in the Main University aula, an important venue for events of this dignity. There were keynote speeches by prominent scholars: Galia Golan from Israel, Christine Sylvester from Australia, Hanne Petersen from Greenland, and Hilary Rose from Great Britain. The following two days engaged fifty-nine scholars, all with paper contributions, in five parallel workshops. The event was acknowledged by the head of the University, Boel Flodgren, the first woman in that position in Swedish academic history, who told the audience her personal story of becoming, first as a professor, then as a university chancellor. We were ecstatic over the success of the conference. It raised our self-esteem and gave us enough support and courage to feel we have a place in international relations and political science. The enormous support we got from those who attended affirmed this. At the same time it seemed to be the culmination of the collective activities on our part, as many had to turn their attention to individual dissertation work. We published a summary of the proceedings and selected papers in a special issue of the Swedish journal of political science (Statsvetenskaplig Tidskrift 1997). It felt like a great acknowledgement.

CONCLUDING REFLECTIONS

Through the analysis of institutional practices in this chapter by way of my own experiences we can conclude that institutional change is a problematic and complicated process. Agents are both enabled and restricted by the embedded institutional norms handed down and reproduced in the organization over time. It was argued that a focus on micropolitical processes is one approach in trying to understand the complexities of institutions. I did this by first focusing on the seminar room as an important site where institutional practices are reproduced. Although the institutional norms were based on male-as-norm and resulted in the sensation of homelessness among the women, there were simultaneously certain elements in the opportunity structure that worked to benefit women's agency. These elements were the particular position of daughters in a paternal organization, equity norms in society, and pluralist norms in academia. The major conclusions were, no doubt, that the rapidly increasing number of women entering the department over a short period of time, beginning in the early 1990s, was a crucial element. So were these particular women's ambitions of shaping the discourse on political science and desires to create a space for themselves through homesteading practices. I argued that it was clearly facilitated by the fact that these young women were initially relatively unaware of the oppressive institutional structures. However, in attempts to change the institutional setting, the women's own agency was partly based on the study of feminist theory and practice was essential.

We may ask ourselves what lasting impact beyond the conference did homesteading have? Do feminists now have a home in the department? There seems to be a space for feminism and gender studies. Feminist topics have become acceptable in the seminar room, and they are no longer seen as controversial or irrelevant, but appear to be part of the agenda. Gender issues have been put on reading lists of courses both at the introductory and more advanced level courses. A number of the scholars originally engaged in the feminist homesteading process are working on research projects and are teaching in the department. A number of graduate students have decided to make gender or feminist issues part of their thesis work. These tendencies notwithstanding, it might be still too early to assess whether the home is permanent or still to be considered temporary.

NOTES

1. Here I have been inspired by Frigga Haug's (1992) and Karin Widerberg's (1995) approach of using memory work as a base for arriving at an understanding of gender politics.

2. Although I rely mainly on my own interpretation of this process and my own experiences of it, for the analysis I feel indebted to all who participated in the process because the insights have come over the years through our many conversations where the issues raised in this chapter have been discussed extensively. Yet, I take full and sole responsibility for what is written here.

3. The way we applied the concept of homelessness to our experience of the daily activities within the academic institution was not identical to the way Sylvester uses the concept in her book on feminist theory and international relations. The concepts of *homelessness* and *homesteading* were used as metaphors to name and describe the sensations we felt as women researchers and gave us tools to understand how to improve our situation—how to create a place for ourselves within such a setting.

4. Obviously, seminars can be very different. The characterization of the seminar chosen in this analysis is associated with the male-as-norm and isolates practices related to those norms and values.

5. I like to point out that many men in this particular academic setting also felt uncomfortable and have pointed out that they did not like the "cock-fighting" atmosphere.

6. Another practice that underscores this claim is the persistent practice of seating arrangement at institutional festive gatherings. Clearly the main and overriding principle for seating arrangements is the heterosexual couple. Why heterosexuality should be such an important principle for every festive occasion is part of the complex puzzle of body politics and gendered institutional practices.

7. Disciplinary practices are understood here along the line of Sandra Bartky's 1990 work.

8. Rather than simply rely on a gender category man/woman it is useful to talk about masculinity, particularly as some men were also expressing discomfort with the setting and its practices. Hegemonic masculinity in Connell's terms implies the dominant model of masculinity; hence, suggesting that other types of masculinities can be discussed within the broad category of woman. I don't make the distinction here but assume that some women might be very comfortable in the seminar room described and that the degree of discomfort may have varied among the women.

9. This is likely a much more general problem, i.e., any researcher interested in a "new" field or perspective may be expected to be "bi-textual".

10. Some recent studies in the field of medical research have shown that women who receive research funding have to show far more publications and merits when applying for and receiving the same research funding that men do (SDS 2001, April 25).

4

Feminism and Interdisciplinarity

Sharlene Hesse-Biber

FEMINISM: RESTRUCTURING THE ACADEMIC DISCIPLINES

Feminist scholarship holds the promise of providing a major challenge to the disciplines. Feminist writings since the second wave of the philosophy in the 1960s have placed women's issues at the center of disciplinary concerns. These writings began calling for a major reassessment of concepts, theories, and methods employed within and across the academic disciplines. Kate Millet expressed second wave feminism's vision for women's studies scholarship at the close of the 1960s:

It may be that a second wave of the sexual revolution might at last accomplish its aim of freeing half the race from its immemorial subordination—and in the process bring us all a great deal closer to humanity. It may be that we shall even be able to retire sex from the harsh realities of politics, but not until we have created a world we can bear out of the desert we inhabit (Millet 1969, 363).

Women's studies, the key academic arena of feminism—like black studies, gay and lesbian studies, and cultural studies—is not confined to a single discipline. Feminists cross disciplinary boundaries borrowing widely from ideas at the borders of multiple disciplines; this contact has made a significant impact on the traditional disciplines of history, sociology, the humanities, and sciences, as "feminist scholars pose new questions and arrive at new interpretations of accepted knowledge"(Klein 1990, 93–94; Stanton and Stewart 1995, 3).

In 1960 there were approximately sixteen courses devoted to the topic of women and gender, and the first women's studies program in the United States was approved in 1970 at San Diego State University (Stimpson 1992, 257 as cited in Klein 1996, 115). The field has grown steadily since then. A recent study conducted by the American Council on Education found that 68 percent of American universities offered courses in women's studies, 48.9 percent of four-year colleges, and 26.5 percent of two-year colleges (Women's Studies 1990, 214; as cited in Klein 1996, 116). Yet while all of the programs were founded on the mission of forging an interdisciplinary feminist perspective, such a goal remains illusive and difficult to achieve, with feminists often practicing "multidisciplinarity" instead of "interdisciplinarity."

Over the past four decades, feminism and women's studies scholarship increasingly have sought to forge an interdisciplinary perspective, but not without challenges. Those involved in interdisciplinary teaching or research claimed they were conducting interdisciplinary work, but this was often done from a multidisciplinary perspective. Multidisciplinarity connotes the "juxtaposition of disciplines," with little interaction or transformation—additive, not integrative or transformative in approach" (Klein 1990, 24). Courses labeled "interdisciplinary" are thus often taught from a multidisciplinary perspective, adding a "speaker a week" or a reading a week from a different discipline, with little integration of topics or issues occurring from week to week. Moreover, much women's studies research and scholarship is in an equally disparate position as it too often masks interdisciplinarity with mere multidisciplinarity (Allen and Kitch 1998). Scholars conducting research from their disciplinary standpoints consult with their colleagues from other disciplines, but little substantive change in disciplinary approach emerges. Such multidisciplinarity, both in and out of the classroom, maintains loyalty to a given discipline, leaving disciplinary boundaries unchallenged:

This model has the virtue of recognizing that women's studies scholars were always/already trained in, and thus never "outside of" the disciplines, but it emphasizes the need to gain the trust of disciplinary gatekeepers and to work for change from within what are still viewed as bounded and unchanging fields. This modified version does not, then, challenge disciplinary privilege or the concept of disciplinarity. On the contrary, it sacralizes the disciplinary department as the site of the production of scholarship. In this scheme women's studies is not the intellectual base for generating new knowledge and for demonstrating the weaknesses of various disciplinary paradigms; it constitutes an ancillary system for ensuring better disciplinary knowledge. (Stanton and Stewart 1995, 2)

Early feminist scholars adopting a multidisciplinary approach made significant strides within their own disciplines. Feminist critiques within the disciplines acknowledged feminism's contributions to the "deconstruction of error" within the traditional disciplines by identifying androcentric bias and addressing the invisibility of women's issues and concerns (Stimpson

1978, as quoted in Schuster and Van Dyne 1985, 25). Some classic examples of this work include anthropologist Emily Martin's feminist analysis of medical discourse, which revealed the sexist attitudes of the medical profession toward the female body and its reproductive processes (Martin 1999). Martin analyzed the language used to depict the sperm and the egg in medical journals and its role in promoting an image of female inferiority. She exposed the negative stereotyping regarding gender in the medical sciences. She further suggests we become more aware of the cultural images we project in our own research, and by doing so, we can "rob them of their power to naturalize our social conventions about gender" (Martin 1999). Feminist philosopher Susan Bordo's (1999) analyses provide another example of exposing androcentric bias. She underscores women's exclusion from philosophical discourse and notes that the "history of philosophy" may be typified as "male."

Yet while these discoveries conducted under a feminist framework did much to enhance the knowledge of certain disciplines, it is imperative to recall that it was the academic fields of anthropology and philosophy that were advanced, not that of women's studies. These studies merely gave a feminist attitude toward their disciplines, rather than interweaving feminism into their disciplines. Yet the lack of synthesis among disciplines within feminism is not necessarily the fault of the feminist researcher. Rather the historical structure of women's studies programs has caused the field to be established as, and to remain, multidisciplinary. Three specific historical factors are to be noted. First is the nature of the feminist journal. Feminist journals and anthologies tend to be collections of often unrelated, discipline-centered studies. Rarely are journals collections of themed works that integrate discipline-based knowledge by formulating new concepts, theories, and epistemologies (Allen and Kitch 1998). A second barrier to the development of interdisciplinarity within feminism is the location of women's studies programs within the academy. In most instances the women's studies major is housed within a pre-existing department. Thus rather than having a unique women's studies department, faculty often have joint appointments with women's studies and additional departments. In this instance, jointly appointed faculty in search of tenure and funding may have little motivation to concentrate their energies on the non-departmentalized and fiscally non-rewarding women's studies program. This practice has an additional byproduct in that this leads to a lack of a research conducted solely within the context of women's studies. This in turn causes women's studies to become a site throughout which funding is not possible, perpetuating the cycle expounded upon above. Finally, while the nature of women's studies programs as "outside" of the traditions of the academy has allowed for the field to become a venue for autonomous and alternative instruction and education, it has left it a poor competitor for scarce resources and institutional status. Again, this leaves faculty members dependent upon traditional disciplines for sources of funding and tenure.

Women's studies faculty must increasingly become jointly appointed, reducing their attention to feminist curriculum, at best, to a mere 50 percent (Allen and Kitch, 1998).

THE MOVE TOWARD INTERDISCIPLINARY FEMINISM

To work from an interdisciplinary framework implies that one is working at the borders or crossroads of the disciplines. Paula Gunn Allen (1992) uses the term "border studies" to describe the work of scholars whose research crosses the borders of multiple disciplines. Higonett employs the anthropological term "contact zone" to describe engagement at disciplinary borders:

A border is a complex construct that defines and localizes what it strives to contain or release. It is rarely a smooth seam; an edge may ravel, gape open at interstices, or leak in both directions. Borders mark sites of rupture, connection, transmission, and transformation. Rather than understand them as static lines of demarcation, margins or impermeable walls; therefore, we might want to examine them as what anthropologists call "contact zones." Since the work of cultural transmission in contact zones is improvisational and interactive, the literary critic who examines such process of transmission can move beyond one way questions. (Higonett 1994, 2–3)

Arabella Lyon (1990) views interdisciplinarity as "giving up territory" in favor of a "tribal approach to knowledge." Working from an interdisciplinary perspective often requires creativity and risk-taking as scholars negotiate a "delicate balance" between being "at home" and being "in exile." Teresa de Lauretis describes the process of feminist theory-building as one of giving up a "place that is safe," where one feels at home with a variety of dimensions ranging from one's epistemological viewpoint to one's basic sense of emotional well being:

A feminist theory begins when the feminist critique of ideologies becomes conscious of itself and turns to question its own body of writing and critical interpretations, its basic assumptions of terms and practices which they entail and from which they emerge. This is not merely an expansion or a reconfiguration of boundaries, but a qualitative shift in political and historical consciousness. This shift implies, in my opinion, a displacement and a self-displacement: leaving or giving up a place that is safe, that is 'home' (physically, emotionally, linguistically, and epistemologically) for another place that is unknown and risky, that is not only emotionally but conceptually other, a place of discourse from which speaking and thinking are at best tentative, uncertain, and unguaranteed. But the leaving is not a choice: one could not live there in the first place. (de Lauretis 1988, 138–139)

Gloria Anzaldua's *la frontera* describes the geographical border between the United States and Mexico and provides us with a graphic image of the perils entailed in the crossing the boundary between what is native and foreign. The borderland is an area:

set up to define the places that are safe and unsafe, to distinguish us from . . . a vague and undetermined place created by the emotional residue of an unnatural boundary. It is in a constant state of transition. The prohibited and forbidden are its inhabitants. . . . Trespassers will be raped, maimed, strangled, gassed, shot. (Anzaldúa 1987, 3)

Jane Marcus's (1989, 23) view of border work is akin to Anzaldúa's notion of "the frontier," in that the feminist scholar occupies a position of exile "aware of her own estrangement from the center of her discipline . . . negotiating dangerous identifications with her subjects, edgily balancing on boundaries and testing limits." Deborah Steinberg argues that feminists working at the intellectual borders of their disciplines do not find their "home" disciplines necessarily places that are "safe," but instead sites of "profound estrangement and considerable danger":

Most of us who are feminists forging interdisciplinary scholarship and pedagogy, I imagine, find it more the case that 'home' is a place of profound estrangement and considerable danger. A place where our work is systematically disproportionate and undervalued, where kinship is a battle we rarely win and our custodianship of teaching and learning, can be as much a bitter as a joyous issue. Indeed, the metaphor of 'home', if we consider the conventional sexual politics of home, is unfortunately appropriate. (Steinberg 1997, 201)

Interdisciplinarity is a process that calls for the combining of knowledge from one or more disciplines. Interdisciplinarity occurs when a scholar interacts with the goal of synthesizing new knowledge from other disciplines in his or her approach to a given problem; for example, a sociologist who uses economic theory to understand the rates of violence against women, creating innovative theory of violence not found within sociology. Interdisciplinary teaching would position student and teacher around a set of topics approached from a range of disciplines, with student and teacher engaging each other in an interdisciplinary dialogue. This dialogue would comprise a concerted effort to explore and understand the ways of thinking among the disciplines under study.

Working from an interdisciplinary perspective requires caution when borrowing concepts from other disciplines: Is one using these concepts uncritically? Has one gained enough expertise in the disciplines at hand? Patai and Koertge (1994) strike a cautionary note when they call attention to the problem of interdisciplinary "opportunism"—those scholars who appropriate work from another field in a random and uncritical manner. While they apply this idea to scholars working within women's studies, their concerns apply to all scholars who work at the borders of multiple disciplines.

Interdisciplinarity allows " 'the space between' for debate, contention, and disagreement" (Stanley 1997, 1). Working at the borders presents feminist scholars "with the task of learning how to use [their] own conflicts constructively, affiliatively, and pleasurably—as sources of pleasure precisely because they can be tools for forging new understanding and new forms of affiliation" (Hirsch and Keller 1990, 379). Feminism in the 1970s and 1980s embraced a sense of idealism and optimism. Marianne Hirsch and Evelyn Fox Keller note that it was a period "sustained by the 'dream of a common language.' "

For the most part, feminists of the seventies wrote, and tried to think, of conflict as operating between feminism and its alternatives—be it Marxism, militarism, racism, heterosexism, capitalism or even the academy—not within. Those of us participating in the development of feminist theory at the time surely had to be aware that this was an illusion, for conflicts were everywhere among us, often explosively so. For the most part, however, we saw these conflicts as minor squabbles, and sought to contain them. (Hirsch and Keller 1990, 379)

Feminism's interaction with post-colonialism, as well as post-structuralism and postmodernism, transformed feminist scholarship and launched a powerful critique of dominant scholarship's emphasis on abstract universals (Waugh 1992). This interaction led to a realization that much of feminist scholarship was racist and ethnocentric and often excluded issues of difference regarding race, nationality, ethnic background, sexuality, and class. It also led to the realization that much of feminist scholarship failed to examine the important interconnections among these categories within specific historical contexts (Mohanty, 1988; hooks, 1984; and Anzaldúa, 1987). As Hirsch and Keller observe "feminists of color have revealed to white middle-class feminists the extent of their own racism" (1990, 379).

Sociologist Patricia Hill Collins (1999) developed a black women's epistemological standpoint, the "outsider-within" which, allowed for the recovery of black women's subjugated knowledge. She provides a strong critique against the hegemony of traditional disciplines, as well as challenging the tendency of white middle-class feminists to over generalize in their knowledge building without reference to the diversity of women's standpoints. Likewise, feminism's border crossings with post-modernism and post-structuralism had the effect, in the words of Barrett and Phillips, of "destabilizing" feminist engagement in grand theorizing by stressing an analytical shift in feminist theorizing to more "local and specific" analyses:

Much of the work is "deconstructive" in character, seeking to destabilize, challenge, subvert, reverse, overturn some of the hierarchical binary oppositions (including those implicating sex and gender) of western culture. Thus we have a developing feminist theory whose intention is to destabilize. (Barrett and Phillips 1992, 1)

CHALLENGING DISCIPLINARY CATEGORIES AND STANDPOINTS

Working from an interdisciplinary framework calls into question disciplinary categories of analysis as they become disrupted by the rich meanings brought to them. A few important examples come to mind: Monique Deveaux's work (1999) demonstrates how Michel Foucault's (1979, 1981) concepts of "power" and "resistance" are transformed when feminists begin to "historicize" them via their grounding in the varieties of women's daily lives (including their experiences of dominance and violence). Historian Kandiyoti (1999) reminds us of the problem of "universalizing" disciplinary constructions and how Western feminists often fail to recognize the ethnocentrism hidden within important concepts like patriarchy. She stresses the need for a historical-comparative approach in analyzing patriarchy across Western and non-Western societies. In the same vein, historian Joan Scott (1999) criticizes the use of "personal experience" as historical fact and asks historians to view experience discursively as a socially constructed "linguistic" event.

Feminism's interaction with post-modernism and post-structuralism also provides a useful theoretical framework for understanding the body. More particularly, this interaction has led to a view of the body as a site of political struggle. In Michel Foucault's (1979, 1981) writings, the body becomes a site for power and control; a surface upon which cultural norms are encoded, but also a site that allows for the possibility of female resistance. Just as feminism's interdisciplinary approach encourages the disciplines to reassess their theoretical constructs, it also encourages important methodological questions for conducting research from an interdisciplinary perspective: how tightly bound is one to his/her own discipline and its methods? For example, does one conduct research as an insider, an outsider, or both? If one adopts the standpoint of outsider, does one become overly identified with the other's viewpoint? If one adopts the role of insider, does one allow oneself to take risks, to challenge one's disciplinary standpoint?

Sociologist Lal's (1999) work, for example, challenges the binary opposition "insider/outsider," a central concept used in conducting sociological research. Lal's Indian heritage does not necessarily guarantee a privileged "insider's" view when interviewing Indian factory women. Her other positions—for example, her class standing and perceived Western status—can undermine her presumed insider status. Adopting an interdisciplinary perspective, then, is often a process in which one becomes both an insider and an outsider, taking on a multitude of different standpoints and negotiating these identities simultaneously. This is aptly expressed by Minh-ha's concept of multiple subjectivities:

Working right at the limits of several categories and approaches means that one is neither entirely inside nor outside. One has to push one's work as far as one can go: to the borderlines, where one never stops, walking on the edges, incurring constantly the risk of falling off one side or the other side of the limit while undoing, redoing, modifying this limit. (Minh-ha 1991, 218)

POLITICAL ACTIVISM

Feminist interdisciplinary scholarship advocates a breakdown of the border between knowledge and social activism. Its interdisciplinary inquiries are answered with action-based research (Allen and Kirch 1998). It is bell hooks (1990) who observes that to work at the borders allows one to conceive of "politics of location," a place from which one participates "in the formation of counter-hegemonic cultural practice":

I am located in the margin. I make a definite distinction between that marginality which is imposed by oppressive structures and that marginality one chooses as site of resistance—as location of radical openness and possibility. This site of resistance is continually formed in that segregated culture of opposition that is our critical response to that domination. We come to this space through suffering and pain through struggle. We know struggle to be that which pleasures, delights, and fulfills desire. We are transformed, individually, collectively, as we make radical creative space which affirms and sustains our subjectivity, which gives us a new location from which to articulate our sense of the world. (hooks 1990, 153)

Susan Bordo acknowledges that there are many differences among women; however, she argues for the strategic use of minimizing these differences to promote the political agenda of women in general. Bordo suggests that the determination of whether to rely on homogeneity (generalizability) or heterogeneity (difference) should be determined "from context to context, not by methodological fiat." She notes that "too relentless a focus on historical heterogeneity . . . can obscure the transhistorical hierarchical patterns of white, male privilege that have informed the creation of the Western intellectual tradition" (Bordo 1990, 149). Spalter-Roth and Hartmann's (1999) work on social welfare policy provides a good example of what Bordo is advocating. They argue for a "dualistic perspective" on social policy research that combines the range of women's "lived experience" with research that is grounded in standards of scientific method. Mohanty (1999) argues for the "strategic use" of essentialism among Third World women by having them organize around their shared material interests and identity as "workers" despite differences in nationality, race, and class backgrounds. Drawing on three case studies of Third World women involved in the global division of labor, she analyzes how ideologies of domesticity, femininity, and race are used by capitalists to socially construct the "domesticated woman worker" and that they are "dependent house-wives" justifies paying low wages. She calls for a re-conceptualization of Third World woman as agents rather than victims, and she argues for polit-ical solidarity among women workers as a potential revolutionary founda-tion against re-colonization.

INTERDISCIPLINARITY AS PROCESS

Klein observes that while there is a paucity of research on how interdisci-plinarians actually conduct their work, there are personality characteristics that have come to be associated with interdisciplinarians: "reliability, flexi-bility, patience, resilience, sensitivity to others, risk-taking, a thick skin, and a preference for diversity and new social roles"(1990, 182). Interdisciplinar-ity requires good communication skills among colleagues from different dis-ciplines and, within the classroom setting, between faculty and students. The wider the gap between disciplines and the larger the number of disciplines involved, the wider the potential communication gaps (Klein 1990, 183).

I conclude this chapter with some practical suggestions for students and faculty engaged in interdisciplinary pedagogy and research. Sjolander's ten-stage analysis of the evolution of an interdisciplinary project is useful in stressing that interdisciplinarity is a process that can unravel at any time (Sjolander 1985, as cited in Klein 1990, 71). I adapt Sjolander's stages and Klein's (1990) account of them to the practice of interdisciplinary teaching, but these steps can readily apply to interdisciplinary research as well. Stage one is *singing the old songs*. Faculty and students will naturally approach course readings from the perspectives of their individual disciplines. Stage two claims that *everyone on the other side is an idiot*. As time passes, stu-dents may experience problems cropping up when others' disciplinary points of view are taken into consideration. At this point some students may become uncomfortable, some may become disenchanted, and some may even drop the course. Stage three is *retreating into abstractions*. Abstractions provide a safe route of agreement among students from dif-ferent disciplines. Consensus may fizzle, however, as students are asked to provide concrete information about a given topic and realize what little course progress they have made. Stage four is *the definition sickness*. This may take effect as students begin holding others accountable for defining terms they are using. Agreement on how concepts should be used by the group is often characteristic of this stage. Stage five consists of *jumping the tussocks*. If participants pass through the first four stages, they may begin to have more fruitful discussions around a set of areas. "The areas are usually quite disparate . . . discussion will tend to jump from one area to another" (Klein 1990, 71–72).

Stage six is characterized as *the glass bead game*. In this stage, students continue to work on the common language they have created, one term ("bead") at a time. Stage seven is when *the great failure* surfaces. After rounds of dealing in abstractions and playing "glass bead" games, students tend to feel that they have failed to come to terms with each others' disciplines. This stage is crucial for moving to a more transformative one for the student. Stage eight will ask *what's happening to me?* This stage is reached when students feel that they have changed their perspective more than they realized. This insight may come when they have contact with individuals in their own discipline and begin to relate their classroom experiences. They may also have a better appreciation for the scholarship "of the disciplines with which they have interacted, strengthening and rekindling interest in further interdisciplinary work" (Klein 1990, 72).

Stage nine involves *getting to know the enemy.* Here students begin to proceed toward more "in-depth knowledge of others' disciplines" (Klein, 1990, 72). There is a conscious effort to explore and understand "general structures, principles, and ways of thinking in other disciplines" (Klein 1990, 72). Lastly, stage ten is considered *the real beginning*. After "a long period" of course meetings, individuals within the course, as well as the course itself, have the potential of becoming truly "interdisciplinary."

5

Women in Art:
A Continuing Controversy

J. Susan Isaacs

Perhaps no other course in the art history curriculum has caused so much discussion in the last thirty years as one devoted exclusively to the role of women in art that is variously taught as "A History of Women in Art," "A History of Women Artists," and "Women in Art." The reasons for the debate are many and usually begin with the general concern within academic communities about offering such a course at all and, once added to the curriculum, how this course should be presented and to whom it should be addressed. As an academic discipline within art history, feminist art criticism is a relatively new field, paralleling the history of the women's movement. Certainly, the history of women artists can be traced back to the ancient world, but it has only entered the art history curriculum as a specific course since the advent of the women's movement. Moreover, two main approaches to the topic have emerged that are at times in conflict with each other: (1) the history of women artists and the images they produce and (2) the discipline of feminist theory and criticism. These may include discussions about images of women and about visual culture rather than those centered on works made by women artists. Another conflict includes questions related to the production of art designated as "feminist" or "feminine," an issue that especially arises when separating out women artists into their own special category.

While many universities and colleges offer such a course today, there is historically some disagreement within the academic community and within the art community about whether to include a course that specifically segregates the work of women artists from mainstream art history and criticism. Not all universities and colleges offer it, even those with strong women's studies programs and large art history departments. Some simply lack faculty interested in the field. Others have been opposed to including a course that essentially teaches a history of the "other," believing, rightly or wrongly, that doing so "ghettoizes" the subject. The same discussion is often visited when suggesting courses related to African-American art. However, because of the impact of post-modern relativism some of this concern has lessened in recent years.[1] Nonetheless, everyone agrees that the ultimate goal is to have work by women and artists of color mainstreamed into the regular curriculum. The question is how to achieve this lofty goal. Many women artists share this concern, too, but also believe that considering them as women first and artists second only continues to marginalize their contributions. Some feminist scholars assert that teaching a history of women artists merely reinforces the impoverished approach of teaching about artists as heroes and geniuses, disguised as heroines and earth mothers, further perpetuating a paradigm that is essentially useless, false, and outdated.

The traditional Western canon of Classical and Renaissance art has had a tremendous hold on the field of art history. Most art history faculty were initially attracted to the discipline while students in general Western survey courses or through visits to museums where such art remains the centerpiece of important collections. In recent years, post-modern critical theory has profoundly influenced the field, providing a new way of looking at traditional bodies of work. Still, the fact that the majority of position advertisements in the College Art Association publication, *Careers,* remains oriented toward traditional categories indicates that little real structural change in art history departments has been made.[2] Many university and college faculty feel that it is important to contain the core curriculum first comprised of Ancient, Medieval, Renaissance, and Baroque, etc., choosing to add other, seemingly more esoteric fields once the fundamentals have been satisfied. It is a reasonable plan. However, not all departments have the luxury of adding more faculty or courses, though clearly a course related to women in art has become much more commonplace in recent years. Others support the idea of mainstreaming women artists into the core curriculum rather than creating a separate course to showcase or segregate their work. Critical theory provides faculty with a new vocabulary for deconstructing visual images, but the additional inclusion of images specifically by women artists or by artists of color does not always take place. Many art historians are simply not aware of these artists and images, not only because they were not taught them when they themselves were students, but also because only a handful of token images by women artists and artists of color have entered the survey textbooks and major museum collections. Moreover, much of the work created by women artists resides in the modern period when women began to have greater access to training and to the exhibition of their work, which is also the period of the survey most often rushed through or omitted at the end of the semester. There are also problems when teaching an upper division course devoted to modern and contemporary art where key texts often include few works by women artists, even though that period of art history includes many more women.[3] The great repository of modern art, the Museum of Modern Art (MOMA) in New York City, also reflects this imbalance. MOMA, like so many museums, includes very little work by women artists, i.e., less than 10 percent of the collection. Kirk Varnedoe, Chief Curator at MOMA, states that "modern art, which is what this museum is about, began largely as an endeavor of white European males . . . I'm not sure which woman painter in those galleries I'm betraying the mission of the museum by not showing."[4] Art Historian Linda Nochlin responds directly to such claims by stating that "the whole notion that the only artists ever worth looking at, or thinking about, are giants is so boring.[5] Nonetheless, teaching a chronological march through history—the history of major monuments and "important" artists—leaves scant time to even cover all of the so-called "famous" individuals, and lesser-known figures continue to be left out. Consequently, few women artists appear in general survey art history classes or even in courses concentrating on twentieth century art. Despite this fact, some university art and art history departments argue against offering a separate course specifically centered on women artists and their work, believing that it demeans women by separating them from the mainstream. Academe is not alone in this opinion. Contemporary women artists often agree with this view, finding not only the idea of courses on women's art marginalizing, but also seeing gender specific art organizations and museums of art for work by women artists only similarly confining. The most obvious example of this is the National Museum of Women in the Arts in Washington, D.C. It was organized in part to balance the collections of mainstream museums like MOMA, and it is the only museum in the world that focuses on art made exclusively by women artists. Founded in 1989, it remains controversial among contemporary women artists who often would prefer a show of their work at MOMA or the Hirshhorn, rather than the National Museum of Women in the Arts. Susan Bee, a painter and book artist living in New York City, represents this point of view when she writes, "younger women artists want to make it in the mainstream, if possible, and not languish on the fringes or in the past, where many perceive the feminist movement to reside."[6] In a 2001 *New York Times Magazine* article, critic Deborah Solomon comments on this very issue in relation to the vast numbers of successful contemporary women photographers working today:

Most serious artists are loath to speak about their work in terms of gender, and for good reason: it is all too easy to fall into reductive stereotypes. And yet among female photographers, whose field was once as welcoming to gender diversity as the trucking industry, a sense of triumph prevails. (Solomon 2001)

Despite taking a careful stance away from aligning oneself with other female artists or any kind of particular women's vision, many successful women photographers are delighted with their successes. Some art historians agree with the concern for gender stereotyping, seeing the idea of a course devoted to the history of women artists as representing an old approach to feminism and art history, one that easily falls into gender stereotyping and that does not take into account the more recent theoretical developments in art history, which address issues of visual culture within a larger context and which shy away from any kind of gender stereotyping.

In 1971, when Linda Nochlin, credited with the first contemporary feminist inquiry in art history, wrote her now-famous article "Why Are There No Great Women Artists?" she proposed a paradigm shift away from the basic premise of art history as a litany of geniuses, because few, if any, women were included in that history and because she believed that the story of art history was more complex and richer than merely a recanting of the work and lives of great geniuses. She determined that there were no female equivalents to Michelangelo or Paul Cezanne, not because women were untalented but, because they were denied access to academic training, which in the eighteenth and nineteenth centuries meant studying the male nude; consequently, they were condemned to secondary fields like portraiture and still life. She wrote this article at a time when most women artists and their works were unknown, so the first art historical approach that followed her milestone article was to identify these lost artists and locate work by them. This was followed by active documentation of women artists, and a great number of books identifying and examining the rediscovered artwork emerged. However, this approach to art history still operated within the traditional hierarchy of exploring great artists and their works, if not women artists (Nochlin 1971).

So the first step of revisionist history was to rewrite the litany, only now doing it with a new group of women artists who would replace the old group of male artists. This historical survey of women artists forms the foundation for most courses on women in the history of art. The goal of many of these classes is to introduce students to artists and works with which they are probably not familiar, many of whose careers have been reconstituted in the last thirty years. It is this approach that has drawn criticism from feminist scholars because of its apparent furthering of the traditional art historical paradigm: a review of great geniuses and their works. Scholars see one of the problems with this desire to prove that there have been women of great accomplishment even if their accomplishments are not as outstanding as those of men as that of creating a canon of white female artists nearly as restrictive as its masculine parallel (Gouma-Peterson and Matthews 1987). British art historian, Griselda Pollock, finds that this revisionist approach creates a competition between men and women that women artists cannot win. Pollack notes that "as early as 1971 Linda

Nochlin warned us against getting into a no-win game trying to name female Michelangelos" (Pollock 1988, 1).

Pollock proposes a new model, one that unites the recovery of historical data about women producers of art with the deconstruction of the discourses and practices of art history itself.[7] In 1981, Pollock, along with her co-author Rozsika Parker, contemplated a fresh approach to evaluative surveys of art, one that looked at the relationship between women and artistic and social structures, analyzing how women "negotiated their particular position" as artists, rather than trying to identify who was the greater genius (Pollock and Parker 1981, 328). In a much later article, Pollock asks the question: "Can the neglected women artists of the past function for me as a narcissistic ideal? Do I want to set them up as semi-divine heroines?"(Pollock 1996, 17). She finds that she does not and suggests an approach that is not based on biography or formal analysis, but is grounded instead in a careful examination of subject and culture. Neither, she states, is she interested in art historical theory, finding it to be an invention of the "Right" and that, "theories are but one face of what we actually do: practices" (Pollock 1996, 20). She wants the field of art history to be a practice committed to critical self-analysis and to the "necessary tension" between what "the mind invents in the way it thinks and the political effects of the logical structures we produce for representing the concrete, social world and analyzing historically those representations" (Pollock 1996, 21).

American critic Lucy Lippard, emanating from a much different scholarly model, decided early in her career to concentrate on images produced by women: "My own choice has been to spend my time on images of the world *by* women rather than on images *of* women by the world." She does not negate all theoretical approaches to the topic of women and art, but finds that the rejection of the spiritual by some deconstructivists and socialists disturbing (Lippard 1989, 31). She would like to see a middle ground where feminists can come together: "I fear the 100% sensuous, sentimental anti-intellectualism that is the worst of essentialism, and I fear the 100% academized intellectualism that is the worst of postmodernism."[8] Helen Molesworth, a scholar of contemporary art and visual culture, also dislikes the split between the disparate practices of feminism, and she describes the argument as that between essentialism and elitism, between a naive view of the body versus no ability to image the body (Molesworth 1999, 20).

While Pollock, who most would see as representing the elitist point of view, states that she is opposed to theory, her ideas in fact depend very much on an understanding of post-modern structuralism. She is particularly interested in the psychoanalytic interpretations of Freud and the historical proposals of Marx. She believes that an "engagement with the legacy in the tense interaction between Marx, Freud, and Saussure,[9] theorizations of the social, of the historical, of the ideological, of the textural, of the sign, and of the subject, is only a matter of art history moving into its own modernity and out of the nineteenth-century intellectual tradition in which it was initially forged" (Pollock 1996, 21). In her interpretations of works of art she closely follows this premise and does indeed examine works based on their subject, historical context, and their psychological possibilities.

In her well-known essay, "Modernity and the Spaces of Femininity," Pollock discusses the use of space in the works of Mary Cassatt and Berthe Morisot in an effort to determine if the socially contrived orders of sexual difference in the nineteenth century structured the lives of the two artists and if it effected what they produced (Pollock 1988). Here she looks at how women artists of the Impressionist group ignored the cafes, bars, and other public spaces of leisure activity that were open to their male contemporaries, depicting instead the scenes of domesticity accessible to women of their social class. Pollock goes beyond the historical and social context, however, examining the spatial order within paintings as well, determining that manipulating spatial structures was one of the defining features of early modernist paintings. She ascertains that both Cassatt and Morisot used proximity and compression in a way that is not typical of the male artists of the Impressionist group and sees a correspondence between the social space of the represented and the pictorial space of the representation. Pollock concludes that the "spaces of femininity," the scenes depicted by the women artists, operate not only at the level of what is represented, but also as a "positionality in discourse and social practice." In other words, she finds the represented scenes a product of mobility and visibility and concludes that femininity is both the condition and the effect (Pollock 1988, 65–66). What Pollock does is connect the content, form, and context by neatly linking the paintings' compositional constructions to issues of social interaction and gender identification. By doing this, she sets out a model for teaching the various women in art courses, one that incorporates both the particular history of women artists and the new theoretical approaches to examining the way in which social and historical structures impact upon art.

One of the most contentious assertions that was certainly raised by Pollock in regard to art of the nineteenth century is the question of a female aesthetic. Is there such a thing as a uniquely feminine point of view? Do women artists see the world differently in terms of subject matter and/or formal elements? Believing that women have a different view of the world, one that materializes in their subject matter and their visual vocabulary, can be hugely polemical. This is an issue that emerges throughout the "Women in Art" course because, historically, that is exactly what men have said of women's work when discounting it—it is specifically feminine and, therefore, less important. Considering women to have a distinctively feminine view is what made Georgia O'Keeffe deny any sexual imagery (vaginal forms) in her floral paintings.[10] She did not want her work to be seen as "feminine." In 1971, Nochlin contended that there are no common qualities of "femininity," that the styles of women artists generally seem closer to other artists and writers of their own period and outlook than they appear to each other (Nochlin 1971, 24). However, a number of artists and critics connected to the women's movement have asserted that there is a particular female vision.

While Pollock suggests subtle subconscious differences between the art of men and women when looking at the work of the Impressionist artists, many of the first generation of artists of the women's movement searched for overt imagery that specifically connected to the female experience. This exploration for a subject matter that responded to the content of their lives with an aesthetic form connected to the female body was blatant and political. Artists like Judy Chicago and Mirium Shapiro and critics likes Lippard believed that they could recognize female sexual body imagery, called "central core imagery," in art created by women artists (Gouma-Peterson and Matthews 1987, 335).

Today, many artists and critics see this approach to a female sensibility as socially constructed rather than biologically inherent (Gouma-Peterson and Matthews 1987, 335; Lippard 1989, 29). Art historians have looked at the nature of women and creativity and generally moved away from essentialism toward an examination of gender construction, avoiding an analysis of specifically female imagery (Gouma-Peterson and Matthews 1987, 336). Nonetheless, this issue is central to any dialogue on the impact of the women's movement on women artists. Often this interchange takes place in a "Women in Art" course when examining Judy Chicago's archetypal piece, *The Dinner Party*, 1979. In it she wanted to convey a history of women's struggles through the use of gender specific materials—ceramics, china painting, and needlework—and by employing vaginal or "core" imagery (Chicago 1982, 143, 208). Although this work is illustrated in a number of mainstream art history texts, it has never found a permanent home in a museum. Many scholars and critics, like MOMA's Varnedoe, see this work as too specific and narrowly political:

The nature of art is by definition somehow to exceed intention, exceeds the intentions of the artist, exceeds the understanding of its immediate context and has a life beyond it, and I find *The Dinner Party* more like agit-prop, that it's a text based art. It's out to prove a didactic point. It's an element to be used in a political struggle. (Varnedoe 1999)

Varnedoe is not alone in his negative opinion of art connected to political struggle, at least in terms of a literal feminist political view.[11] Johanna Drucker, a writer of visual poetry and critic of contemporary art, believes that it is better to achieve a position of maximum freedom of aesthetic expression rather than putting one's aesthetics at the service of an agenda (Drucker 1999, 14). For her the goal of feminism is to include work that does not have overt feminist agendas but that has the capacity to challenge received ideas, thereby becoming implicitly rather than overtly feminist.

Her feelings represent the current, younger generation of artists and writers. Faith Wilding, an interdisciplinary artist and writer, also believes that "feminist ideals can be perpetuated without writing about or representing women, gendered practice, or gendered identity" (Wilding 1999, 28). This is an opinion shared by many women artists whose work might be considered feminist. They are apprehensive of falling into didactic categories and eschew the term "feminist" (Pollack 2001, 134). New York based artist Kim Sooja states that "Feminism is part of my nature as a woman artist, but I never wanted this to be my only intention."[12]

When University of California art historian Amelia Jones organized the exhibition "Sexual Politics: Judy Chicago's Dinner Party in Feminist Art History" for UCLA/Armand Hammer Museum of Art in 1996, she encountered a tremendous amount of hostility from some segments of the feminist community, raising the specter again of the two opposing views of feminist theory. She came to the conclusion that the most interesting thinking in feminism and art today is being done through art practice rather than through art history and theory. Tremendously disappointed with the reception of the show, she deemed that as art historians and feminist scholars we have theorized ourselves out on a limb and don't know where to go next. For Jones, contemporary artists were exploring ideas about gender and identity in ways that were much more interesting and vital than were scholars (Jones 1999, 18).

Students of the "Women in Art" course are largely art and art history majors, those very audiences addressed by Jones, though in the beginning of their chosen professions.[13] Their response to feminist issues is interesting and perhaps upsetting to older feminists. They have grown up with feminism and have internalized many of its lessons, but they don't know its history. Artist and teacher Emma Amos believes that every first-year class needs to learn about just how recently women have entered the mainstream (Amos 1999, 9). Drucker is troubled by the historical amnesia of her students with regard to political background. While she finds that they have tremendous self-confidence and can assert their gendered, gay, ethnic, or otherwise once-marginalized identities, they also need to be pushed to think beyond their own individualities (Drucker 1999, 15). Jones sees the same kind of problem, "the obviousness of feminist argument to younger generations of women and men coexists with their complete ignorance about the history and subtleties of feminist arguments about visual culture. She states that "feminism is at the same time both naturalized into popular culture and invisible" (Jones 1999, 18). Wilding agrees, concluding that there is still a great deal of work to do in terms of raising gender consciousness (Wilding 1999, 29).

My own experience teaching this course supports these conclusions. Almost all of my students are female studio or art history majors who have taken the general art history survey before enrolling in the "Women in Art" course offered at our university. Occasionally, students who have not had an art history survey but who are well versed in feminist ideology, though not always its history, come over from the women's studies program. For the most part, all of the students are unfamiliar with any women artists beyond Mary Cassatt and Georgia O'Keeffe. They have little knowledge of the history of the women's movement, but most all the students feel that they have equal rights and can operate as independently thinking artists, unhampered by sexism.[14] Most do not consider themselves feminists.[15] My course is an elective, and it does not fulfill a general education university requirement. Students still elect to take it, and it almost always fills to capacity. However, in a class of forty-five, there may be only one or two young men who choose to take it, generally because it is the only class that fits their schedules, not because of any interest in the topic or desire for personal growth.[16] Student evaluations at the end of the semester demonstrate that for many of the students the course is a turning point in their lives. They are excited about learning all of the new artists and their works and often they express anger that this work was not introduced to them before in their survey classes. Still, they remain uncomfortable with any personal identification with the term "feminist." They are also motivated to look more closely at visual images and to decode them in ways that never occurred to them before taking the class. This, too, fascinates them as they are used to accepting visual imagery for its superficial content.

I teach the course very much as a composite of the various approaches discussed above. As such, it is both an examination of images made by women artists throughout history and a deconstruction of images of women by male and female artists, as well as an examination of work from various theoretical points of view, using many of the avenues open to post-modern scholars. While we do move through images in a chronological fashion, for example, beginning with *The Woman of Willendorf* and ending with the nudes of Jenny Saville, throughout the course we examine the period and the individual images using a number of different approaches and theories. I teach three related courses, "Modern Art," "Visual Culture" and "African-American Art" as well and find that the four classes intersect in ways that inform each other.

My own teaching has been tremendously affected by my study of visual culture. I do incorporate work by women and artists of color into my Modern survey, and I do help students learn to decode the visual images that they see, very conscious in a post-modern way of the distortion of my own decoding. In a perfect world more than a few token images by women artists and artists of color would be mainstreamed into the standard survey courses. But, it is not a perfect world. Faith Wilding has written: "Going far beyond instituting sexual anti-discrimination rules, teaching girls to use power tools, or mentioning a few women artists in art history courses, feminism still calls for nothing short of a complete overhaul and restructuring of the obsolete sexist and racist educational systems still in place everywhere" (Wilding 1999, 29). I believe that in the last thirty years we have taken those first steps towards this overhaul and that the "Women in Art" course represents but one of the early phases in the process of that restructuring.

NOTES

1. In a post-modern world, hierarchies have been demolished thus encouraging a move away from absolutes and universal rules in art. If there is no good or bad art, then one is able to study art that is not considered the work of genius and that has not traditionally entered the art history lexicon. This previously considered "lesser" art has become worthy of study despite the fact that it has not entered museum collections until quite recently, if at all.

2. "Careers" is the publication sent out to members by the College Art Association in which prospective academic jobs in the arts are listed. It is published about four times per year. Most advertisements call for specialists in Ancient Art, Medieval Art, Renaissance Art, Baroque Art, etc. Currently, Asian Art is a "hot" field, and in recent years one can find a call for individuals who can also teach histories of film and/or photography as well as art of the African Diaspora or Women's Studies.

3. The key texts of this course are usually H. Harvard Arneson's *History of Modern Art: Painting, Sculpture, Architecture and Photography* or Sam Hunter, Daniel Wheeler, John M. Jacobus's *Modern Art: Painting, Sculpture, Architecture.* They each contain only a small percentage of images by women artists. Once one moves to a post-1940 text like Jonathan Fineberg's *Art Since 1940: Strategies of Being,* the percentage number of women artists increases, supporting Kirk Varnedoe's contentions about the role that women artists have played in twentieth century art made in *Women Artists: The Other Side of the Picture,* Princeton, N.J.: Films for the Humanities and Sciences, 1999, videocassette.

4. Interview with Kirk Varnedoe in *Women Artists: The Other Side of the Picture,* 1999, videocassette. Varnedoe does state in this film that once the renovation and additional space to MOMA is completed, he expects to include more women in the collection of post-1960 work. But he is not going to rewrite early twentieth century art, and he believes that it is false to look for correct balances and artificial percentages of work by women artists. He also points out that the art world is tough for all artists, male and female. He finds that "good will and virtue" should not necessarily be rewarded. In other words, artists and their works should be rewarded by entry into the collection because they make significant contributions, but not because they are earnest or work hard or because including their work balances some ideal proportion of male/female artists.

5. Interview with Linda Nochlin in *Women Artists: The Other Side of the Picture,* 1999, videocassette.

6. Essay by Susan Bee included in Schor, 1999.

7. See Pollock 1988, 55. Pollack is grounded in a Marxist point of view and thus sees women artists as workers, as producers of art. The word "discourse" is often found in the critical theory, and it refers to a verbal presentation or dialogue. It is connected to the ideas of the philosopher, Michel Foulcault, who see discourse as a loosely assembled set of features that define commonly held assumptions that are specific to the viewer or reader rather than universal, thus preventing the idea of absolute truths. It is a post-modern concept that pushes us to realize that the old way of looking at art as a series of absolutes of good and bad is no longer relevant or even possible (Homer 1999, 120–121).

8. See Lippard 1989, 32, 34. Essentialism refers to the belief by a group of feminist women artists that there is an essential core imagery particular to the female

gender. Lippard wrote this article in 1987, and in 1989 when it was published, she added a postscript, finding that the dialogue between the two sides had progressed in the interim.

9. Fernande de Saussure was a Swiss linguist whose ideas have strongly impacted upon art historical theory and criticism, especially feminist criticism. Saussure's system is called *semiology*. He believes that language, in this case visual language, is a system of signs and that meaning results from the relationships between these signs.

10. O'Keeffe did not like the personal nature of the art reviews of her early floral images, which characterized them as the highly emotional expression of a sexually obsessed woman and as a revelation of female sexuality. In response, she created a series of images of New York City skyscrapers, a subject considered by Alfred Stieglitz, her husband and dealer, and the other artists of his circle, as inappropriate for a woman. New York was probably seen as a man's subject because of the phallic form of the buildings and because of the feeling that men should control civic space (Lynes 1992, 43; Chave 1992, 74; Peters 1991, 277).

11. MOMA certainly owns work by a number of the Mexican artists, like Diego Rivera for instance, whose images are directly connected to the political struggles of the peasants of Mexico. I venture that Varnedoe would argue that Rivera's work transcends its specific political statement while Chicago's does not.

12. See Barbara Pollack 2001, 134.

13. The make-up of the student population for this course seems to vary depending upon whether or not it fulfills some sort of requirement. At Towson University, it is an elective course that attracts a specific audience of women in the arts.

14. Most of my students are white and also believe that there is little racism left in the world today.

15. Towson University is a suburban campus just outside the borders of the city of Baltimore, which primarily serves students from suburban high schools. Consequently, students are perhaps more conservative than those found on big city campuses.

16. This is actually a concern to me, though I recognize that not all professors consider it a problem when few, if any, men take women's studies classes. Should these courses be exclusively directed toward women? I don't believe so.

Radical Learning: A New Vision of Feminist Pedagogy

Peggy Douglas

INTRODUCTION: GETTING PAST THE "F" WORD

First of all I must say I'm a feminist.[1] It is obligatory. I resent having to do it, but it is mandatory. It is a required preface for the context of my work to be accepted as good or bad. That I must qualify myself before I speak seems absurd in this day and age. That I must state publicly that my pedagogy is not mainstream brings up all sorts of questions that, alas, I must address before getting to the content of my ideology. Sometimes, pondering why we have to ask certain questions is more profound than the answers themselves, even though part of me just wants to get on with it. Why must I first say that I'm a feminist? I suppose it's because my pedagogical frame of reference is nonconforming. Not only is it abnormal (meaning out of the norm), it is considered by many of my more traditional colleagues to be substandard. Some would even say feminist critical thought is illegitimate. So again, I ask myself, why must I engage in self-discrimination?

I'm not the only woman who has struggled with the question of why "gender matters." In her book, *A Room of One's Own*, Virginia Woolf questions herself in the process of creating the fictional character, Mary Carmichael, her archetype for the feminist writer. We as feminist writers chastise ourselves for our preoccupation with our gender and for our painful compulsion to identify ourselves again and again. As Simone De Beauvoir revealed in *The Second Sex*:

First of all, I must say I'm a woman. A man never begins by defining himself as an individual of a certain sex; it goes without saying that he is a man. On the contrary, women have never constituted a closed and independent society; they form an integral part of a group, which is governed by males and in which they have a subordinate place. (De Beauvoir 1963, 562)

That explains it, I thought as I read *The Second Sex*. The male experience has been traditionally written about and accepted by society as being the norm or representative of all "mankind." Thus when a woman speaks of the human experience, she must state explicitly that her frame of reference comes from the margin or outside of what is perceived to be standard reality. I must begin by saying I'm a feminist just so we can get beyond it. I have found that when I do not explicitly identify myself as coming from a feminist perspective that my work is automatically discounted by patriarchal standards to be deficient. This phenomenon slapped me with cold reality when I was working on my doctoral dissertation in the late eighties. I was defending my thesis proposal to my committee members, specifically my design to survey residents of a rural county as a means of estimating the social costs of siting a solid waste landfill on a ridge above the community water supply. "Social costs, what kind of nonsense is that!" exclaimed the head of the economics department.

I remember that pivotal moment when I almost capitulated and apologized for my silly notions. However, the "warrior woman" in me emerged just in time to reply in which I told Professor Anderson that a new methodology has been developed in the field of environmental economics allowing the researcher to obtain non-market (intrinsic) values of clean air, water, and other natural amenities through the use of a contingent valuation survey. Two other of my committee members jumped on the bandwagon and objected to the "non-scientific" approach, stating that I would only derive the "perceived" social costs of the dump rather than the "actual" costs.

I argued that their perception is their reality. "Nonsense," they responded. They then told me that the market is the only true indicator of a person or object's real worth. Human emotions and subjective values have no place in determining public policy. Fortunately, my major professor saved me by interjecting that I am a feminist and that I have a different way of looking at the world. I never asked exactly what he meant by his reference to my "difference." His remark solved the problem by evoking the F-word, and I decided to accept my good fortune without question. The two dissenting committee members resigned. Their replacements acquiesced to the idea that non-market values should be included in the cost-benefit analysis of putting a dump on top of the major water source in a rural community.

Feminist (Value-Laden) Research

I realized later that the professors who resigned from my dissertation committee were programmed to reject my idea of including human values and beliefs in public policy decision-making. In their minds, research and public policy should be value-free, and I was boldly proposing to break a time-honored patriarchal commandment. They had no choice but to resign or accept a method of research that is qualitative and value-laden—a methodology that been condemned by traditional academic scholars as lacking in rigor and reliability.

On the contrary, feminist research can never be objective and value-free. Women scholars such as Dueli-Klein (1983) insist that teaching and research should employ the radical notion of including intuition, emotions, and feelings in teaching pedagogy and scientific research methodology.[2] Not only is feminist research value-laden, but it also has a political agenda. By its very nature, it explores the human experience in a way that questions a patriarchal society characterized by gender, class, racial, and other forms of human oppression. As Kathleen Weiler points out in *Women Teaching for Change: Gender, Class and Power,* the pedagogy and methodology of feminism takes a side that is contrary because it does not insist that objective criterion serve as the "ultimate test for rigorous research," but whether such research results in the transformation of the individual and progressive social change (Weiler 1987).

Feminism and Teaching

Since the eighties, a great deal of progress has been made in the academic acceptance of feminist research. Contingent valuation methodology is considered mainstream, and value-laden research has been validated in scholarly journals. In addition to broadening the scope of research methods, feminist academicians in the last two decades also brought about changes in educational curriculum and content. Courses and programs have been created to address women's history, psychology, art, literature, and multicultural disciplines. However, progress in diversifying the curriculum has been both slow and painstaking. Consider the following case in point. When I took English literature in 1970, I had a progressive professor who started the class by apologizing for the content of the course. She explained that she was constrained by departmental policy that required her to teach the canonical writers such as Theodore Dreiser, John Cheever, and John Updike to the exclusion of women, people of color, and writers from different class and ethnic backgrounds. As I listened to her confession, I was thunderstruck. The notion that I was being exposed exclusively to white, male, middle-to-upper class thinking was unsettling, to say the least. Hearing my professor name such a deliberate omission in my education made me feel ignorant. The thought that I was purposely miseducated made me livid!

Fortunately, Professor Smith (Gloria, as she told us to call her) assigned some reading material that was not included on the syllabus. Excerpts from Zora Neale Hurston, Virginia Woolf, and Langston Hughes let me know that my education could not be fully realized in college classrooms. Gloria had primed a thirst for knowledge within me. My radical education had begun. Because of the bold and self-sacrificing actions of feminist teachers like Gloria, English literature and other required courses had been multiculturalized. Furthermore, entire academic programs have been developed to study the history, language, art, and literature of traditionally marginalized groups of people. Gloria, however, was denied tenure because of her "unprofessional" teaching methods.

Parity at Last

Some critics now argue that feminism is no longer relevant. Some argue that women have reached parity with men in higher education. An anecdote that bears witness to this attitude involved a faculty senate meeting several years ago at the college where I taught. We were facing severe budget cuts when the president of the faculty senate made the suggestion that the women's studies program be discontinued. He stated that it was unfair that there should be a women's studies program and no men's studies program—a statement that was confirmed by several other male faculty members in the room. I told myself to bite my tongue even though I wanted to shout that didn't these tenured dinosaurs realize that every other program in the college is, in essence, a men's studies program. Fortunately, I remembered something Gloria told me almost thirty years ago. Sometimes educating an uninterested audience is not worth the effort, especially considering the payoff. So rather than engage in theoretical discourse, I decided to save my energy for my male students who are more open to diversity and pluralism.

Several of my women colleagues have had similar encounters with their male counterparts. In addition to anecdotal stories, recent trends in higher education give rise to the need for continued efforts to promote feminist pedagogy and curriculum. Colleges and universities are becoming more technocratic. The promotion of distance learning degrees with no face-to-face contact between teacher and student is increasing in public and private schools. Larger class sizes and more reliance on standardized testing are becoming the norm. Interdisciplinary and multicultural classes are being questioned as insignificant and lacking in rigor. Many faculty advocate the elimination of these programs with a public cry for "the basics" in education. Basics from a male perspective, my cynical side might argue. I not only feel that feminist research and curriculum development are still relevant, I believe that they should be further developed and evaluated. In the eighties, feminism evoked imagery of women's liberation. In the nineties, many feminist scholars questioned these images as being too white, too middle class, and too heterosexual. As a result, feminism was broadened to include all aspects of human liberation. Race, sexuality, ability, spirituality, and other forms of oppression were included in the struggle for pluralism. Feminism now strives to be a symbol for people to understand their history, to redefine themselves, and to become self-determining.

This brief synopsis of feministic thought and accomplishments in higher education leads to the question: "where do we go from here?" My answer begins where the word "radical" enters the definition of my teaching pedagogy, and I expect the word might also require some additional explanation. Thus, in the remainder of this chapter I explain why "radical" is an essential component for a new vision of feminist pedagogy.

WHAT IN THE WORLD IS RADICAL PEDAGOGY?

Pedagogy is more than a style of teaching—it's the art of teaching. And the point is, teaching is an art. Radical teaching pedagogy is grounded in a concept called "popular education," a creative learning process that began in adult literacy programs and community organizing for social change. Traditionally, higher education pedagogy is quite different from radical teaching. Some people say that radical pedagogy has no place in the college classroom. Others, like Professor Ira Shor (whom I discuss later), have been using radical teaching pedagogies in higher education with great success. One of my colleagues recently remarked to me that trying to use a teaching pedagogy in a college classroom that has its roots in civil disobedience is crazy; it might incite rebellious behavior in students. I could only grin. Others also wonder where I get my crazy ideas about how students should learn to think critically about themselves and their place in the world. But, contrary to popular interpretation, radical doesn't mean wild and crazy. Radical comes from the word "root".

I subscribe to radical pedagogy because I want to get at the root of the problem, i.e., the education problem of why students are not learning, not persevering, and not succeeding in becoming self-determining and happy people. My experience leads me to believe the root of the problem is a prevailing educational consciousness that treats students like empty vaults to be filled with knowledge. With this "banking method" of education, information is deposited into the students and withdrawn at exam time. There is no two-way dialogue, no opportunities for critical thinking, and no transformation of the student.

Contemporary education is narrative. The narrator (teacher) leads students to mechanically memorize content. The more completely the teacher fills the empty vaults, the better teacher she is. The more passively the students permit themselves to be filled, the better students they become. Therein lies the problem. Students are not taught how to think. They are not taught to critically question norms, values, and beliefs. They are not given the motivation and skills to solve life struggles and transform their lives. I've been teaching freshman students since 1993. Much to my chagrin, I realize that students coming out of high school, as well as non-traditional students, enter the college classroom as passive learners expecting to be enlightened by an expert. If you doubt this fact, begin a freshman class by telling students that you believe they are the best teachers in their own lives. Challenge them to identify what they want to learn about themselves and take note of the silence that transpires. This phenomenon strikes me as not only tragic, but also horribly oppressive. It reminds me of my former organizing work with poor Appalachian communities characterized by a deep sense of self-doubt and hopelessness.

Maybe my angst over teaching in the current educational system is the result of my twenty-year history as a social activist and community organizer whose purpose in life is to help people (including myself) become self-determining. I want to be a consciousness raiser, not a consciousness-maker. Consciousness-making would mean that through my role as a teacher I make students conscious of their ignorance; I impose on them my norms and values; I project my reality onto them; and I manipulate them into looking at life from my beliefs and convictions. Consciousness-making education also means that I don't have confidence in my students; I see them as objects, not as intelligent human beings in their own right; and that I don't understand and accept their reality. It also means that I will only reward them if they obey my rules and accept my ideas and concepts. If I teach how conventional educators expect me to teach, there will be no space for students to discuss their own ideas, set their own boundaries, develop their own solutions, and make transformative decisions. In response, I say *NO, I am a consciousness-raiser.* I must take a radical stand and address the root of the problem. I am convinced that students need a learning experience that is liberatory and transformative. An authoritarian teaching approach is not appropriate for this goal. As an alternative, I adopted a problem-posing pedagogy and developed a college-level radical learning course.

A RADICAL LEARNING CLASS

The content of my radical learning class emanates from the life situations and reality of the participants. Their life struggles are the basis for the curriculum. The problem-posing pedagogy shows students that they have the right and the responsibility to question the causes and influences on their identity, to develop their own values and beliefs, and to take positive steps to improve their lives. I want them to question me, their teacher, and take responsibility for co-designing and directing the content of the course.

I use three techniques to facilitate the radical learning process in my classroom: creative writing, experiential exercises, and horizontal dialogue. Readings are used as a motivational story-telling tool for students to write and tell their own stories. Horizontal dialogue means that the roles of the teacher and student are interchangeable. I learn as much from the students as they learn from me.

I had to write my own radical learning textbook because one didn't exist. It was designed both as an instructor's manual and a student workbook.

There are no secrets or hidden agendas kept from students as to the theories and methods behind the content. No confidential lesson plans or test banks are given to other instructors. And instructors are expected to be co-learners in classroom exercises and activities. The goal of the radical learning class is for the teacher and students to discover reality together, to liberate each other from false myths and oppressive ideas, and to evolve as individuals and community-members. This goal is achieved through a commitment to rigor, not in the conventional educational sense that is inflexible and permanent.

With radical pedagogy, rigor involves uncertainty. For many educators, walking into a classroom without a preset agenda is frightening; some may even say too loose to be academically rigorous. Others, like renowned educators Ira Shor and Paulo Freire, define academic rigor as "a desire to know, a search for an answer, a critical method of learning" (Shor and Friere 1986). Rigor is also a form of communication that challenges participants to express their true identity, honor differences, and form democratic communities. It is subjective. It is value-laden. It is feminist.

Fundamentals of Radical Feminist Pedagogy

Every summer, I instruct teachers how to incorporate radical feminist pedagogy in the academic classroom. I personally have no list of do's and don'ts. We learn to teach by engaging in a weeklong mock classroom environment. Our experience as students in a radical learning class forces us to develop a more dialogic, multicultural, student-centered approach to teaching. In addition, the process of becoming radical forces us to examine personal issues that block our ability to be creative and effective communicators.

In these workshops, I have been asked to list the ABC's of Radical Feminist Pedagogy, but I just can't do it. It would go against the grain of the pedagogy to give another person "my" answer. So, I compromise and tell stories about my favorite radical feminist teachers. I offer the same to my readers, noting for the record that three of my favorite mentors are male—a fact, which surprised even me when I was in my semi-final analysis of deliberation.

MENTOR ONE: JOLENE THE UNION QUEEN

My first vision for developing a radical teaching pedagogy came from a profound experience that I had with a union organizer named Jolene. For decades, she had been helping Appalachian coal miners unite against unsafe working conditions. For her dedication, hard work, and compassion for the working poor, she had gained the respect of many Appalachian communities. The mine owners didn't exactly love her, but they sure did listen up and take notice when Jolene came around.

One Saturday morning in 1989, Jolene called to invite me to a town meeting in Logan County, West Virginia, a community that was being environmentally blackmailed by a hazardous waste company. I had just finished my Ph.D. in environmental economics and rural sociology, and my doctoral dissertation focused on the social effects of hazardous waste dumps. Jolene wanted me to be available to provide the townspeople with any technical assistance they needed to solve their problem. I jumped at the opportunity to watch Jolene the Union Queen in action.

On the drive from Knoxville to Logan County, Jolene briefed me on the facts. The County was full of towns whose economies were built by coal mining companies. The companies had depleted the coal resources several years prior to our meeting. When the coal was gone they took their operations elsewhere, leaving behind a scarred, polluted valley and a number of out-of-work miners who were suffering from black lung disease. The town officials had tried unsuccessfully to attract other industries, but no businesses were interested in inheriting the environmental problems left by the coal barons.

Finally, a large hazardous waste corporation approached the town with a promise to provide plenty of jobs, as well as funding for new schools and recreation centers. Having been out-of-work for such a long period of time, many of the citizens were anxious to welcome the company and all it had to offer. Just as many folks were concerned because the corporation had a reputation for creating environmental disasters. The deal was on the table. The waste management company wanted to inject hazardous waste into the old mine shafts. Company officials claimed they would take measures to contain the waste so that no pollution would occur.

From my doctoral research, I knew that the company's claim was bogus. Injecting hazardous waste into the karst terrain of the Appalachian Mountains was like putting heroin in a vein. It wouldn't take long before all the groundwater in Logan County was full of toxic chemicals. I was outraged. I screamed that we have to stop the company and its environmental blackmail.

Jolene told me to hold on, that we are not doing anything of the kind because this is their problem and they have to be the ones who come up with the solution. I replied that this isn't funny and that we can't let the town be blackmailed. Jolene responded to me by telling me that I didn't know much about community organizing and that my job was to be a resource, an educator, but not the know-it-all expert. I then told her that I thought educators were experts. Jolene told me that that's where I was wrong and that I've obviously been dumbed down by all my prestigious education.

I was a little offended, but nevertheless, intrigued. Jolene was considered to be the best organizer in the business, so I decided to listen to what she had to say. She explained that education that empowers people to transform their lives is, unfortunately, quite different from public education. Then she educated me on how the system that had schooled me for twenty-one years dumbed people down. I felt ignorant. Jolene went on to say that popular education or "education by the people not for the people" created long-lasting personal and social change. The first step in solving a problem is for the affected people to name it. An outsider (educator) can't do this for them. She went on to teach me that the role of the outsider (educator) is to provide the insiders (students) with resources and support to solve their own problems. I didn't really understand what she meant, so she told me just sit quietly when we got there and watch.

The memory of the meeting is branded in my brain. We arrived at the meeting early. I sat peacefully, but with dismay as I watched people come in pulling their oxygen tanks that fed life to their damaged lungs. Many of the people who were dying from exposure to toxic work environments of the coalmines wanted to accept the hazardous waste company's offer. They felt they had no choice. They were proud people who hated living off of government assistance. They wanted jobs, any job, at any costs.

Other folks wanted to hold out for clean industries. They knew that once the hazardous waste company moved in, Logan County could abandon any hopes of recruiting environmentally-friendly businesses. The lines were drawn, and the debate became heated. At one point the group was so divided and frustrated that someone turned to Jolene and screamed just tell us what to do. I was ready and willing, but Jolene gave me her look and I knew to become invisible. She explained that she didn't know what to do and that this was their community and their problem. She told them that she trusted that if they keep discussing the issue and coming up with ideas, they would arrive at the best solution for their community; they were the experts since it was their problem. Finally popular education was starting to make sense to me.

The group continued to debate the issue and develop alternative solutions. By two o'clock in the morning, a consensus still had not been reached. In fact, the situation was getting more contentious by the minute. The biggest guy in the room was so aggravated that he finally jumped up and put his fist right in front of Jolene's face and told her to tell them what to do or get the hell out. I wanted to tell them all to hold out for clean industries. My head was screaming for them not to let themselves be blackmailed by sleaze-balls, but Jolene gave me "the look." I was frustrated but remained silent while Jolene remained calm. She looked the guy square in the eye and said to him that she would leave if this were the consensus of the group, but that she would also stay as long as it took them to reach a group decision.

Thankfully, the group calmed and finally arrived at an agreement. Its not the outcome that stands out in my mind, but the process. What had a momentous effect on me was Jolene's commitment to the principles of true education—a belief in the inherent wisdom of all people; a resolve that the educator's role is to empower people to name and solve their own problems; and a trust that given the proper support, people can transform their lives. I decided I would use Jolene's principles when I started teaching college that same year. Fifteen years hence, I'm still convinced that Jolene's philosophy of education holds true.

MENTOR TWO: MYLES HORTON

Another extraordinary educator that embodied the core values of radical education was Myles Horton, who founded the Highlander Folk School in 1932 to help working class people in some of Appalachia's poorest counties become self-reliant. In the preface to Horton's autobiography, *The Long Haul: An Autobiography,* Bill Moyers had this to say about the radical educator:

Myles was beaten up, locked up, put upon, and rallied against by racists, toughs, demagogues, and governors. But for more than fifty years, Horton went on with his special kind of teaching—helping people discover within themselves the courage and ability to confront reality and change it. (Horton et al., 1998, Preface)

Horton was not just about ideology; he was a catalyst who made things happen. Highlander was not only the training ground for labor organizing in Appalachia, it also provided a education center that civil rights activists like Martin Luther King, Rosa Parks, Andrew Young, Julian Bond, and scores of others attended to develop their community leadership skills. One of Highlander's most famous stories is about a young black woman from Montgomery, Alabama whose friend talked her into attending a Highlander workshop in 1955. The workshop was filled with other black and white individuals who were concerned about the growing violence and discrimination against African Americans in the South. This young lady listened respectfully to other people's struggles and plans for creating social change. When it was her turn, she related her own experiences as a black woman living in a white racist town. However, when it came time for her action plan, she humbly admitted that she was a follower and not a leader.

The other people at the workshop wouldn't accept this shy but eloquent woman's humility. They encouraged her to act as a leader and to support others in leading movements for change. After a weekend of radical education, this woman got in touch with her inner strength and will to take action. Within a few weeks, she refused to give up her seat to a white man on a city bus. Rosa Parks was arrested and taken to jail, but her heroism became the catalyst for the Montgomery Bus Boycott and an inspiration for many generations of civil rights activists.

In the 1950s and 1960s, Highlander became one of the primary targets of southern bigotry. The state tried to close it down for being a "communist school." The Klan constantly harassed whites and blacks for gathering together, and the FBI investigated Myles Horton for his subversive ideas. It's interesting that the government believed that Horton's ideas on radical education were threatening to the security of the United States. In his autobiography, Horton explained that the essence of radical education was not about "teaching or techniques," but about loving people first. He also explained that it was about having that belief in people and their ability to learn and to show respect for their own experiences (Horton 1998). Even though Highlander has been raided, shut down, and burned to the ground, it continues to survive and grow with the needs of the people it serves. Today, Highlander has the reputation as the most effective radical education school in the world.

MENTOR THREE: PAULO FREIRE

Paulo Freire was a Brazilian educator who was exiled from his native country for his educational ideas about helping the urban poor overcome their sense of powerlessness so they could make improvements in their lives. In the early 1960s, Freire was responsible for bringing adult literacy programs to thousands of impoverished Brazilians. His literacy programs, also known as popular education, were radical and unorthodox. Rather that teaching just basic reading and writing skills, Freire's popular education schools taught literacy to the poor as a means to enable them to participate in the political process. Through his efforts, the passivity and fatalism of the working poor diminished as they developed the literacy tools and confidence that were required to question their oppressors.

In 1964, the military became threatened by the success of Freire's popular education programs, and they had him thrown in jail for his "subversive activities." During his imprisonment Freire began his work on radical pedagogy. After spending seventy days in jail, Freire was exiled to Chile. Eventually, Freire was recognized throughout the world for his pioneering work in the field of adult education. His most famous book, *Pedagogy of the Oppressed* (1976) is a classic treatise on radical pedagogy. Before his death in 1997, Freire taught and served as a visiting professor at Harvard University and as the Secretary of Education of the World Council of Churches. He eventually returned home where he became the Minister of Education for the City of Sao Paulo. In this position, Freire was responsible for guiding school reform within two-thirds of Brazil's public schools.

Freire's radical teaching pedagogy represents a departure from what he termed *conventional banking education*. The implication of banking education is that students are uneducated and in need of knowledge that can only come from the teacher or expert. In contrast to education where information is deposited in the student, radical education is problem-posing teaching. Radical pedagogy is designed to help students realize that problems may arise as a result of circumstances, but solutions arise as a result people understanding their problems and acting (sometimes collectively) on their own behalf. The role of the educator is that of a facilitator who helps students learn to think critically and creatively. The underlying belief behind Freire's radical pedagogy is that students become empowered to be successful if education values their existing knowledge and experience. The instructor accomplishes this objective by motivating students to define and express their reality, to identify aspects of their life that are problematic, and to work with others on developing practical solutions to their problems. The Freirian Principles of a Radical Teacher can be summarized as follows. First, *believe in the student*. Regardless of the beliefs and behavior of students at any given time, the teacher must hold the belief that each student has the potential to solve her or his own problems. Second, *listen and ask questions; don't give answers*. If a student is struggling with a problem or failing to realize her or his potential, the role of the teacher is to help the student clarify the problem and creatively find solutions. Third, *create a dialogic learning environment*. The teacher should create a safe and supportive dialogic learning environment. The value of a dialogic pedagogy is that students can exchange information in a way that is democratic, multicultural, and community-building. Fourth, *encourage reflection, analysis, and action*. Students must be allowed to reflect on their own experiences, move from reflection to analysis, and move from analysis to individual or collective action.

MENTOR FOUR: IRA SHOR

Ira Shor is an English professor at Staten Island Community College in New York. He has written several books on his experiences in applying radical pedagogy in the college classroom. In the early seventies, Shor began to experiment with "student-centered" teaching. In *Empowering Education: Critical Teachings for Social Change* (1992), Shor recounts a typical first day of the semester when he decided to make a radical shift in his teaching pedagogy for the remedial English course at the City College of New York. It was the day he decided to include the students in designing the syllabus for the course. Shor's account of the students' reaction was typical in that they all sat staring straight ahead in dead silence waiting for him to arrive. Shor proceeded to ask his students to pair up and tell their partner something about themselves so they could introduce one another to the class. When it came time for sharing, no one would cooperate. They were resisting his dialogic pedagogy. When he tried other icebreaker exercises, the class increased their resistance with sneering looks and snide comments. Although Shor admits to becoming impatient, he persisted in his commitment to a radical teaching pedagogy. He decided to pose a question and asked what was going on and why did they not like him without even getting to know him first. Finally, after an uncomfortable period of silence elapsed, one outspoken guy said to Shor "we hate that test." Shor asked the student what test he was referring to. The student told Shor "the writing test we had to take for college." The other students chimed in with comments like "its not fair." The topic of New York State's imposed standardized proficiency exams for entering college freshmen was not in Shor's lesson plan for the first day of class, however, Shor realized that the students' concern was an opportunity for a learning moment and he ran with it. He asked them to tell him what was wrong with the test and why they thought it was unfair. The class responded to his questions. Students were talking so loud and fast the classroom had shifted from no participation to a runaway discussion. They voiced their frustration at having to spend extra time and money on remedial classes that didn't count towards their degree. Shor decided to push their critical thinking skills a little further. He told them that they had a valid point about the proficiency exam, but that yelling and complaining was not enough. He explained to them that they needed to come up with an alternative solution that would make more sense (Shor 1992).

Shor then challenged his students to write two pages about their ideas on the proficiency exam. To his delight, they willingly agreed. He then asked them to read their drafts in groups of three, to discuss their ideas, compare their criticisms, and formulate a group analysis. The group analyses were shared with the class as a whole. Shor then asked the students to take their papers home and rewrite their essays based on the discussions with their classmates. In the ensueing classes, Shor took notes as the students read the second, third, and fourth drafts of their essays. He presented to them again some of the key issues so that each student could reflect on the collective thoughts of the class. By the third week, the class had come up with an alternative policy for the proficiency exam that they thought was more sensible and equitable. Their ideas included three recommendations. First, rather than having a fifty-minute time limit, students should have as long as they need to write the best essay they could. They pointed out that the time limit benefited the proctors not the students. Reflecting on the work they had done in the first three weeks of Shor's class, the students justified their opinion based on the knowledge that a developmental writing process requires time to think over the issues, discuss them with other people, take notes, write drafts, share them with peers, get feedback, do relevant reading, and make revisions. Second, the students thought they should not have required topics, but that they should be free to pick their own themes. Some students may need prompts for topics such as "Does TV make children violent"? Third, the students suggested that the timing of the exam was problematic. It was given in the spring of their senior year when they had "senioritis." They thought the exam should be given in the fall of their senior year while they were still focused on schoolwork (Shor 1992).

Shor was impressed. The student's suggestions made practical sense. As he reflected on their ideas, he had to admit that his students had been unable to pass an apparently simple writing test, but in a student-centered classroom, they were able to critique a long-standing bureaucratic policy and develop viable options. The students also learned that when they are angry about a situation, it's important to reflect on and discuss the problem.

They also realized that anger could be transformed into creative solutions using a democratic problem-solving process. By reflecting critically on the problem, the class developed a response that was not only intellectually astute, but also empowering as individuals and as a group.

CONCLUSION

I'm now faced with trying to make some concluding remarks and realizing that I really have no answers—only questions like the ones that Ira Shor poses to his readers. What kind of learning process can empower students to do their best? How can I promote critical and creative thinking so that students can become effective learners, communicators, and citizens? What are the conditions in schools and society that limit the development of students? How can they be changed? My attempt to conclude this chapter is further hindered by my preoccupation with the historical significance of today, Monday, October 8—the holiday that commemorates Columbus and his "discovery" of America. Memories flood my mind with images of elementary school teachers and their bulletin boards with the hero Columbus and crew on the Nina, Pinta, and Santa Maria. We traced his voyage. We celebrated the landing of Columbus in the new world and his brilliant foreign policy.

I played an Indian girl in the Columbus Day pageant, with feathers pinned to my barrette and a smile plastered on my face that showed my gratitude for the saviors who crossed the ocean to deliver us. The pilgrims brought us presents and religion and promises of a better life. Columbus was our hero. When I was a child I bought this miseducation without question. When I became an adult, a more enlightened teacher gave me the critical questions that were omitted in my formal education: How could Columbus say that he discovered America when the Native Americans were here first? How could Columbus justify kidnapping people and sending them back to Spain? How might these individuals have felt being ripped away from their families, their homes, and their heritage?

Thanks to a story that I remember reading about a radical Columbus Day Tribute, this anniversary is no longer depressing to me. I used to subscribe to a journal called *Radical Teacher*. Unfortunately it went out of business due to a lack of demand. Nevertheless, I have kept every issue. The Winter 1993 Quarterly featured an account of a radical teacher's lesson plan called "Rethinking Columbus," which was designed to commemorate Columbus Day at Jefferson High School in Portland, Oregon in 1992. The following summarizes the story:

When the morning school bell rang, Linda Christensen's students invaded other class-rooms, stealing teachers purses, and other students' pencils, claiming ownership over all bounty they could grab from others. With permission from school officials, Ms. Christensen's students then gave presentations and led discussions that addressed traditionally taboo topics such as racism, imperialism, genocide, and the story of Columbus from a Native American perspective. The point of the radical exercise was to provide more than a critique of unjust foreign policy. The aim of the lesson was to encourage students to listen for and appreciate other voices, especially the voices of those who have been silenced by those in power. Furthermore, students at Jefferson High that day were encouraged to question and analyze the way in which political, social, and economic power influences norms, customs, and historical references.[3]

Critics of radical pedagogy such as the one used in the Columbus lesson argue that such questioning of traditional educational values and archetypes will rob us of our heroes, our historical roots, and our identity as Americans. I must agree with them. Using radical pedagogy, I do seek to redefine history. I want to give my students a chance to choose their heroes. And yes, some might decide that the Mother Theresa or Che Guevarra is more of a historical hero to them than George Washington.

However, the point of radical pedagogy is more than a substitution of heroes; it's aim is to encourage students to imagine alternatives and determine the nature of a society they would like to create and to individually and collectively work towards their goals. Lastly, for those who are frustrated with my endless stories and are still waiting for the ABC's of radical pedagogy, I will acquiesce and give you the definition of a *radical teacher* as defined by Pam Ennas. A radical teacher is one who provides a student-centered rather than a teacher-centered classroom. A radical teacher is also

- One who shares rather than transmits information.
- One who aids in student growth and empowerment by drawing out what is already there and latent.
- One who respects and believes in students.
- One who possesses the capacity to listen well and the self-control not to fill silence with the sound of her/his own voice.
- One who believes that theory and practice are inseparable.
- One who is as concerned about process as about content (and maybe more so).
- One who knows that good intentions are not enough to create a radical teacher.
- One who understands the power of language.
- One who believes in a pluralist, multicultural, and holistic approach to teaching.
- One who allows a safe place for students to name and deal with all forms of prejudices.
- One who demands a lot from students by refusing to accept passive, obedient learning in favor of critical thinking.
- One who does not assume s(he) knows it all.

As I reflect on Pam Ennas' last criterion for a radical teacher, I must humbly submit to the reader that this chapter is merely an account of my continuing story as a student of radical learning. I am not an expert, but a journeyer. I trust that others will find their own path and that our combined efforts will radicalize public education for the benefit of many generations to come.

NOTES

1. Reference is made to the classic line, "First of all I must say I'm a woman." In Simone De Beauvior. 1963. *The Second Sex.* New York: Bantam Books.

2. See page 83, Renate Dueli-Klein. 1983. *Theories About Women's Studies.* London: Routledge and Kegan.

3. *Radical Teacher.* Boston Women's Group, Inc. P.O. Box 169, W. Somerville, MA.

7

Beyond Gender and Heterosexuality: Teaching Virginia Woolf and Jeanette Winterson in an Undergraduate Classroom

Justyna Kostkowska

I have been teaching a "Women and Literature" course for several years. This course is the last of four required English courses and is the finishing touch of the English education for the non-English majors, who are the majority of my students. Mostly, but not exclusively, they are female between nineteen and thirty years old and mostly working, paying their own way through college.

A feminist and a Woolf scholar, I have focused the course around the issues of gender, sexuality, and their impact on our lives that Woolf raises in *Room of One's Own*. The course covers over two hundred years of literature by women, starting with Wollstonecraft's *Vindication of the Rights of Woman,* and ending with Alice Walker, Toni Morrison, and Jeanette Winterson's *Written on the Body*. Over the years, I occasionally had a student come to share the impact the class had on him or her. They would tell me how the class was "surprisingly interesting for a required class" or that it was "fun . . . easy to engage in . . . close to their experience." But it is only recently that I heard a comment that made me realize how important this course may potentially be in my students' experience. The comment came from one of my best students, a considerate and intelligent reader, and one of those students we rely on to start a class discussion. One day she came to class and said: "I've been reading this last novel and it made my face so red my mother asked me what I was reading and it made her face red, too."

No, I was not teaching a pornographic novel. The text that generated this response was Winterson's *Written on the Body*. My student's comment reminded me of something I have grown to forget, lulled by the progress and prevalence of feminism in general, and feminist pedagogy and criticism in particular. It reminded me of the educator's responsibility of constant eye-opening, of provoking self-exploration, thinking out of the boxes of gender and sexuality, of building individuality, diversity, and tolerance of difference. It confirmed the importance of texts such as *Room of One's Own, Mrs. Dalloway,* and *Written on the Body*—texts that challenge gender and sexual stereotypes. From then on, I have been on a quest to make my students blush. What is it about those three texts that contain the precious "shock" value for our students?

A ROOM OF ONE'S OWN: "AM I PART MALE, PART FEMALE?"

Examining the history of women's writing in *Room of One's Own*, Woolf ponders what seems to be a question very deeply rooted in gender difference: "What does one need to be a successful writer, and why have so few women, compared to men, become writers through history?" Her investigation leads her back to one basic reason—poverty. She concludes that to be a writer one absolutely needs two things, which are money and a room of one's own. But Woolf also points out that what has hampered women as much as their social status as nurturers without any personal rights, such as owning property, are the rigid standards of morality that have required women to be chaste, virgin, and unknown—therefore respectable. The requirement for chastity and respectability stifles creativity and makes the woman writer pre-censor self-expression. According to Woolf:

That woman . . . who was born with the gift of poetry in the sixteenth century, was an unhappy woman, a woman at strife against herself. All the conditions of her life, all her own instincts were hostile to the state of mind which is needed to set free whatever is in the brain. (1957, 52)

Given these handicaps, Woolf says it is important for women to assert themselves, to "write like a woman" and to create a sentence that is a "woman's sentence" (1957, 95, 80). At the same time, she realizes how much a writer would benefit from the other gender's perspective when she writes that "perhaps to think . . . of one sex as distinct from another is an effort . . . it interferes with the unity of the mind" (1957, 100). She continues "but there may be some state of mind in which one could continue without effort because nothing is required to be held back" (1957, 101). Then she moves to pose her famous definition of an androgynous mind:

In each of us two powers preside, one male, one female . . . the normal and comfortable state of being is that when the two live in harmony together, spiritually cooperating. If one is a man, still the woman part of the brain must have effect; and a woman also must have intercourse with the man in her. . . . Perhaps a mind that is fully masculine cannot create, any more than a mind that is purely feminine. (1957, 102)

Woolf's way of thinking raises a set of questions that deal with self-definition. She starts out with the familiar in which everyone is either a man or a woman; where women have historically been disadvantaged, they need to assert themselves and their rights. This is the feminist argument that most of my students have learned to understand and support. Put in Woolf's elegant and witty language, it does not threaten anyone's identity. But her androgynous proposition does. Why is that? It is because she is asking us to step out of our gender identity, all male or all female, and allow a part of "the other" in. She challenges men to find in themselves the woman and for women to find the voice that is male. She encourages us all to be what Glen McClish calls "androgynous communicators":

With Woolf's help, the androgynous communicator can be seen not merely as a man or woman alternatively choosing strategies from the male and female repertoires, but as a person who transcends such binary oppositions altogether in the pursuit of a more profound mode of communication—and gender equality." (McClish 1995, 61)

Put more crudely, Woolf's text encourages us to be open to the possibility that we are not wholly and completely male or female, that it is not only "ok" to act out of the gender role we were socialized into, but it is a prerequisite to being creative. As McClish puts it, "Woolf creates transcendent spaces that empower men and women to imagine and produce the richest literature [and, I would add, lives] possible" (1995, 57). Asking such questions as "what would I be like if I were a man/woman? Would I be that much of a different person? What has made me believe that I should only think and act as a man/woman? What would happen if I allowed the male/female side of me to speak out?, starts the self-exploration and an awareness of the limitations we often willingly accept with our gender identity.

MRS. DALLOWAY: "WAS SHE A LESBIAN?"

Mrs. Dalloway is a book my students complain about. It is not "reader friendly." It does not lend itself to being put down to make a cup of coffee. If you do so, you find yourself leafing back to "hook" back into it. It trains its readers to slow down and patiently go with its flow, the flow of a thinking mind. I tell my students to let it take them, to not try and force it to yield information that they want because what they want may not prove as important as what they ignore. The novel speaks indirectly, metaphorically, about what critics have called "a lesbian suicide," about a woman in her fifties who has lived her entire life in the prison of social expectations because security and conformity became her core values. But my students do not read feminist criticism. They tell me that Clarissa marries a successful politician because he offers her a luxurious house and no "danger" of intimate sharing. It is clear to her that she must reject her two soul mates. The first, Peter, because he demands intimacy that she says would "destroy" her and the second, Sally, because she flourishes on rebelliousness, non-conformity, individualism, and sexuality. In short, its all that Clarissa has to suppress to have the life she thinks she wants. Thirty years later, we meet the lonely, introspective Clarissa, and feel free to judge her. It is easy for my students to see that she is unhappy. They see through the front she puts up as she tries to convince herself that she made the right decision. They are also quick to attribute her unhappiness to her choice of husband; had she married the one she loved, she would not be lonely, they say. It's her fault, they determine. This is the time to ask if it is her fault entirely. What makes Clarissa so determined to have a husband with money? How does her gender limit her options? What options does she have after she finds herself unhappy with the "respectable" Richard? Can she divorce him? What would she do if she did? In this way we get to our focus, which is how gender consciousness limits and regulates individuals and their life choices. Why are women putting security over a fulfilling partnership? Why is intimacy such a low priority, even a threat?

It is interesting that Clarissa's sexuality almost never gets any attention from the class. References to her "narrow bed" (1981, 31) and her nun's quarters in the attic are read in the context of Clarissa's mysterious illness and her aging. She is simply not perceived as a sexual being. Part of that reading is justified in the way Woolf creates her character. Clarissa is mainly a thinker, not an action heroine. She is introspective, analytical, pondering. But she feels very strongly and has a great passion for life, a dedication to live every moment to the fullest. She thinks:

In people's eyes, in the swing, tramp, and trudge; in the bellow and the uproar; the carriages, motor cars, omnibuses, vans, sandwich men shuffling and swinging; brass bands, barrell organs, in the triumph and the jungle and the strange high singing of some airplane overhead was what she loved; life; London; this moment in June. (Woolf 1981, 4)

A character so passionate about life surely must be equally passionate in love. But still we dismiss Clarissa as a sexual individual for reasons, this time, independent of Woolf's intention, if not directly contradictory to it. The problem lies in the fact that because Clarissa's passion is not directed towards either of the men in her life, we simply assume that it does not exist at all. One of the most puzzling things about my students' reception of the novel is their almost total ignorance of the nature of Clarissa's relationship with Sally. After all, the most sexually charged scene of the entire novel is the memory of Sally's kiss (1981, 32). Clarissa thinks about it on several occasions, remembering how happy she was around Sally " . . . the charm was overpowering, to her at least, so that she could remember standing in her bedroom at the top of the house holding a hot-water can in her hands and saying aloud, 'She is beneath this roof. . . . She is beneath this roof' " (1981, 34). And again:

She could remember going cold with excitement, and doing her hair in a kind of ecstasy . . . and feeling . . . 'if it were now to die 'twere now to be most happy.' That was her feeling—Othello's feeling, and she felt it, she was convinced, as strongly as Shakespeare meant Othello to feel it, all because she was coming down to dinner in a white frock to meet Sally Seton! (Woolf 1981, 35)

How do we get programmed to ignore the significance of that memory and subordinate its importance to Clarissa's heterosexual life? The reason is a simple and pervasive denial of difference. We would take any opportunity not to acknowledge the existence of "alternative" sexualities. Yes, progress has been made to integrate alternative sexuality into the mainstream culture. But why is it that despite the presence of homosexual characters on every television sitcom, my students still do not see Clarissa's suppressed homosexuality, and do not simply ask, was she a lesbian?

From my students I hear "could it be that she was . . . (the unspoken "l" word) no, they were just friends." And "they were teenagers—the 'close girlfriends' phase." I ask them why they think so and why we undervalue the significance of that kiss? I ask them if it is because we judge a relationship between two women as less important because it could not lead to marriage or family? Why do you think women were not able to build a life with the women they loved? We are back to the gender limitations, but I press the sexuality issue with another passage from Clarissa's thoughts "Miss Kilman has become one of those spectres with which one battles in the night; one of those spectres who stand astride us and suck up half of our life-blood, dominators and tyrants; for no doubt with another throw of the dice . . . [Clarissa] would have loved Miss Kilman. But not in this world. No" (1981, 12).

There are many ways to read this passage, but intolerance of sexual difference is one. How many people still feel this way almost a century later? Why is a homosexual lifestyle still so much harder to live freely than the heterosexual norm? We end the discussion agreeing that the problem starts with our blindness, our ignorance of difference; that our first instinct is still to make the assumption of uniformity, similarity with the majority rather than individuality. Embracing difference is not yet our comfort zone.

WRITTEN ON THE BODY: "COULD IT BE THAT I AM A LESBIAN?"

Of all the three texts, Winterson's novel is perhaps the most overtly shocking. What we could have overlooked or underestimated in Woolf because of the distance between her experience and ours is now right in front of our faces. Winterson speaks the language we speak. And we listen, even though her honesty makes us uncomfortable. She is contemporary, young, confident, direct, and frustrating. She detests compromise. Although as poetic as Woolf, she is much more blatant with her tone, and she has a way to bring her points about loyalty, integrity, self-exploration, and growth almost too close to home.

Written on the Body is a novel about love. Most of my students agree that it is the kind of love a lot of us dream about, one that is intense, passionate, and true. But with that love come challenges because it is anything but easy. To begin with, neither of the lovers is single when they meet. Each has to acknowledge the meaning of the new love and embrace it as the top priority. Each has to step out of his/her comfortable, stable relationships and risk starting a life anew. "What you risk reveals what you value," the nameless narrator says to Louise, continuing . . . "you set before me a space uncluttered by association. It might be a void or it might be a release. Certainly I want to take the risk. I want to take the risk because the life I have stored up is going moldy"(Winterson 1994, 81).

Winterson challenges the core values we have adapted for ours without question, such as love as the foundation of relationships and the stability of marriage as an institution. The narrator states:

No-one can legislate love; it cannot be given orders or cajoled into service. . . . Love is the one thing stronger than desire and the only proper reason to resist temptation. There are those who say that temptation can be barricaded beyond the door. . . . Marriage is the flimsiest weapon against desire. (Winterson 1994, 78)

To hear this is disturbing because we find ourselves agreeing and strongly siding with the narrator, a person whose moral ethics do not necessarily coincide with ours and who breaks up a marriage in an initially adulterous affair. We are forced to reevaluate our definitions of loyalty and love or perhaps admit that there are no such definitions. We realize that the manuals we grew up with are good for nothing because they were written about someone else's life, not our own.

It is also, therefore, a novel about personal growth. What is disturbing about that? Perhaps the fact that growth is painful. Growth is about taking the risk of letting go of old beliefs and facing the unknown. Winterson's narrator first outgrows the skin of a casual lover. S/he understands that relationships with married women are a set-up for disappointment, as well as a way to avoid commitment. S/he also matures into recognizing the deceptive comfort of the life with Jacqueline when she describes. " . . . Jacqueline was an overcoat. She muffled my senses. With her I forgot about feeling and wallowed in contentment. Contentment is a feeling you say? Are you sure it's not an absence of feeling?" (Winterson 1994, 76).

We find ourselves pausing and asking similar questions about our own lives. The growth process never stops—in the book or in life. The narrator plunges into the unknown terms of the new love and asks him/herself, "I've been through so much I should know just what it is I'm doing with Louise. I should be a grown-up by now. Why do I feel like a convent virgin?" (1994, 94). Then she grows through self-righteousness and the desire to control Louise's life to letting go and taking life a moment at a time, even though it comes without guarantees about the future.

But the most frustrating part of Winterson's novel is her ungendered narrator. We are allowed into the depths of his/her soul without knowing that basic, required fact—the gender. A good question to ask here is why this information seems so basic and required. My students tell me they spent up to three quarters of the book looking for gender clues before they gave up. I ask them if it was not a waste of time and what more would you know about the narrator if you knew if he or she were male or female? I continue to ask what the author's point is in purposefully and methodically hiding the narrator's gender from us? My students agree that, frustrating as it is, Winterson's narrative strategy is effective in showing how much we have in common as people, and how little gender really tells about a person. When asked, most of my students said that they imagined the narrator to be a man, some of them, mainly women, said they imagined a woman. They all noticed that the novel's truth about embracing life with no guarantees remains unchanged, regardless of gender. To learn to be comfortable with the ungendered narrator is to learn the meaninglessness of gender markers. It is to see our common basic humanity as foremost and most important.

One more aspect of Winterson's play with gender is how the narrator's unknown gender opens the possibility of a homosexual relationship. The narrator we have grown to like and sympathize with may well be a woman, which makes her . . . a lesbian. That unspoken "l" word again. So if we are a part of the heterosexual majority, we are faced with a choice. We can reject her as someone we cannot relate to, or we can acknowledge what we have been feeling all along, that we understand her. We understand what it is like to be a lesbian! How can that be? This realization makes many of my students uncomfortable, and that is why they prefer to read the male gender into the narrator. The same comfortable blindness that made them ignore Clarissa's lesbian passion in *Mrs. Dalloway* now governs their choice of the narrator's gender in *Written on the Body*. The denial of difference appears to be a very deeply-rooted mechanism that texts like Woolf's and Winterson's seek to undermine. The value of ambiguity here is the value of diversity because in that basic unanswered question, "male of female?" resides the essence of our humanity, stripped of social norms and taboos.

Teaching texts like Woolf's and Winterson's brings up questions crucial to critical thinking and self-questioning. What is the difference between being male and female? Why does gender seem so important in social functioning? Why are we so intolerant of other sexualities? Texts such as these develop openness to difference and an acknowledgement, if not always tolerance, of diversity. Students often start the course with preconceived ideas about gender and sexual difference, but as the course progresses the "male" and "female" and "straight" and "gay" camps move closer together. The defensive boundaries drop lower as students, inspired by the texts, share stories of their partners, families, and friends, only this time with a better understanding of their particular individuality. Virginia Woolf's point about thinking about "one sex as distinct from the other as an effort" once again rings true (1957, 100). If anything, to hear my students say the course made them blush is reason enough to teach it.

8

A Model for Evaluating Gender Equity in Academe

Kenneth L. Miller and Susan M. Miller

INTRODUCTION

Gender inequities persist in higher education. Without ignoring the difficulties that men may encounter, women confront the day-to-day consequences of these inequities. The focus has moved from confronting gross manifestations of inequity to detecting and remedying the more subtle forms of gender inequity that permeate a range of domains relevant to life in academe. As Sandler noted: "many of our gender expectations are subtle" (1997a, 4). Thus we can expect that manifestations of these differential expectancies will also be subtle. This chapter begins with five challenges to gender equity on college campuses: (1) equitable access to institutions/programs, (2) equitable campus climate, (3) equitable access to instructors, (4) equity in instruction, and (5) equitable employment practices. Although discussed separately, these challenges interact to produce micro- and macro-experiences and consequences of gender inequity. The chapter concludes with an evaluation model that addresses these challenges.

Institutions of higher education hold a unique position in society. Their role in sustaining democratic ideals is supported by federal laws that prohibit discrimination. Although rooted in meritocracy, institutions of higher education have come to be viewed as essential for a democratic society and as a gateway to "the good life." Institutions of higher learning are viewed as promoting the social good, not only for individuals who attend, but also for society at large (Moses 2001). As vehicles for social justice, universities are charged with preparing students to live successfully in a diverse society (Stake and Hoffman 2001) and with personal confidence and self-determination (Moses 2001).

The academy can provide individuals with the opportunities, resources, and impetus to reach their professional and personal potential. It is the responsibility of institutions of higher education to ensure that these opportunities and resources are available and that impediments to growth are minimized. A review of the literature suggests that many institutions have made good faith efforts to conduct self-evaluations regarding impediments to equity. These studies have typically examined some aspect of gender inequity in campus climate or discrepancies in faculty salary. In contrast, the authors propose an evaluation model that can be used to evaluate gender equity across the five domains previously mentioned. It is based on Maslow's Hierarchy of Needs that provides a humanistic and hierarchical perspective in which to frame problems of gender inequity.

Maslow's Hierarchy of Needs (Crain 1992; Maslow 1954, 2001) describes a five-phase model where human needs and motives are arranged hierarchically. In general, individuals can more easily achieve higher level needs when lower level needs have been satisfied. Meeting *physiological needs* for food and sleep are primary to individuals. *Safety and security needs* are associated with a sense of security and freedom from danger. Once these needs are met, *belongingness needs* can be addressed. Belongingness involves the need to affiliate with others and be accepted. *Esteem needs* are met through accomplishment and achievement with approval and recognition from others. Finally, individuals strive for *self-actualization* when growth and development are self-directed and opportunities exist to achieve full potential.

Challenges to Equitable Access

One of the most common approaches to studying gender equity in higher education is access. Access involves equitable admittance to institutions as well as equitable entrée to specific programs and disciplines within the institution. It includes not only access to opportunities, but also to equitable results or outcomes (Toutkoushian 1999). Thus an examination of access equity addresses the numbers of women entering academia, as well as differences in their experiences and outcomes.

Currently more women than men attend institutions of higher education, a positive sign in light of the belief a century ago that educating women was equivalent to creating "monstrosities" in years when only 19 percent of college graduates were women (Sadker and Sadker 1994). The greatest gains in enrollment for women occurred between 1970 and 1985 (Chamberlain 1988). In the early 1980's women slightly surpassed men in the number of undergraduate and master's degrees earned, a trend that continued in the 1990s (National Center for Education Statistics 1994).

However, challenges to equitable access are evident in a more detailed examination of enrollment patterns. These patterns are based on (1) perceived value and prestige of institutions or discipline areas, and (2) within-group differences based on race, income, or age. Women, including a disproportionate representation of minority women, are enrolled in two-year rather than four-year institutions (Lee, Mackie-Lewis, and Mark 1993; National Center for Education Statistics 1992). In turn, they earn less than their male counterparts (Lin and Vogt 1996).

Paralleling the over-representation of women in less prestigious institutions, women are more often employed in less prestigious disciplines. This subtle and easily overlooked challenge of equitable access is captured by Sadker and Sadker's notion of the "glass wall" that separates the education of women from men (1994, 17). Women continue to enroll in disciplines such as education and communication, and are under-represented in the hard sciences (Barber 1995; Chamberlain 1988; National Research Council 1991; Sadker and Sadker 1994; Seymour 1992). Between 1960 and 1974, the number of women earning bachelor's degrees in science and engineering, relative to men, increased. However, Barber (1995) noted that these gains were not sustained, nor was there a pattern of gain at the doctoral level. Indeed, the higher the degree, the lower the gain (Ware, Steckler, and Leserman 1985). Despite the increased number of women earning doctorates between 1974 and 1985, segregation of disciplines by sex actually increased (Ransom 1990).

The recruitment and retention of women at the doctoral level in sciences is of concern, and robust evidence suggests that the major variable in this under-representation is gender-related (Barber 1995; Kahle 1988; National Research Council 1991). The disciplines of engineering, sciences, and math continue to be perceived as "masculine" domains (Leder 1986; Seymour 1992), and the phenomenon of female students who "leak" from the educational pipeline is now part of the discussion within the scientific and educational communities (Alper 1993; National Research Council 1991; Kahle 1988; Ware, Steckler, and Leserman 1985). As part of this dialogue, it should be noted that female students entering the sciences receive less financial aid than male students. Yet female students who receive financial aid at the undergraduate level are more likely to persist to advanced degrees (National Research Council 1991).

Challenges of Equitable Campus Climate

The term *chilly campus climate* refers to a collection of behaviors and institutional actions that create an environment where women are treated differently in ways that adversely affect their personal and professional development. Devaluation, stereotyping, gender expectations, harassment, and faculty bias are elements that contribute to the chill (Sandler 1997b).

Rape is the most extreme form of harassment faced by women on campus. Surveys suggest that the number of rape victims vary from 1-in-4 to 1-in-20 (Koss and Harvey 1994) and most occur with acquaintances or dates. However, most rapes are not reported as revealed by disparities between crime statistics and survey data. Other forms of harassment range from sexist jokes to *quid pro quo* threats. Approximately 20-to-50 percent of female faculty members have faced sexual harassment, including hostile work environments and *quid pro quo* (Fitzgerald 1996; Sandler and Shoop 1997), of which only 22 percent make a formal report (Seals 1997). A similar number of female students also experience harassment, although only 3-to-5 percent formally report it (Truax 1996). Many female students avoid sexual harassment by not enrolling or by dropping a course (Fitzgerald 1996). These career sacrifices are compounded by emotional consequences that include disbelief, guilt, and self-reproachment (Dziech and Weiner 1990).

Challenges to Equitable Access to Instructors

Components of campus climate include relationships among students and between faculty and students. The faculty transmit values and beliefs about the world and expectations about students' potential places in that world. Beneficial out-of-class interactions have the potential to acculturate students in the values and norms of academic and professional communities. Poor or absent interactions can leave the student "out in the cold."

There is robust evidence that the number and kinds of out-of-class interactions between student and faculty influence academic performance, intellectual development, personal development, academic persistence, and career goals (Lamport 1993; Terenzini and Pascarella 1980). Additional evidence suggests that these informal interactions with faculty play a more pivotal role for female students, particularly in the early stages of their academic tenure (Nora, Cabrera, Hagedorn, and Pascarella 1996).

For students in disciplines such as science, mathematics, and engineering that employ more masculine-oriented pedagogical strategies, out-of-class interactions take on greater importance. Thompson (2001) found that informal interactions were significantly related to students' efforts in science courses, as well as to science and mathematical gains. However, female students reported fewer informal interactions than did their male counterparts.

Challenges to Equity in Instruction

Challenges to equity in instruction include the nature of interactions that occur in the classroom, the type of instructional strategies that are employed, and curriculum content. Evidence suggests that these factors are interwoven to produce a classroom that often provides inequitable instruction for women.

Gender differences in the classroom behaviors of male and female students, and of their instructors, are well documented. Male students control the flow of information in classrooms, talk longer and more frequently, and are rewarded by faculty who give them more attention, eye contact, and difficult challenges (Sadker and Sadker 1994). These gender differences are found not only in K–12 classrooms, but thrive in college classrooms in both traditionally "feminine" and "masculine" disciplines.

The importance of instructional methods lies in relationships among pedagogy, the promotion of egalitarian worldviews, and instructional strategies favored by female and male students. The latter factor gains importance in fields such as science, mathematics, and engineering (SME) where women are typically under-represented. Strategies that promote collaborative learning, critical thinking, and a sense of personal confidence are associated with women studies' courses (Stake and Hoffman 2001) and are typically absent from courses in SME disciplines.

Instructional strategies and classroom experiences are important because they are predictive of the types of courses that students will select. Ware, Steckler, and Lesserman (1985) found that enjoyment of a freshmen science class was predictive of selecting science as a major; however more male than female students found the introductory course enjoyable. SME courses are characterized by "masculine" pedagogical strategies that include competitiveness, use of masculine examples, and verbal interruptions (Kahle 1988) compared to a more collaborative and cooperative pedagogical model (Rosser 1995; Seymour 1992b). Therefore, pedagogy plays a role in challenges to equitable access for women in the disciplines of science, mathematics, and engineering (Rosser 1995).

Paralleling the challenge to equitable instruction based on the use of masculine-oriented strategies is curriculum content. What is being taught is as important as how it is taught. Curricular issues have received considerable recent attention in disciplines where women are under-represented. In her five-phase model for evaluating and changing SME curricula, Rosser (1995) observed that SME curricula nationwide are at phase I—not yet at the point of noticing the exclusion of female scientists in the curriculum or in the field. However, the absence of women from the curriculum is not restricted to disciplines in which women are under-represented, but permeates the general curriculum in higher education (Schmitz and Williams 1983). Even in disciplines such as communications (Rush 1993) and education where women dominate, there is a history of under-representation of women in textbooks and curricular materials (Campbell and Sanders 1997; Sadker and Sadker 1994; Titus 1993).

Challenges to Equitable Employment Practices

Employment patterns in academe continue to reflect gender inequities. Women are more likely to be hired at less prestigious institutions. Approximately 46 percent of faculty at two-year institutions are women (Sax, Astin, Arredondo, and Korn 1996), whereas only 10 to 13 percent of faculty at elite institutions are women (Freeman 1977; Sadker and Sadker 1994). Tout-koushian (1999) noted that a greater number of female faculty are concentrated at two-year and liberal arts colleges than at Research I and II institutions.

Female faculty are concentrated in lower academic ranks, with more women working as instructors and assistant professors compared to male faculty, who are more likely to be full professors (Sax, Astin, Arredondo and Korn 1996). Although there are increasing numbers of women earning doctorates, this increase is not reflected in the number of females in full-time positions (Toutkoushian 1999). Similar nonrepresentation is found in the type of discipline in which female faculty are employed. Female faculty continue to be under-represented in engineering, natural sciences, and social sciences (National Center for Education Statistics 1994), and more women than men are in lower, untenured ranks (National Research Council 1991). A variety of researchers (Balzer et al. 1996; Boudreau et al., 1997; Looker 1993) using different methodologies to examine salary equity found that female faculty earn less than their male counterparts.

Differential hiring and promotion patterns are compounded by policies and practices that fail to support the unique circumstances of female academicians. For example, dual career marriages and parental leave (Norrell and Norrell 1996) are issues that differentially affect the potential for female career success (Freeman 1977). Limited parental leave combined with child-rearing demands may explain findings of a gender difference in research productivity, with males out-producing their female counterparts. This difference persists even after relevant variables are taken into account (Toutkoushian 1999).

EVALUATION MODEL

The proposed model for evaluating gender equity in academe incorporates the five major challenges to gender equity discussed previously in the context of Maslow's hierarchy of needs (Crain 1992). In this model shown in Table 8.1, equity challenges are listed in the far left column and needs are identified in the top row. Basic human needs are hierarchically ordered to illustrate that lower order needs must be met before higher order needs can be expressed or satisfied. From lowest to highest order, these include physiological, safety, belongingness, and esteem needs, as well as a need to develop one's full potential or self-actualization.

At the intersection of each challenge to gender equity and level of need are target conditions that university administrators, faculty, staff, and students can develop and evaluate to determine progress toward creating a gender equitable institution. In the figures and discussion that follow, the authors have identified a representative list of target conditions. Although not intended to be comprehensive, these conditions may serve as departure points for discussion, elaboration, and identification of additional targets that may reflect unique institutional circumstances and needs.

TABLE 8.1   Model for Evaluating Gender Equity in Academe: Challenges to
Gender Equity in the Context of Maslow's Hierarchy of Needs

Maslow's hierarchy of needs					
Challenges to gender equity	Physiological needs	Safety needs	Belongingness needs	Esteem needs	Self-actualization
Equitable access to institutions/ programs	Target conditions	Target conditions	Target conditions	Target conditions	Target conditions
Equitable campus climate	Target conditions	Target conditions	Target conditions	Target conditions	Target conditions
Equitable access to instructors	Target conditions	Target conditions	Target conditions	Target conditions	Target conditions
Equity in instruction	Target conditions	Target conditions	Target conditions	Target conditions	Target conditions
Equitable employment practices	Target conditions	Target conditions	Target conditions	Target conditions	Target conditions

Samples of target conditions that address the challenge of equitable access
to institutions/programs by hierarchical needs are presented in Table 8.2.
These conditions represent both implicit and explicit guarantees of institutional commitment to gender equity to both potential applicants and current
members of the academic community. The benefits of evaluating these conditions and communicating findings in campus publications and admissions
materials are evident in light of increasing diversity at most universities, as
well as student, parental, and societal expectations.

Under the heading of physiological needs, target conditions include provision of adequate financial resources to meet daily living needs. Such
resources could be offered in the form of direct aid, scholarships, grants, or
assistantships. Special attention should be given to providing assistance in
disciplines where women are under-represented and under-financed compared to their male counterparts.

Target conditions associated with safety needs must include a publicly
stated and rigidly enforced university-wide policy of intolerance for gender
bias, discrimination, and/or sexual harassment. To insure equitable opportunities for access, participation, and acceptance, institutions must actively
recruit students for nontraditional disciplines (e.g., women in engineering,
men in elementary education). These efforts provide strong evidence of the
institution's commitment to gender equity by promoting acceptance of students' unique interests, desires, and abilities. By insuring equitable access to

TABLE 8.2   Equitable Access to Institutions/Programs and Hierarchical Needs

	Physiological needs	Safety needs	Belongingness needs	Esteem needs	Self-actualization
Equitable access to institutions/ programs	Financial aid	Zero tolerance for gender bias, discrimination, and/or sexual harassment Secure parking Advocacy for gender equity in university policies and programs	Recruitment of students for non-traditional disciplines Equal opportunities to relate with same and opposite-sex peers, faculty and staff Mentoring programs for females	Equal access to scholarships, and other rewards Treatment as a valued member of the academic community by administrators, faulty, staff, and students	Equal opportunities to achieve full academic and personal potential

scholarships, grants, assistantships, jobs, and other rewards, institutions communicate the value they hold for all people, regardless of their sex. If this message is reinforced in the words and actions of administrators, faculty, staff, and students, needs for esteem may be satisfied. Target conditions associated with self-actualization are necessarily ambiguous. Because the process is unique to individuals, universities must first insure that equity targets at all lower levels have been achieved. They must then insure equity of access to institutional and programmatic resources that may serve to facilitate full academic and personal potential for all in the university community.

   Table 8.3 contains representative target conditions associated with the challenge of creating an equitable campus climate. In order to equitably meet the physiological needs of all persons in the university community, administrators must insure that males and females have equal access to quality meals and housing. This includes students, but extends equally to administrators, faculty, and staff. To insure a climate of physical and psychological safety, a well-trained security staff (preferably with expertise in university issues) of sufficient size must provide twenty-four-hour protection throughout the week. All persons in the university community must know that escort services are readily available and that a sufficient number of appropriately placed and functional emergency telephones provide immediate access to security officers. In addition, all in the university community must understand that rape is a criminal act that will be prosecuted to the fullest extent of the law.

TABLE 8.3   Equitable Campus Climate and Hierarchical Needs

	Physiological needs	Safety needs	Belongingness needs	Esteem needs	Self-actualization
Equitable campus climate	Healthy meals and adequate housing for all students	Zero tolerance for gender bias, discrimination, and/or sexual harassment Adequate security staff, escort services, and emergency telephones Strict enforcement of date rape laws	Equal opportunities to participate in student government, sports, and campus organizations University support for a women's studies program, a women's center, and a sexual assault education program	Professional development and leadership training opportunities for women Respect, acceptance, and encouragement by same and opposite-sex peers, faculty, and staff	Equal opportunities to achieve full academic and personal potential

Target conditions that address belongingness needs include the provision of equal opportunities for all students to participate in campus organizations, sports, recreational activities, and student government. By supporting women's studies programs, a sexual assault education program, and a women's center, university administrators actively demonstrate commitments to meeting the affiliation needs of women in the university community. Campus climate targets associated with esteem needs include leadership training and professional development offerings, to which women have historically had limited access. Self-actualization targets should be identified by a cross-section of the university community. They may include acquisition of funds for special programs (e.g., women's lecture series) and activities (e.g., international travel) that promote full academic and personal growth.

Because instructors play a critical role in the academic, professional, and career development of students, access to them is an important equity challenge. It is created by a history of university life dominated by male faculty and students. Although the past fifty years have witnessed sweeping changes in enrollment patterns by sex at American universities, this trend continues in many of the physical and natural sciences. Similarly, females are over-represented in disciplines such as education and communication, where male students may be reluctant to approach or work with female faculty or advisors. Students enrolled in opposite-sex-dominated programs

TABLE 8.4   Equitable Access to Instructors and Hierarchical Needs

	Safety needs	Belongingness needs	Esteem needs	Self-actualization
Equitable access to instructors	Zero tolerance for gender bias, discrimination, and/or sexual harassment	Equal opportunities for formal and informal meetings with instructors Access to same-sex advisors	Equitable challenges and encouragement for plans and successes	Equal opportunities to achieve full academic and personal potential

must be assured of equal access to instructors, who provide the same levels of challenge and encouragement they do for same-sex students. University administrators and faculty should make every effort to recruit and hire non-traditional (i.e., opposite-sex) faculty in such programs in order to assure access to same-sex advisors and instructors.

Table 8.4 contains target conditions that address this challenge along the continuum of human needs. Safety in accessing instructors must be assured by university policies that prohibit gender bias, sexual discrimination, and sexual harassment. Students and faculty must further understand that violations of these policies will result in swift disciplinary actions. Beyond the belongingness targets identified above, instructors must provide appropriate challenges and encouragement to students, regardless of sex, as they make academic and career plans. In so doing, students' esteem needs may be met. Self-actualization targets related to access may include opportunities to meet or work with instructors informally (e.g., brown bag lunches, department-sponsored picnics), on faculty projects (e.g., art exhibits, symphony performances), or through travel (e.g., international study programs, participation in faculty research projects).

Table 8.5 includes representative target conditions for the challenge of equity in instruction. This challenge is based on a long and well-documented history of unequal treatment of males and females in instructional settings. Students' physiological needs can be met by providing equitable facilities, including equipment, heating and cooling, lighting, and maintenance in both male- and female-dominated disciplines. Target conditions for safety needs are consistent with previous challenges. Belongingness needs are achievable when learners have equal opportunities to participate in learning activities and experiences, regardless of their sex. Inclusion of gender issues in discussions of theories, perspectives, practices, and applications further enhance opportunities for the attainment of these needs. To meet students' needs for esteem, instructors must provide equal time, attention, challenge, and praise to females and males. As noted previously,

TABLE 8.5   Equity in Instruction and Hierarchical Needs

	Physiological needs	Safety needs	Belongingness needs	Esteem needs	Self-actualization
Equity in instruction	Sanitary, adequately heated, and well-lighted facilities in both traditionally male and female disciplines	Zero tolerance for gender bias, discrimination and/or sexual harassment	Equal opportunities to fully participate in learning activities, projects, and experiences Examinations of gender issues in theories, perspectives, achievements, etc. in course content and discussions	Equitable attention, challenge, and praise of male and female students	Equal opportunities to achieve full academic and personal potential

instructors can facilitate achievement of learners' self-actualization needs by equitably providing learning opportunities that extend beyond the boundaries of the classroom.

Table 8.6 contains target conditions for the challenge of equitable employment practices. As discussed earlier, gender inequities exist in the areas of institutional type (two-year vs. four-year, research vs. comprehensive), university quality/prestige, discipline, academic rank, and salary, even when variables that affect these factors are statistically controlled. Safety needs can be addressed by policies that require all administrators, faculty, and staff to receive gender equity training. Additional opportunities to meet these needs can be enhanced by regular (e.g., semi-annual) publications of institutional progress in meeting established gender equity goals.

Belongingness needs are achievable when gender-equitable hiring, tenure, and promotion policies and practices are established and rigorously enforced. Attainment of these needs is enhanced when policies and procedures translate to equitable salaries. Esteem needs can be addressed through equitable representation by sex in university governance and leadership, particularly in senior positions. Universities must also redress the previously discussed problem of inequitable opportunities for female faculty during childbearing years. By establishing paid leave programs for natural childbirth/adoption and reasoned expectations for promotion and tenure during these periods, administrators communicate value for a fundamental life process as well as for the differential biological roles played by women and men.

TABLE 8.6   Equitable Employment Practices and Hierarchical Needs

	Safety needs	Belongingness needs	Esteem needs	Self-actualization
Equitable employment practices	Zero tolerance for gender bias, discrimination, and/or sexual harassment	equitable hiring, tenure, and promotion policies	Equitable representation by sex in governance and leadership positions	Equal opportunities to achieve full academic and personal potential
	Requisite training in gender equity for faculty/ administrators	Equitable salaries Mentoring programs for female faculty	Paid leave programs for natural childbirth or adoption for either parent	
	Publication of annual reports on institutional progress in meeting gender equity goals			
	Gender			

Finally, self-actualization needs related to equitable employment practices can be met when institutions create novel, and even visionary, opportunities for all members of the university community to excel in their work roles. These may include flexible work schedules, campus-based childcare, work exchange programs, and advanced training in areas of specialization.

DISCUSSION

Although the past half-century has witnessed significant progress in reducing the scope of obvious gender inequities in the academy, many persist and exert a powerfully destructive influence. More subtle, and perhaps more deeply institutionalized, these inequities systematically deprive both women and men of opportunities to meet basic human needs. We have argued that the academy must respond. We have offered a model for evaluating gender equity in academe by examining the interface between five major challenges to gender equity and five levels of human needs identified by Abraham Maslow. By working collaboratively to identify equity targets at each interface, administrators, faculty, staff, and students can systematically evaluate progress toward creating a gender-fair academy that will, in turn, empower all women in higher education.

9

The Transformative Leadership of Women in Higher Education Administration

Margaret Madden

In July of 1993 I participated with seventy-six other feminist psychologists in a working Conference on Education and Training in Feminist Training Practice in Psychology, in which we collectively explored the issues and future agenda of feminist psychology. As a social psychologist and faculty member at a small undergraduate college, I was in a working group on curriculum development (Chin et al. 1997). When the groups convened in plenary sessions to discuss feminist assumptions topical areas, there was a striking similarity in the principles each group identified as important. The conference resulted in a book, *Shaping the Future of Feminist Psychology: Education, Research and Practice,* edited by Judith Worell and Norine G. Johnson (1997), which has, indeed, had an impact on psychology.

That fall I moved to a new college and began my first full-time academic administrative position. While I continue to use the framework we developed for feminist psychology when I teach psychology of gender, the conference had the more profound effect of giving me a framework to understand and develop my identity as a feminist-social-psychologist-academic-administrator. This chapter represents my current thinking, combining values articulated at that conference with my experience since embarking on a full-time career in higher education administration. I use the feminist principles for psychology as a framework for a feminist analysis of higher education administration. Conceptually, this transition was easy for me, as I now think of myself as an "applied social psychologist," employing the worldview of my original academic discipline to understand the very real group and individual dynamics faced by academic administrators at all different kinds of institutions of higher learning.

I do not intend to debate whether these assumptions are correct, although one could assemble psychological research to support them (Worell and Johnson 1997). Rather, I use them to begin articulating a philosophy of higher education administration that can be implemented by others. Because of the absence of role models in much of higher education, I and others I know who have moved into administration recently are experimenting with strategies that permit us to be effective in our organizations in a way that supports our feminist principles. The principles are as follows:

- *Principle 1:* Individuals are located in a sociocultural context that creates differences in perspectives based on cultural, racial, and other dimensions.

- *Principle 2:* Peoples' perspectives are a function of their power in a sociocultural structure.

- *Principle 3:* People are active agents who use diverse behaviors and strategies to cope and grow within various environments.

- *Principle 4:* Multiple perspectives are more useful than dichotomous ones, which are both ineffective and unrealistic.

- *Principle 5:* Connection is the basis for human interaction, and collaboration is important.

HIGHER EDUCATION ADMINISTRATION

Higher education management is, in fact, just that, management of people, resources, and ideas. As a manager, one's role is to make things happen to support the mission of one's institution, which requires exploring whether the institutional mission is one that supports feminist values on some fundamental level. Since most institutions and organizations have histories of conflict around values that may call into question their compatibility with feminist values, those of us who have made conscious decisions to remain at our institutions have explicitly chosen to work within a system, despite ambivalence about doing so. The "transition from activist to administrator" alters one's perception of what one's role should be, putting one in a different, though not necessarily always better, position to facilitate social change (Zalk 1997). Therefore, understanding that others might criticize my decision, I have chosen the tactic of trying to "be at the decision-making table" and work within my organization, rather than the more radical choice to dismantle the United States educational system entirely (Kettle 1996).

Examining the literature on higher education leadership I found a number of models that are compatible with the feminist principles although their authors may not explicitly define their ideas as feminist. Astin and

Astin's (2000, 2001) report for the Kellogg Foundation, *Leadership Reconsidered,* outlines principles of "transformative leadership," leadership that transforms higher education institutions. Because transformative leadership is so consistent with the feminist principles that I wish to articulate and explore, I will describe its components. Astin and Astin define leadership as fostering change, "a purposive process which is inherently value-based" (2001, 8). Therefore, a leader is a "change agent" who involves others in a collective process. People in all strata of colleges are potential leaders.

In higher education, leadership development should enable all constituents—students, staff, faculty, and administrators—to enhance institutions' missions of student learning and development, knowledge generation, and community service. Purposive leadership encompasses the values of creating a supportive environment, promoting future sustainability through harmony with nature, and constructing communities based on reciprocal and shared responsibility. The relationship between leaders and followers should be collaborative, guided by shared purpose, enable respectful disagreement, have clear divisions of labor and responsibilities, and create a learning environment in which individuals develop. Leaders, therefore, display self-knowledge, authenticity and integrity, commitment to the collective effort, empathy and understanding of others, and competence. Astin and Astin's monograph outlines strategies for implementing transformative leadership and implications for the various stakeholders in education.

Taking an explicitly feminist standpoint, Regan and Brooks (1995) propose a model of relational leadership characterized by five attributes: collaboration, caring, courage, intuition, and vision. Regan and Brooks regard gender as a category of experience that influences women to develop feminist leadership values. Women may not envision themselves as leaders because they have not conceptualized or articulated the value of the relational leadership on which they rely. Barriers keep these attributes of leadership invisible, unspoken, and inaccessible. Regan and Brooks talk about intuition as an important feminist attribute, defined as "the ability to give equal weight to experience and abstraction, mind and heart" (Regan and Brooks 1995, 33). Women they interviewed talked about wanting to be able to articulate their feelings, their sense of things "on a gut level." While empirical evidence does not necessarily show that women are more intuitive than men (Graham and Ickes 1997), it is possible that women are more inclined to listen to and articulate concerns that result from how things "feel." My own experience is that, when a situation doesn't "feel right," it is well worth taking the time to explore why. Often those feelings occur because others are being ignored or treated unfairly and, if I keep inclusive values in the foreground, I can think of a better way to handle the situation.

In her book, *Failing the Future: A Dean Looks at Higher Education in the Twenty-first Century,* Annette Kolodny (1998) outlines some of the challenges and likely changes faced by higher education in the future and describes her experience implementing a feminist agenda as a humanities dean. She predicts the future will involve interdisciplinarity, education for a leisured society, and internationalization. Interdisciplinarity demands pattern-seeking and comprehensive analysis, flexible curricula, collaborative learning and research, and receptivity to emerging disciplines. Education for a leisured society will need to meet the needs of a new constituency of learners seeking new educational services. And internationalization will be demanded and facilitated by trends such as a unified Europe, global technology, and interactive learning.

Kolodny believes the humanities curriculum has been made more rigorous through the impact of feminism, multiculturalism, and postmodernism on disciplines and textbooks, despite attempts to demonize these trends. Traditional authors and texts remain, but others are added. Understanding literature from other cultures is more demanding and difficult than reading only in one's own culture. Learning to read a variety of texts is challenging, requiring more complicated tools for judgment. Students are often more inclined to stray outside of disciplinary boundaries than faculty members. For example, doctoral students ask difficult questions about how society is organized and dislike being told to stay within disciplinary boundaries.

Kolodny speaks of institutional characteristics that contribute to the context of the administrator's job. The hours of time spent double-checking budget numbers from central bureaucracies could be better spent on curriculum renewal, mentorship programs for students, recruiting new faculty, and other important matters. Most academic administrators lack support staff or funds for minimally satisfactory performance. Being in an organization in which "critical decisions were made in all the wrong places by all the wrong people" (Kolodny 1998, 28) is wearing and leads to problems, such as resources not matched to decisions about class sizes or teaching loads.

The nature of students is also changing, with many more who are ethnic minorities or from poor families and school districts. Students also see new technologies as a way to transform learning and their lives. Faculty may be more resistant, but Kolodny says it is inevitable that technological innovation will transform teaching and learning. Institutions must provide incentives and continuous support to faculty members to help them teach new student populations in new ways. Of her tenure as dean, Kolodny says, "I hoped to test my hypothesis that, once given a position of recognized decision-making authority, a feminist committed to both equity and educational excellence could prove an instrument for progressive evolution" (Kolodny 1998, 8).

Many of the notions presented here are consistent with discussions of higher education management that are not avowedly feminist. Indeed, writers who discuss higher education in light of management theories such as organizational development, strategic planning, and total quality management espouse principles very much like those discussed here. Differences tend to involve the degree of emphasis on the impact of power and context variables in institutions.

For example, in their book about strategic planning in higher education, Rowley and Sherman (2001) contend that strategic planning can help colleges improve community, be more student-centered, and respond to the fast-changing demands of the information economy through inclusion, caring, and sharing. They argue that the tradition of shared governance, most normative at small colleges but ostensibly valued at all kinds of institutions, lends itself to participatory, consensus-based decision-making. Shared governance, team building, and empowerment of employees are very compatible with organizational development models. Leadership, then, involves promoting effective communication and trust, listening, open processes, and creating interdisciplinary, self-directed teams. It is useful to identify who is affected by change and attempt to respond to those outcomes.

In all institutions, students expect more influence over programmatic and pedagogical matters, particularly at private, tuition-driven colleges that espouse the importance of teaching. The shift in language that focuses on learners rather than students, or the imagery of students as consumers demanding excellence inherent in the total quality management movement in universities and colleges, speak of empowering subordinate groups.

Yet, Rowley and Sherman say, notions of shared governance frequently fall short in usual administrative processes. Budgeting processes, which determine priorities for all practical purposes, are rarely collegial or participatory, despite pretenses of shared governance. And faculty development is often overlooked in strategic planning. If colleges want faculty to change, they must supply training and incentives. Rowley and Sherman assert that colleges planning strategic shifts must build trust, political support, and training before beginning planning processes, as these signal intentions to produce change inclusively. Employees who trust their managers convey vital information, facts and feelings, and are receptive to influence and interdependence. Trust and openness are essential to successful strategic planning; without them the implementation of plans will fail. Implementation must continue incrementally, with ample communication and honesty, assessment of progress, and reports of successes and problems. In the remainder of this chapter, I describe how feminist values can clarify and expand these attributes of good administration.

PRINCIPLE 1

The prominent influence of sociocultural context on individuals' perceptions and behavior is a tenet of much postmodern thought, including most versions of feminist and multicultural theory. Critics of this "cultural relativism" have argued that this assumption leads to an inability to distinguish right from wrong because all perceptions are equally valid. I believe that feminist principles require the articulation of very clear statements of right and wrong, or acceptable and unacceptable behavior. However, making decisions based on those values should not prevent one from attempting to understand the context that leads people to perceive their situation as they do, nor from understanding the context and variables that influence one's own perspective.

Astin and Leland's (1993) analysis of three generations of women leaders in academe, whom they name the Predecessors, the Instigators, and the Inheritors, illustrate the impact of historical context. The Predecessors were those who came of age during the Depression and World War II. In interviews, they emphasized education and its value for achieving equality for women. They were "solo" leaders who often adopted male models of leadership in their highly masculine environments and felt they achieved through hard work and high standards of performance. They saw empowering other women as important goals, but tended not to describe themselves as feminists.

Instigators came of age during the 1960s and became leaders of the wave of feminism that followed the civil rights and anti-war movements and early experiences of discrimination. Issues of female identity became important as women collectively began to understand the political dimensions of their personal situations, served on committees on the status of women, and experienced strong connections with networks of other women and the effectiveness of collective action. They focused on concerns about opportunity in education and other work settings and the inclusion of women in scholarly and curricular concerns. Awareness of discrimination leads to concerns about access to education and opportunities within education, and eventually to the emergence of fields of inquiry such as women's studies and the examination of women and issues of importance to women within all academic disciplines. Inheritors are those who were ascending to leadership position in the 1990s. Recognizing the role of the Instigators in shaping their vision, they often mentioned important role models, but have extended the vision and values as they begin to articulate alternative visions of leadership. Along with appreciating collective action and friendships, awareness of power dynamics and political savvy also characterize their view of leadership.

Discrimination and Stereotyping

While those who write about women in higher education acknowledge progress towards equity, no one argues that women have achieved equal status with men. Discrimination may be subtler, but it is still common in economic, political, and educational realms (Goodwin and Fiske 2001). An

American Psychological Association Task Force on Women in Academe (2000) noted discriminatory practices in regard to start-up funds for new faculty hires, bias against certain kinds of research, overburdening women with committee and other service obligations, and the underrepresentation of women in senior administrative positions. Ethnic minority women are affected most strongly in these areas. Women are often aware of the discrimination, but it frequently takes forms so subtle that it is hard to redress (Carli 1998). For instance, behaviors of men who are uncomfortable with achieving women may impact women's behavior by making them also feel uncomfortable and self-conscious, or women may stay in mid-level administrative positions for a longer time than men before they are tapped for promotion.

Indeed, much of the mechanism for this discrimination may derive from unconscious stereotyping. Goodwin and Fiske (2001) indicate that the dimensions of sociability and competence often underlie stereotypes of outgroups. Stereotypes about women interact on these dimensions in the form of the false dichotomy of housewife vs. career woman. Furthermore, "feminist" and "career woman" are implicitly synonymous, based on stereotypes of being "not nice" and "not feminine enough." Hence, Fiske sees the "housewives vs. feminists" dichotomy as central. Feminists are seen as competent, but not likable because they threaten the status quo power structure. Given that women in higher education administration are, by definition, career women and frequently self-identified as feminist, these stereotypes probably impact them even more than other employed women. Furthermore, gender stereotypes undoubtedly interact with other stereotypic perceptions such as those for ethnicity. The limited research on gendered ethnic stereotypes suggests that African-American women are considered more aggressive and hostile and Asian, Native-American, and Hispanic women more deferent and passive than European-American women (Task Force on Women in Academe 2000).

Situational power, when one group has situational control over another group, aggravates stereotype use (Goodwin and Fiske 2001). Those with power attend more to stereotypic information about their subordinates than to information that contradicts stereotypes, affecting their behavior and setting up self-fulfilling prophecies that impact the behavior of everyone involved. Although stereotypes are activated automatically and perceivers are usually unconscious of them, awareness of biases can mitigate their effect. Paradoxically, women often deny the influence of bias on their own outcomes, which may reduce their ability to enact this protective mechanism. Accountability to third parties also reduces the impact of stereotypic biases, especially when higher-level authorities explicitly refute biases and act fairly themselves. This underscores the importance of having college administrators who explicitly acknowledge the effects of biased perceptions and consistently administer policies that counteract stereotypic expectations.

Hierarchical Organization

The hierarchical nature of postsecondary education in the United States is indisputable. Colleges vary in prestige and reputation, administrative layers reflect stature, disciplines vary in status, tuition is equated with value, and faculty prominence is correlated with salary. While higher education may not have as strictly linear organizations as other businesses, every college has its own internal hierarchy and a sense of its status in relation to other educational institutions. These affect the perceptions and actions of all constituents on a campus.

Although it is simplistic to equate hierarchical and masculine values, feminist writers often note that organizations change when a critical mass of women employees, particularly women leaders, is reached (Kanter 1977; Regan and Brooks 1995). Certainly women are in the minority in higher education. According to Glazer-Raymo (1999), 15 percent of college presidents, 25 percent of board members, 15 percent of chief academic officers, and 25 percent of dean-level administrators were women in the mid-1990s. Women were more likely to hold these positions at less prestigious institutions, e.g., religious colleges, and two- and four-year colleges, or in disciplines that are lower status, such as schools of education. While proportions have changed modestly in twenty years, change has been neither dramatic nor proportional to changes in gender-balance in other campus constituencies, such as students, mid-level administrators, or faculty. Glazer-Raymo discusses the masculine nature of academic organizations, noting that boards of trustees, which influence institutional climate from the top down, are usually predominantly male and, by their selection for status and wealth, tend to be people who are accustomed to dominating agendas. When women constitute a majority of board members (as they may at women's colleges), presidents note that the climate changes, with less emphasis on personal agendas and ego gratification.

In a feminist analysis of pragmatic liberal education, Crumpacker, McMillin, and Navakis (1998) maintain that feminist thought has begun to influence the management of colleges. Through promoting integrative models of education, feminist thinking leads to questioning traditional disciplinary boundaries and hierarchies, including the top-down administrative structure of colleges and universities. However, collaborative leadership that facilitates involvement by those who implement decisions requires privileged people to give up power. For example, senior academic officers need to risk giving up their absolute control over resource allocation, and senior faculty need to give up power and privilege they feel they have earned. Therefore, resistance to consultative leadership is to be expected (Crumpacker et al., 1998; Regan and Brooks 1995).

Leadership in Masculinized Context

Yoder argues "how women enact leadership is inextricably intertwined with being female" (2001a, 2), and leadership occurs in social contexts that vary in how congenial they are to women. Highly masculinized contexts are those in which men are the numerical majority, tasks are stereotypically masculine, the main goal is task completion, and hierarchy and coercive power are stressed. Leadership in masculinized contexts depends on status and autocratic, self-promoting behavior, all of which are viewed negatively when engaged in by women.

Academe is a masculinized context. Most university regulations do not permit active discrimination against women, yet women still are in lower status positions. Women administrators interviewed reported that the power structure was dominated "by what was described as a team, but was really a group of competing individual men" (Kettle 1996, 55).

Amey and Twombly's (1993) discussion of women presidents at community colleges vividly illustrates a masculinized leadership context. Historical accounts of leaders in the community college arena focus on a few "great men" who have shaped the role of these colleges in higher education. These descriptions are often couched in terms that evoke pioneer, athletic, and military images. To the extent that leadership is seen as comparable to the role of military officer, the leadership styles of women and ethnic minorities are seen as problems, rather than as offering diverse strengths. Thus ideologies reflected in language used to describe leadership underscore how philosophies of leadership limit access to leadership positions.

The frequently noted political character of academe also illustrates its masculinized nature. Kolodny (1998) describes the political nature of the dean's role at length. While she tried to model management based on cooperation, consultation, and team building and asked it of others who reported to her, she found that institutional conflicts forced her to become territorial and entrepreneurial in relation to other colleges in the university. She reports often analyzing the politics of a given situation as she tried to identify effective strategy. For instance, she says she learned not to permit a conversation to "get to 'no' " with a superior, but rather withdrew agenda items that seemed headed for a negative decision so she could consider other strategies. Similarly, Dawson (1997) argues that African-American women must understand academe as political and strive to understand the politics of their own institutions to prepare for administrative positions.

Interactions of Gender with Other Identity Factors

Little is known about the interaction of gender with other cultural status variables (Carli and Eagly 1999; Goodwin and Fiske 2001; Madden and Hyde 1998). To the extent that ethnic stereotypes promote status differences in social role, similar dynamics surely impact members of non-white ethnic groups and interact with gender in complicated ways. Moses contends, "racism and sexism may be so fused in a given situation that it is difficult to tell which is which" (1997, 15). All women, but especially black women, are treated as superficial or in terms of sexuality, their accomplishments ignored or perceived as moving too fast. Moses believes that people are more uncomfortable with black women who are powerful, assertive, ambitious, and or achieving than they are with similar white women. The expectations placed on black women academics are higher. Not only does being a token lead to unrealistic expectations, but also the visibility can result in burnout and exhaustion. For these and other reasons, she argues that black women are less likely to seek the highest administrative positions than either white women or black men. In contrast, Wolfman (1997) feels black women are less threatening to white men than black men and are less often viewed as sexual objects than white women. Instead, their prospects are restricted by lack of information. In addition to "trying to understand the puzzles of the more esoteric and subtle aspects of polite racial hostility" (Wolfman 1997, 163), they often have to learn an institutional culture through observation, guile, and intelligence, rather than information from internal mentors.

The types of colleges where black women are concentrated as administrators affect their actions. Discussing challenges of administration at a historically black college, Shields (1997) notes that lack of resources lead to particular problems, such as absence of large office staffs or assistant or associate deans. However, the experiences of working with multicultural groups found at such colleges and developing new leadership styles may prove useful as models for administrators at other kinds of institutions.

Focus on Structural Change

Understanding the context of higher education is a necessary precursor to implementing an administrative principle based on the recognition that people's behavior is a function of their context in reference to sociocultural variables. Many writers maintain that good administrators monitor the complex environment in which they operate to gauge the motivations of various stakeholders. Astin and Astin (2000) talk about the context in which college presidents operate as consisting of the type of institution and its mission and the immediate circumstances in which the president operates, such as external mandates from governing bodies or internal factors like the college's financial stability. They maintain that institutional leaders must understand the culture of the institutions or the groups within it to facilitate change. Arguing that transformative leaders are collaborative, authentic, and self-aware, they point out that "top-down" strategies in which the president orders others to change their activities are the least effective way to transform institutions.

Changing organizational structure is easer than changing individuals' long-standing habits and dispositions. In other words, one can change the structure and processes at work in a particular situation more readily than one can change peoples' behavior directly. By altering the contingencies, as a behaviorist would say, one modifies rewarded behaviors. The feminist models described promote this approach to change. To use Astin and Astin's (2000) term, the administrator is a "change agent" who focuses on process and structure rather than the force of personality to alter her organization.

Astin and Astin (2000) call this transformative leadership because it not only accomplishes immediate goals, but also transforms the institution. Nearly every article on women in higher education administration cites institutional transformation as the ultimate reward for women's persistence in academic administration. While some decry the glacial pace of change and express weariness from constant vigilance and repeated battles (McKay 1997), most conclude that they have created a more congenial environment for future generations of administrators. In the metaphor used by the Task Force on Women in Academe (2000), we have gone beyond trying to level a male-designed playing field and now are thinking about changing the rules. The task force lists more than sixty ways various academic constituencies can enhance climate, achieve equity, and ensure accountability.

More specific examples of ways to change organizations are detailed by several writers. Kolodny (1998) describes how she modified faculty governance within her school of humanities and changed the tenure and promotion review process to make it fairer for all candidates. Green (1997) discusses responsibilities of institutions to maintain a friendly climate, equity in compensation, accountability of chairs and others, mentoring for teaching, fair evaluation, equitable support for research, and recognition of service. Each of these administrators derives satisfaction from having transformed an institution by changing the rules applied to future faculty and staff.

PRINCIPLE 2

Emphasis on the central, pervasive role of power in human interactions, particularly in hierarchical organizations, is a major difference between a feminist analysis of higher education and other discussions that might be characterized as humanist. The importance of understanding power relationships derives from the feminist concept of positionality, awareness of how one's position impacts one's perceptions. To develop alternative models of power distribution, people need to understand how their position and relative power in an organization affect their own behavior, as well as that of others (Crumpacker et al., 1998). A related concept emphasized by feminist theory is status, the ranking one holds by virtue of characteristics such as gender, social class, ethnicity, ability, and sexual orientation (Grumet and McCoy 1997; Madden and Russo 1997). Many feminist administrators have trained and taught in feminist pedagogies that are sensitive to power dynamics in the classroom and discuss the exploitation of teachers of various statuses. Thus they bring the values of feminist pedagogy to their administrative positions.

Many writers also note that women must be politically attuned to these power dynamics in their institutions (Lindsay 1997; Maguire 1996; Moses 1997). Johnson (1993) asserts that feminist administrators are seldom concerned with obtaining power or establishing strong personal claims to authorship, but, nevertheless, they need to understand the leadership culture of their organizations, since the masculinized context so frequently found in higher education includes the assumption that effective leadership depends on status and power manifested through autocratic behavior (Yoder 2001b). Another common observation is that administrators must understand the political nature of the academy and the interaction of gender with politics. Understanding politics essentially means understanding the nature of formal and informal power in academe in general and in a particular institution, as Dawson (1997) says when she notes that African-American women aspiring to advance in administration must study and understand the politics of power in their institutions. Gender is related to power, and power is further reduced when a woman is a member of another minority as well (Gibson 1996; Lindsay 1997; Maguire 1996; Moses 1997). Citing organizational literature, Lindsay notes that racism and discrimination serve to maintain the power of the privileged in an organization. Assuming that feminist values also dictate a desire to change dynamics, it is vital that administrators explicate the redefinition of leadership as collaborative and consultative, turning power into empowerment of those who share decision-making and implementation (Crumpacker et al., 1998).

Even the most powerful body in academe, the board of trustees, is affected by gender status. Lay boards of trustees or directors are inherently conservative because they exist to perpetuate the institutions they govern (Chamberlin 1993). Because of their function to protect the institution, their self-generating recruitment, and the origin of individual board members from among the privileged and powerful, boards have little inclination to support empowering underrepresented groups. In 1985, only 20 percent of governing board members were women and only 10 percent were nonwhite. Furthermore, board committee service is gendered. Even women who are business leaders are more likely to serve on student and academic affairs committees than on finance, budget, or development committees. Hence, governing boards mirror the masculinized contexts of higher education administration and are perhaps even more inclined to resist change than the broader institution. But women's presence on boards does make a difference. They have more liberal attitudes than their male counterparts and frequently raise issues of concern to women students. They also raise issues concerning board functioning, a desire for more consensus building, and integration of new and underutilized board members.

Leadership as Empowerment

A difference between women leaders in ascendancy in the 1990s and their predecessors interviewed by Astin and Leland (1993) is awareness of the role of power dynamics and politics in higher education. As more women moved into positions of authority, they could use power to support their values and goals. The women academic leaders interviewed in Baker's (1996) qualitative study developed consultative leadership styles, actively engaging others in processes, recognizing interdependence on constituencies, possessing purposive vision, drawing on the talent of others or collecting their visions, and moving people forward to a shared vision. These women are consciously and deliberately reconstructing leadership.

It is not easy to simultaneously change a masculinized context while attempting progressive and feminist leadership. Like the women managers mentioned by Hornby and Shaw (1996), women administrators are ambivalent about the perceived need to play power games to advance before being able to change the nature of the game (Johnson 1993), finding it difficult to become assimilated while articulating a critique of male management models. Some may simply choose other careers to avoid the dilemma (Kettle 1996). Kolodny writes that her administrative experience taught her "the agonizing difficulty of acting ethically in ambiguous situations and amid profoundly divided claims on one's time, attention, and budgetary resources" (Kolodny 1998, 51).

Aligning one's leadership values with institutional mission helps to clarify decisions. Astin and Astin (2000) argue that transformative leaders empower groups and that, indeed, an essential goal of the academy should be to promote leadership development in students so they become agents for social change in the wider community. Therefore, the curriculum and co-curriculum should provide opportunities to develop the leadership skills and the requisite personal characteristics of authenticity, empathy, self-knowledge, and respectful disagreement.

Aligning one's leadership values with other higher education traditions can also make them less threatening. The tradition of governance shared by faculty and administration relies on the assumption that groups, the faculty as a whole and its committees, make wise decisions. While one might argue that this tradition has been muddied by various trends in higher education such as the growth of huge and complexly organized university, faculty unionization, and the commodification of higher education (Humm 1996), most institutions still strive to maintain some form of faculty governance and accrediting bodies continue to assert the importance of faculty control over academic standards and curricula.

Successful institutional change reported by women administrators often involves using existing structures. Stallings (1997) discusses the power of the search committee, arguing that the tendency to hire people like oneself is not necessarily overt discrimination. As dean, she required college and department search committees to include women, ethnic minorities, and representation from more than one department. Describing their experience of successfully instigating greater sensitivity to gender issues at a polytechnic university in the United Kingdom, Price and Priest (1996) present a model for organizational change initiated by a group of women faculty members with little formal power and no structure for networking. Higher education involves dispersed decision-making, meaning that women and other underrepresented groups need to gain access to key decision-making committees and senior administrators. Among the strategies Price and Priest suggest are making sure that the problem is defined by the change agent, gathering information through actively listening to the stories that are circulating, taking part in task forces or other groups designed to study relevant issues, planting seeds to shift the meaning of the stories that comprise institutional history, gathering data, collecting political information about "existing stakes" in the issue, and selling the project. Next is coalition-building through finding allies, setting up teams of task forces, making sure that senior managers know about the project (even if they do not approve), lining up supports at all levels of the organization, and formalizing the coalition. Finally, mobilization involves handling the opposition, maintaining the momentum, redesigning systems, and external communication. The influence of collective action by less powerful members of the staff is often underestimated. Lott and Rocchio (1998) make similar points in their description of a successful effort to influence the administration of their university to develop and enforce a comprehensive sexual harassment policy.

Effective strategies vary with the historical and current culture of an institution. McKay (1997) argues that one of the advantages of having separate black studies departments in the early history of the discipline is that it permitted the field to develop its own academic and political agendas. Now that the discipline's existence is established and that faculty members have made it into the ranks of the tenured, they must form alliances with other ethnic studies areas to actually change the curriculum.

Finally, groups' self-attributions may restrict their vision, as they frequently accept the conventional perception of their relative positions (Astin and Astin 2000). For instance, student affairs professionals have accepted the assumption that institutional leaders are those with formal power, particularly those in the academic hierarchy, missing the opportunity to exert leadership in collaboration with other administrators and faculty who recognize that learning occurs outside the classroom and teaching is not the sole province of faculty.

How, then, can leaders empower groups? At first glance, the notion of transformational power may seem to deny the real, hierarchical power structure of institutions. After all, it seems naïve to ignore the reward and punishment contingencies that operate in institutions. Administrators do serve at the pleasure of the president, presidents do serve at the pleasure of the board, tenured faculty and deans do make life-changing decisions about junior faculty members' tenure, faculty do give students grades that have consequences for students' future options. Astin and Astin never deny these realities, but instead argue that those with institutional power must be aware of how contingencies influence transformative leadership.

Recounting their own experiences, women deans describe similar strategies. Kolodny believes that her most significant contribution to her school was to democratize the decision-making process, dismantling old power alliances, despite the conflict generated by the threat to established ways of doing business. If she were to return to administration, she says she would focus on restructuring the university to introduce an information-rich, decentralized environment and inclusive decision-making. Faculty and staff should be fully informed in shared administration as true partners, sharing information and negotiating priorities. Administrators should "build community without silencing debate or disagreement . . . be comfortable with diversity and inclusivity . . . [and have] the tact to ensure that a few prima donnas or enlarged egos (including her own) do not dominate decision making for selfish or parochial purposes" (Kolodny 1998, 30).

Recognizing that deans are seen as having formal and distant relationships means it is incumbent for the dean to reach out to get to know people on a personal level (Stallings 1997). Direct communication with faculty, listening to concerns of lower status groups, and responding to them are essential, along with building a team of people who will share one's philosophy. However, change agents should appreciate the long-term investments in the institution of senior people, who may react to loss of personal and professional prestige or financial advantages.

PRINCIPLE 3

One of the most misrepresented aspects of feminist psychology concerns understanding how victims of difficult circumstances respond. Feminist psychologists maintain that people use active strategies, rather than being the passive victims feminism is often accused of encouraging. Indeed, apparently dysfunctional behavior often is an attempt to actively control a negative situation, as when an abused person attempts to please her abuser. Academic reward systems sometimes encourage behavior that may seem unhealthy, but is a way to cope with an environment that does not permit more functional behavior. The faculty member at a research university who treats teaching duties perfunctorily is responding reasonably to the reward system in that setting.

The gender differences in effective leadership strategies summarized by Carli and Eagly (1999) may be interpreted as illustrating this point. Women who have succeeded may have developed their leadership styles through trial and error, discovering what works for them through trying various strategies. It is meaningless to ask whether women's leadership styles would have been different if our society were not heavily gendered, but the fact that effective strategies do vary with the extent of masculinization of the context does suggest that women learn to use context-specific leadership strategies (Yoder 2001b). People probably solve problems in ways similar to those that have worked for them previously. When confronted with a new personnel problem, I consciously recall similar situations and plan responses like those that have worked previously. In other words, because of the context in which they are employed, women leaders adopt leadership styles that take advantage of gendered expectations others have for them and perhaps they have for themselves. Thus, gendered styles may represent active and realistic coping with constraints imposed by stereotyped notions of leadership and discriminatory opportunities for gaining experience. In this vein, Regan and Brooks (1995) argue that their feminist attributes of relationship leadership derive from the active experience of women in the world. While men may engage in relational tactics, primarily women practice them because they result from gender-specific experience.

While policies, laws, and cultural norms now offer greater opportunity, women who have achieved also deserve credit for their own agency. The literature on women in collegiate administration describes numerous survival strategies, often in the form of advice to aspiring administrators. One of Regan and Brooks' feminist leadership attributes is courage, defined as "the capacity to move ahead into the unknown" (1995, 29). Women in male-dominated careers have had to risk failure and other problems resulting from being women in a male-based environment. They also have had to take risks when they try to manage things differently from the way men do, to understand and try to change their employment setting.

Astin and Astin (2000) talk about the personal resources that facilitate transformative leadership: autonomy, critical thinking, academic freedom, and a willingness to challenge. Autonomy gives one the freedom to undertake initiatives. Even within the constraints of institutional bureaucracies and externally-imposed mandates, college faculty and staff have a good deal of freedom to organize their colleagues, interpret requirements in their own way, and thereby exercise power. Astin and Astin cite the impact that student activism has had on the development of new curricular areas like women's and ethnic studies as examples of a result of student autonomy. The right to challenge ideas and raise questions is embedded in academic culture and, while they may be used to maintain the status quo, they can be important catalysts for change.

African-American women administrators consistently describe strategies they use to succeed in a difficult environment, active tactics that explicitly acknowledge the reality of ethnic and gender discrimination. Wolfman (1997) contends that self-sufficiency has always been important to black girls. Without mentors, woman managers often have to rely on their own intelligence to understand institutional culture and racial hostility. McKay (1997) echoes this describing strategies used by black women who attended graduate school in the 1960s and 70s, the first generation to make inroads into careers in white academic institutions. She says, "Black women must always weigh the cost of their choices against the balance of energy, will, and the determination to survive with human dignity. Daniel (1997) discusses the coping strategies of African-American nursing administrators, noting that the low status of nursing multiplies oppressions from race and gender. Personal strategies focus on developing a strong sense of one's goals, values, and career plans and attaining the education, skills, and experience necessary to accomplish them. Strategies focusing on institutional change involve lobbying for fair access, suitable protections and grievance procedures, and communication with top administrators. Self-sufficiency and token status may contribute to burnout, with which African-American women must also learn to cope (Moses, 1997). One of Moses' respondents reports that she learned to "maintain a less visible profile as a coping and survival strategy" (Moses 1997, 16).

African-American women presidents are more likely than other presidents to pursue administration because of some personal circumstance of challenge, anger, or frustration (Jones 1997). Jones' respondents, seventeen of the twenty-six African-American women who were college presidents in the United States in 1991, describe gradually evolving leadership styles based on understanding group dynamics, conflict resolution, consensus building, and shared governance. They also emphasize the importance of professional and spiritual role models and family influences more than their white counterparts.

Another theme is self-knowledge. Miller and Vaughn's (1997) respondents counsel emerging African-American women leaders in higher education to develop a strong sense of their own values, beliefs, and abilities. Green (1997) contends that African-American women administrators need to define situations for themselves, rather than letting the situations define them. By understanding institutional history and culture, building collegiality, and listening to others, one can redefine a situation. She advises women to prioritize objectives, use available formal power to its fullest extent, build external support outside of one's unit, develop strong negotiating skills to aggressively cut the best deal to protect one's own interests, and make plans to leave when changes in the institution or its leadership dictate it. And Miller and Vaughn also say, "know that discrimination exists and that nothing is guaranteed" (1997, 187).

Of course, individual survival sometimes involves escaping a difficult situation. Williams (2000) argues that one way that women have coped with the excessive demands of tenure track positions is to choose alternative careers. She also discusses negotiating with one's partner about the division of childcare and housework, job sharing, and part-time tenure track work, but these strategies may be difficult without cooperation from others. Others talk about withdrawing from service to avoid burnout (Moses 1997). Such strategies make good sense, and women who choose them must be respected. Women who do pursue higher education administration often have a sense of mission, deliberately adopting transformational leadership styles. Frequently writers talk about being inspired by a vision of a transformed environment in which future administrators do not have to tolerate the conditions they have experienced.

Price and Priest's (1996) description of ways that women act as change agents in an institution without formal power also speak to the issue of active coping. Many of these strategies, and those developed by leaders studied in other research, rely heavily on forming coalitions. Because collective action is one of the few ways individuals who are members of powerless groups can challenge those with high status, this represents a practical and very active strategy for coping with disadvantage.

The theme of defining situations rather than being defined by them is also important, as it underscores the notion that survival depends on interpretation and the meanings applied to situations as well as on actions. Feminists know that words are important, as Amey and Twombly (1993) illustrate when they show how women community college presidents are discussed in ways that emphasize their problems and marginalize their accomplishments. If, rather than using military, athletic, or construction metaphors to describe leaders, one used metaphors of weaving, cultivating, and networking, how different would be the interpretation of presidents' behavior. Leadership then becomes a process to empower, facilitate, collaborate, and educate rather than a personality characteristic.

Changing Incentives

In addition to being a survival strategy, the importance of agency also forms the basis of a management strategy. Administrators frequently talk about trying to understand the reward system at work in a setting and modifying it to change the behavior of its participants. Astin and Astin's (2000) definition of leadership as purposive and value-based calls for leaders to be thoughtful in their analysis of the values promoted by formal and informal incentive systems in the academy. Because academic reward systems may no longer, and perhaps never did, reinforce the behavior desired in institutions, they deserve careful scrutiny, particularly when constituencies are not behaving as one desires. If an institution really values undergraduate teaching, then successful undergraduate teaching should be rewarded in tenure, promotion, or merit decisions. Understanding and changing these reward systems can empower lower status groups, such as newer faculty members who are interested in curricular reform. If one wants to discourage uncollegial behavior on the part of a spoiled superstar faculty member, one should not reward that person with accolades.

Recent proposals to reevaluate criteria applied to scholarship emphasize the centrality of the teaching mission of most colleges (Boyer 1994). Faculty who do not engage in the work of revising curricula or take faculty governance work seriously may do so because they believe that the administration does not value their expertise and will ignore them, that students are not really interested in learning, or that colleagues are unwilling to change their behavior (Astin and Astin 2000). Disciplinary structures, limited resource allocation, and a belief that separation from administration is necessary to maintain faculty autonomy also contribute to reluctance to become transformative leaders.

Other writers also propose altering reward systems to transform higher education. Because black women are called on disproportionately to mentor black students, Moses (1997) argues that institutional values placed on these activities should be increased, e.g., that teaching, counseling, community work, and advising should be weighed more heavily in promotion and tenure. Kolodny (1998) also suggests that incentives can be used to encourage faculty members who are no longer doing research or enthusiastic about teaching to retool by pursuing new areas about which they can be excited.

Training for leadership should begin with students (Astin and Astin 2000). Working, socializing, volunteer work, team sports, and participation in student organizations provide opportunities for leadership training. Student complaints can be transformed to leadership development. In my experience, when students are complaining about things or attempting to influence school policies, they are often seeking to make changes in the only ways they believe are available to them as a relatively powerless group. Thus the student petition that demands some action on the part of the administration may be seen as an attempt to cope with some problem. Transformative leaders attempt to help students find problem resolution strategies that also develop leadership skills. Astin and Astin argue that any student who seeks to become a change agent can do so if given relevant knowledge and skills. Colleges must foster these abilities. Kolodny (1998) instituted a program to prepare graduate students for nonresearch aspects of faculty life to help them develop skills for committee service, department management, and curricular reform and to encourage them to value these activities.

Similar arguments can be made in regard to faculty. Administrators who model the principles of transformative leadership can also encourage faculty to use them in their teaching. Creating a shared purpose by bringing self-knowledge, empathy, authenticity, disagreement with respect, and collaboration to interactions with students are strategies for effective teaching within and outside of the classroom. Faculty members can learn to use these traits in their campus leadership activities and teach them to students at all levels.

Activism and Social Justice

Agency also underlies another concept that differentiates feminist management theories from others, a commitment to activism and social justice. In a feminist analysis of pragmatic liberal education, Crumpacker et al. (1998) argue that feminist thought contributed commitment to social justice and action to the list of other characteristics encouraged by liberal education, such as competence, knowledge, and ethics. Grumet and McCoy (1997) point out that feminist pedagogies seek to develop students' confidence in their own agency and ability to work collectively for social change in a discussion of feminist impacts on the discipline of education.

Feminist administrators share these values. One of Regan and Brooks' (1995) feminist attributes is "being visionary", i.e., formulating new ideas and enabling others to consider new options and making a commitment to changing the culture. Sometimes this theme is couched in an obligation to give back to the community and mentor others, as African-American administrators frequently mention (Miller and Vaughn 1997). Effective tactics for pursuing social justice probably vary with one's position. Administrators who want to empower other people to make change walk a fine line between encouraging and instigating, which may create reactance or be dangerous politically. Zalk (1997) describes how her own transition from campus activist to senior administrator influenced her behavior and the expectations of others. Yet, despite changes in how she pursued goals, her commitment to social justice remained central to her actions. Strong leaders are guided by values; feminist theory provides a belief system that is the foundation for the values of many higher education administrators of both genders.

PRINCIPLE 4

People who have not spent time in the academy may be surprised at a principle eschewing simplistic analysis. Don't academics spend their time devising convoluted theories to address abstruse problems? Yet people in academic environments often set up false dichotomies and straw arguments, which inevitably involve oversimplification. Complex problems need to be treated as just that, complex. I think of a biologist I know who divided her world into "real science" and "not science," meaning to her "good" and "bad." Any work that did not fit her conception of "real science" was valueless; the opinion of any colleague who did not do "real science" was worthless. The resistance to interdisciplinary studies articulated so clearly by Nussbaum (1997) results from a tendency to dichotomize and essentialize problems.

In his important statement about American higher education, Ernest Boyer (1994) discusses the ways in which rigid disciplinary boundaries limit universities' effectiveness. Boyer's premise is that the United States needs to invent at new model for American education and the professoriate, not derived from the German research university, with its emphasis on the professoriate and the generation of new knowledge, or the American liberal arts college, with its emphasis on general education and loyalty to a campus. Faculty should be encouraged to generate scholarship of integration, cross-disciplinary synthesis, and application. The New American College should respond to the crises of our day, just as land grant colleges responded to the needs of an agricultural economy. In other words, the New American College is an institution that rewards faculty members who teach students to examine problems from multiple perspectives and avoid rigid thinking about issues. In addition to encouraging interdisciplinary analysis, it redefines scholarship as including students and existing primarily for the improvement of student learning.

Interdisciplinarity is an important tenet of feminist theory. Crumpacker et al. (1998) discuss the impact of the collaborative, interdisciplinary nature of feminist theory on disciplines and institutions. They argue that feminist thought and multiculturalism have forced discussion of the limitations of rigid disciplinary boundaries that fragment knowledge and limit students' ability to solve complex problems or relate to the complicated issues of life that require examination from multiple perspectives. Feminist pedagogies encourage students to think critically about their own experiences and express their ideas with confidence (Grumet and McCoy 1997; Madden and Russo 1997).

Astin and Astin (2000) argue that the committee structure of shared governance lends itself well to introducing multiple perspectives if committee heads use transformative leadership techniques. That is, committee chairs should display self-knowledge, authenticity and integrity, commitment to the collective effort, empathy and understanding of others, and competence, just as college administrators should. In their chapter on college presidents, Astin and Astin outline ways chief executive officers can promote expression of diverse viewpoints. The goal is to avoid "groupthink," when the pressure for consensus curtails a group's careful analysis of a problem (Janis 1982). When faculty members do not know the president's agenda or understand the multiple constituencies presidents serve, Kolodny (1998) argues, shared governance is a sham, and faculty take their frustration out on deans, provosts, presidents. To share information and be clear about her agenda as dean, she created a large, inclusive faculty advisory group that met to engage in collective problem-solving.

Kolodny's advisory committee was one feature of her broadly applied collaborative decision-making. Astin and Astin's (2000) leadership through collaborative process is also intended to promote expression of diverse viewpoints. Purposive leadership creates a supportive environment to construct communities based on reciprocal and shared responsibility. Collaborative relationships between leaders are guided by shared purpose, enable respectful disagreement, have clear divisions of labor and responsibilities, and create a learning environment in which individuals develop. In higher education, leadership development should enable all constituents to enhance institutions' missions of student learning and development, knowledge generation, and community service.

Finally, collaboration requires valuing diversity of opinions and, therefore, facilitating the presence of diverse people with diverse viewpoints in decision-making groups. African-American education deans frequently report having their ideas validated only after white colleagues restated them as their own (Lindsay 1997). They also point to a discounting of certain kinds of professional experiences in search processes. That is, administrative experiences in hospital, government, or national associations may be more available to women candidates than line positions in education, but may not be considered relevant to higher education administration.

Outlining elements of a feminist leadership agenda in higher education, Johnson (1993) included appreciating the value of diversity and developing leaders sensitive to diversity. While appreciating diversity is important for the sake of those who are excluded and have no voice, institutions should also value diversity because it makes for better decision-making. In other words, being sensitive to diversity involves appreciating diverse perspectives. Yet, women administrators question whether lip service paid to diversity really reflects an underlying value. For instance, Townsend and Twombly (1998) note that the Total Quality Management movement recently embraced by community college administrators emphasizes conformity rather than difference and is undermined by multicultural and gender inclusion. Perhaps, recognizing that diversity brings better decision-making requires a genuine belief in the value of collaboration.

PRINCIPLE 5

Collaboration is an effective leadership strategy. Collaboration works because participatory and consensus-based decision-making is far more satisfying for participants and produces results and plans that people can buy into readily. Articulating reasons for collaborative leadership as part of shared value system can clarify tactics for participants or skeptical colleagues accustomed to authoritarian modes of leadership. Collaborative decision-making consistently is considered a fundamental tenet of feminist leadership. Johnson (1993) says that feminist leadership emphasizes shared and collective decision-making, inclusion of a range of viewpoints, public priority setting and problem solving, and facilitation rather than domination. Good leadership, then, requires good listening, facilitating effective work of others, promoting interdependence of people and units, and proposing initiatives that others pursue.

Regan and Brooks (1995) identify collaboration and caring as important elements of feminist leadership, in keeping with relational psychology's contention that those attributes are a more prominent part of the experience of women than of men. Collaboration involves inclusiveness, shared ownership, and connectedness with others. Caring translates into a moral commitment to action on behalf of others, promoting human development and respondent to needs.

However, arguments in support of collaboration go beyond its compatibility with feminist values. The pressures faced by higher education today mandate involvement of all stakeholders in decision-making because serious problems and rapid change require a great deal of cooperation among policy makers and policy implementers. Boyer's (1994) thesis about the New American College is based on this notion of connectedness, across disciplines, between faculty and students, and among all features of campus life and curriculum. The College focuses not only on discovery, but also on integration, application and teaching, forms of collaboration among people and between the institution and the world. Astin and Astin's (2000) transformative leadership also assumes that leadership is a collaborative activity. They discuss collaboration among and between students, faculty, student affairs professions, and senior officers of the institutions. Particularly in their discussion about leadership by presidents and other senior administrators, they explicitly talk about how to overcome institutional culture to encourage collaboration.

Writers discussing varied educational settings stress the need for participatory decision-making, one collaborative process. Kolodny (1998) argues that current budgetary realities and structures in public institutions require a risk-taking administrator to develop an inclusive team approach to administration, which she labels horizontal problem solving. Articulating problems, despite causing discomfort to those who lose power, and willingness to explore all possibilities and search for solutions are necessary. Amey and Twombly (1993) argue that traditionally defined leadership in community colleges is noncollaborative in nature and that women's attempts to use collaborative styles are seen as aberrant. But, in fact, alternative leadership styles are needed at a crucial point in the history of community colleges, when they will be either revived or will fail. The metaphors for leadership she invokes, such as weaver, cultivator, networker, and connector all speak to collaborative efforts, combining the activities of groups of people. Leadership, then, is empowering, facilitating, collaborating, and educating—all activities that connect people rather than telling or pulling them along do traditional directive styles.

Women Collaborate

Women use collaborative leadership more often men. They are expected to and, in fact, are ineffective if they choose more authoritarian leadership tactics. Carli and Eagly (1999) show that women are expected to be warmer and more collaborative in their leadership styles than men, who are expected to be more task-oriented. Women also are expected to be more concerned about connections among people. Women are more influential when task-oriented influence is combined with positive social behavior. Women do engage in more positive social behavior than men, presumably because that is what works for them. They use less direct language and combine competence with warmth to overcome resistance to their influences.

Women leaders from the 1960s on, according to Astin and Leland (1993), have understood the necessity of collective action to improve women's positions in all facets of higher education, from opportunities for women students to advancing the careers of individual women leaders. The assumption that lower status people must band together may seem obvious and simplistic, but it provides a *modus operandi* that is explicit for many people trying to change the academy. Women administrators interviewed by Baker (1996) all emphasized their interdependence with followers, their community service orientation, and their ability to create conditions of trust and caring as well as fairness, objectivity, focus, and vision. The skills they relied upon involved empowering, team building, and facilitation, along with problem solving and risk taking.

At the other end of the authority spectrum from presidents, women who lack power must also rely on collaboration to influence academia. Price and Priest (1996) focus on the importance of coalition for promoting change when one lacks formal power, illustrating the point with a case history of an extensive and highly successful group effort to reduce discrimination in their university in the United Kingdom. Price and Priest emphasize the importance of creating informal networks and taking advantage of every institutional vehicle for creating formal networks (e.g., committees). After defining a problem, those seeking to make change should find allies, set up task force teams, communicate with senior administrators, line up supporters at lower and higher levels of the organization, and finally formalize the coalition. Sometimes groups designed to deal with one set of issues can be redefined to deal with another issue.

Collaboration appears to be even more important for members of under-represented groups. African-American women writing about higher education unanimously mention the importance of forming coalitions, networking, finding supportive communities, and seeking support from other members of their ethnic group and sympathetic people from other groups. Shields (1997) argues that deans at historically black colleges have tended to need to be collaborative because they rarely have assistants or adequate support staff. Dawson (1997) contends that success and mobility are based in diverse networking, speaking also of the importance of connections with familial foremothers. Wolfman (1997) points to the importance of cooperation in African-American homes and to collective support from church and extended family as ways to cope with racism. Church and women's groups often prompted girls' pursuit of professional jobs with a service orientation. McKay (1997) believes that black women must cultivate coalitions with those in other ethnic studies, maintaining that the backlash from conservative movements against progressive movements like multiculturalism is a sign of the potential power of such coalitions. Hine (1997) also discusses investing much time in developing community among black historians and women's studies professors, as well as black feminist scholarship. She emphasizes the importance of friendships and support across gender and race boundaries. With the appreciation of the importance of networking comes the obligation to mentor others.

Collaboration Is Not Easy

Despite its value, collaboration is neither easy nor a panacea for leadership problems. Indeed, it may limit women's ability to be seen as leaders. Women presidents may be misunderstood if their methods are so disparate from conventional views of leadership or they may be further marginalized or trivialized by inadvertently reinforcing the stereotype of women as nurturers (Bensimon 1993). Administrators with egalitarian leanings may have difficulty in environments that have relied on authoritarian structure and distance (Stallings 1997). Systems that are inherently conservative and developed for other modes of leadership are difficult to change and current economic stress on institutions makes that challenge greater (Johnson 1993). However, each of these authors contends that insights from feminist analyses should be used to transform the normative models of leadership rather than reverting to authoritarian strategies. While the need to educate constituencies about why certain strategies are being used or, even more fundamentally, about how one defines leadership, can be wearying, it is probably an unavoidable component of being a change agent.

Women have fewer choices in regards to leadership behavior, particularly in masculinized environments (Yoder 2001b). Furthermore, the desire to collaborate and help others may pose career problems for women, who see service to the community and to others similar to them as important. Women believe service is valid and important, but service in academic departments does not necessarily enhance prospects for administrative leadership positions, which may require stellar scholarly work more than administrative experience. Because men spend more time on research than women, and women spend more time on service and teaching than men, men may be seen as more impressive candidates for senior academic positions (Task Force on Women in Academe 2000). Excessive demands for committee work and support of others exacerbate these problems for ethnic minority women (Stallings 1997).

If women leaders are uncomfortable with a double standard about appropriate leadership behavior, there may be two choices—either work to change gender-based expectations about leadership or work to change conceptions of leadership to include more facilitative and socially positive behavior. Some of us are attempting to do both simultaneously.

Mentoring

The importance of mentoring is stressed in virtually every discussion of women in higher education administration. The loneliness and liability of isolation is a common problem for women who are tokens, solos, and barrier-breakers in their departments and institutions (Quina, Cotter and Romanesko 1998). Women in general feel isolated, and isolation is exacerbated for members of ethnic minorities and other underrepresented groups (Gibson 1996; Locke 1997; Moses 1997). Despite the value women place on interpersonal connections, Heward (1996) asserts that women may have benefited less from networks of contacts than men, and these networks become increasingly important in middle and later stages of academic careers. Formal and informal mentoring provides one remedy for women's isolation.

Space does not permit reviewing the rich literature on mentoring, but I will describe a few suggestions dealing specifically with mentoring for and by college administrators. Attempting to address the problem of incompatible matches and unclear expectations observed in intradepartmental mentoring programs, which can create discipleship, rivalry, or hurt feelings, Kolodny (1998) devised mentoring programs for new department chairs and new faculty members based on informal "buddy groups," composed of two buddies, one male and one female. One buddy was male, and one from the mentee's home department but not the same specialization. The mentors served primarily as supportive personal contacts, rather than scholarly collaborators.

Recognizing that few black women psychologists have peers in their workplaces, Jessica Henderson Daniel (2001) developed in intriguing mentoring program for a group of black women who recently received doctorates in psychology. The group meets for long weekends and engages in team-building activities with a professional facilitator and career advising by experienced black women psychologists. After the initial sessions, communication is facilitated through electronic means and additional meetings are held in conjunction with professional conferences that all agree to attend. In a moving panel at the American Psychological Association, participants described the support this group of "sister scientists" has given them in the year since, from advice for professional dilemmas to celebration of each others' successes to collaborations on research projects.

In the absence of formal mentoring programs, women must seek out support networks. In her advice for black women in administration, Dawson emphasizes the importance of supportive relationships, including recognizing that even in discriminatory situations there are people who will support one. She also discusses the importance of realizing that one is charting new ground as a way to understand the situation. She suggests developing collegial relationships with diverse groups of professionals and developing cordial relationships with staff and faculty. She argues that developing conciliatory skills, accepting criticism gracefully even when it is unjustified, and trying to understand rather than to be understood are skills to develop. Miller and Vaughn also (1997) speak to the importance of mentoring and networks. Family networks that promote expectations of accomplishments and success as a means of racial and family improvement are important. Mentoring models that work for African-American women are those that are selective and have assessed similarities. Several authors echo the importance of building networks across one's institution (Daniel 1997; J. H. Daniel 2001; Green 1997; Miller and Vaughan 1997). Daniel (1997) makes specific suggestions about networking for African-American nursing administrators, such as joining national nursing networks, support groups for women administrators, workshops related to administration, forums with top-level administrators, professional organizations that include professionals other than nurses, and committees on professional climate issues and policies.

Given the necessity for mentoring, many writers also stress the importance of serving as a mentor to other women (Miller and Vaughan 1997). Moses (1997) talks about the responsibility of black women to mentor students and other black women in professional and faculty positions. She also mentions that black students and graduate students can also provide support and encouragement for women faculty and staff who may be isolated in their departments. Their isolation may cause them to be left out of the decision-making processes that affect their work directly, so promoting relationships is important in order to integrate them into the mission of universities.

Balancing Work and Family

The need for finding support outside of one's job raises the issue of family life. Several authors advise women administrators to take care of themselves physically and mentally, seek balance in their lives, and get support from their family and friends. But of course, balancing work and family can be a source of stress for many employed people and, because women still bear a disproportionate share of family responsibility and work, they tend to be more impacted than men. Hensel asserts, "Lack of a supportive environment for combining family and work may be the biggest barrier to women's advancement in academe" (1997, 38). Women in high-level administration face even more challenging questions when they have small children or become pregnant. Never-ending work, the availability for early morning meetings, and evening events make the balance difficult. The need for academic administrators to continue to engage in scholarship compounds this problem because their days are filled by administrative duties, and the only time for research may be nights or weekends.

While much is made of the difficulties, it is essential to note the social psychological literature that says that juggling career and family responsibilities is actually healthy for women and their children (Barnett and Hyde 2001; Crosby 1993). Indeed, having multiple roles is psychologically beneficial for both women and men, but produces stress when one of the roles is excessively demanding (Barnett and Hyde 2001). Hensel (1997) argues that deans must set a model for establishing appropriate balance between career and personal life. They should educate employees about the law, but also establish a climate where it is acceptable to use the law, for example, to take family leave. They should set limits on their own work to serve as positive models for all employees. In terms of policy, administrators should do a "family responsiveness audit" to identify whether policies and practices support family situations and care giving and recognize the roles of employees outside, as well inside, the organization. She argues that this will benefit universities in the long run by creating healthier, happier employees who devote adequate time to the next generation, their own children, and their students.

Beyond Equity

Applying principles of feminist psychology helps articulate characteristics of a feminist approach to higher education administration. Understanding cultural context, sensitivity to power and status dynamics, viewing people as active agents capable of responding positively to environmental circumstances, seeking multiple perspectives and solutions to complex problems, and appreciating the importance of collaboration are concerns voiced by women and men writing about higher education administration. Those who identify themselves as feminist tend to emphasize these themes, but many others discuss the utility of strategies rooted in these values.

Because social activism is an important element of feminism, explicating these principles serves to frame and explain strategy for academic institutions. Change agents may have limited time frame in which they can operate effectively (Astin and Astin 2000; Kolodny 1998), so clear values, objectives, and goals are important components of success. Those not in positions of high authority can be empowered by understanding that collaboration can change even inherently conservative organizations like academic institutions. As more like-minded people ascend into positions of authority, the opportunity to work with others with similar views will increase. There is cause for a sense of optimism that higher education will continue its progress towards becoming a working environment that provides opportunity for people from diverse backgrounds, is equitable and fair, and promotes interdisciplinary analysis of complex problems within and outside of its metaphorical ivy walls.

Optimism must be tempered with realism, of course. Strategies focusing only on policy changes have not advanced women in higher education as quickly as is desirable For instance, campus commissions on the status of women have tended to see consensus and equity, but not deal with fundamental change in the organization (Glazer-Raymo 1999). While continual review, making gender impact studies a regular part of planning processes, and developing accountability in regard to women's issues on campuses are necessary, they are not sufficient (Johnson 1993). Instead, it is time to develop a shared belief system that is explicit about the assumptions and values underlying decisions, examines how institutional structures constrain women's leadership, and takes advantages of the gendered experiences of women to transform academe, rather than simply adding women to a masculinized administrative context (Glazer-Raymo 1999; Johnson 1993; Lindsay 1997; Yoder 2001b). There will always be institutional inertia, external pressure, and financial constraints to undermine this kind of change. As Astin and Astin say, "Resistance is a necessary part of the change process . . . and practicing transformative leadership is a never-ending process" (2000, 95). May a shared vision, strong sense of the importance of the mission, and faith in the power of collective action give us the energy and determination to persist.

10

Institutional Barriers for Women Scientists and Engineers: What Four Years of Survey Data of National Science Foundation POWRE Awardees Reveal

Sue V. Rosser

On January 29, 2001, the presidents, chancellors, provosts, and twenty-five women scientists from the most prestigious research universities (Cal Tech, MIT, University of Michigan, Princeton, Stanford, Yale, the University of California at Berkeley, Harvard, and Penn) held a special meeting at Massachusetts Institute of Technology. At the close of the meeting, they issued the following statement:

Institutions of higher education have an obligation, both for themselves and for the nation, to fully develop and utilize all the creative talent available," the leaders said in a unanimous statement. "We recognize that barriers still exist" for women faculty and they agreed to: analyze the salaries and proportion of other university resources provided to women faculty; to work toward a faculty that reflects the diversity of the student body; to reconvene in about a year "to share the specific initiatives we have undertaken to achieve these objectives; to "recognize that this challenge will require significant review of, and potentially significant change in, the procedures within each university, and within the scientific and engineering establishments as a whole." (Campbell 2001,1)

For the first time in public and in print, the leaders of the nation's most prestigious universities have suggested that institutional barriers have prevented women scientists and engineers from having a level playing field and that science and engineering might need to change to accommodate women.

Almost simultaneously, the National Science Foundation (NSF) initiated ADVANCE, a new awards program at a funding level of $19 million for 2001 that has two categories to include institutional, rather than individual, solutions to empower women to participate fully in science and technology. NSF encouraged institutional rather than individual solutions because of "increasing recognition that the lack of women's full participation at the senior level of academe is often a systemic consequence of academic culture" (NSF 2001, 2). Under ADVANCE, Institutional Transformation Awards, ranging up to $750,000 per year for up to five years, promote the increased participation and advancement of women, whereas Leadership Awards recognize the work of outstanding organizations of individuals and enable them to sustain, intensify and initiate new activity (NSF 2001).

Public admissions by the most prestigious and mainstream universities and foundations that the parts of institutions and the particular professions remaining most closed to women must become more women-centered will require significant institutional changes to empower women scientists and engineers. Creating a woman-centered university becomes a daunting task because of the historical, statistical, and cultural traditions that have built the university to fit male needs, developmental stages, and interests. As women have entered the university, we have fought to change these male-centered traditions to make them more female-friendly.

HISTORICAL STATISTICAL PROFILE OF WOMEN IN SCIENCE AND ENGINEERING

Although attempts to produce a more female-friendly environment encountered substantial resistance, the most significant changes have occurred in parts of the university where the most women have been for the longest time. Historically women were not permitted to enroll in institutions of higher education; the first coeducational colleges and universities emerged in the United States in 1833 with many of the Midwest land grant universities established as coeducational from their inception in the 1860s (Solomon 1985). The women's colleges in the East and South provided important opportunities for women students to receive an excellent education; they provided virtually the only opportunities for women faculty to teach and pursue scholarly research (Glazer and Slater 1987). As late as 1966, women constituted 42.6 percent of undergraduates, 33.8 percent of M.S., and 11.6 percent of Ph.D. students (NSF 2000, Table 3-12) in all U.S. institutions.

Currently, 55.9 percent of undergraduates (NSF 2000, Table 1-5) and 54.3 percent of graduate students (NSF 2000, Table 3-12) are women. In these days of attention to statistics and interest in meeting the needs of the student as consumer, universities have accommodated some practices for the statistical majority, who are women students. However, resistance to both curricular and extracurricular changes for equity can be seen, in part, in the struggle of women's studies (Carroll 2001; DeGroot and Maynard 1993; Pryse 1999; Zimmerman 2000) and women's sports (Heckman 1997; Sandler 1997a) to obtain equity and legitimacy.

In some disciplines and whole colleges within the university, women students remain in the minority. While the number of women majoring in scientific and technological fields has increased since the 1960s, reaching 49 percent in 1998 (NSF 2002, Table 3-4), the percentage of women in computing, the physical sciences, and engineering remains small. In 1998 women received 74.4 percent of the bachelors' degrees in psychology, 52.5 percent in the social sciences, 52.7 percent in the biological and agricultural sciences, 39 percent in the physical sciences, and 37 percent in the geosciences, while they received 18.6 percent of the degrees in engineering (NSF 2002, Table 3.4). The percentage of computer science degrees awarded to women actually dropped from 37 percent in 1984 to 20 percent in 1999 (Eisenberg 2000).

The percentage of graduate degrees in these fields earned by women remained lower. While women earned 55.5 percent of the M.S. degrees in all fields, they earned only 39.3 percent of the degrees in science and engineering fields. By specific fields, the percentages were as follows: engineering, 17.1 percent; physical sciences 33.2 percent; geosciences 29.3 percent; mathematics 40.2 percent; computer sciences 26.9 percent; biological and agricultural sciences 49.0 percent; psychology 71.9 percent; social sciences 50.2 percent (NSF 2000, Table 43). Women earned 40.6 percent of the Ph.D. degrees in all fields, but only 32.8 percent of the Ph.D.s in science and engineering. The specific field percentages included 12.3 percent in engineering, 22.4 percent in physical sciences, 23.7 percent in geosciences, 23.4 percent in mathematics, 16.2 percent in computer sciences, 40.7 percent in biological and agricultural sciences, 66.6 percent in psychology, and 58.7 percent in the social sciences (NSF 2000, Table 4-11).

Women faculty still do not represent a statistical majority; data reported in 2000, which is based upon 1995 figures gathered by the Commission on Professionals in Science and Technology, show that women constituted 34.66 percent of faculty overall, with the vast majority holding positions at the lowest ranks in the less prestigious institutions. Women faculty constituted the following percentages of full-time instructional faculty: 50.4 percent of the instructorships, 54.3 percent of lectureships, 43.6 percent of the assistants, 31.8 percent of the associates, and 17.8 percent of the full professorships at all institutions. For academic year 1996–97, 71.8 percent of men faculty and 51.6 percent of women faculty had tenure. At four-year institutions, 70.9 percent of men and 46.9 percent of women held tenure, while at universities, 74.6 percent of men and 47.4 percent of women faculty had tenure (CPST 2000, Table 5-10). With their male colleagues continuing as the majority and in the more powerful positions, women faculty have met considerable resistance to requests for policies to stop the tenure-clock during child-bearing, for on-site daycare, and for dual career hiring to make the university more female-friendly.

The small number of women receiving degrees in the sciences and engineering results in an even smaller percentage of women faculty in these fields. For example, only 19.5 percent of science and engineering faculty at four-year colleges and universities are women; 10.4 percent of the full professors, 21.9 percent of the associate professors, and 32.9 percent of the assistant professors in science and engineering at these institutions are women (NSF 2000, Table 5-15). Although many have read these statistics as suggesting that women will reach parity with men in these fields as they advance through the ranks, other information indicates that more substantial changes must occur to make the climate more female-friendly to retain senior women in these fields.

Perhaps it is not surprising that the male dominance in these fields is reflected not only in their statistical majority, but also in a continued tradition of male-centered approaches in labs, practices, and cultures. The extent to which these approaches, practices, and cultures present institutional barriers for women scientists and engineers has recently been underlined through the MIT report released in 1999 and recent anecdotal reports that some women scientists actively choose to avoid research universities (Schneider 2000) because of the hostile climate. Recent data document that women make up 40 percent of tenure-track science faculty in undergraduate institutions (Curry 2001). Although the bulk of science and technology research occurs at institutions formerly classified as Research I, decreased lab space, lower salaries, and fewer prestigious opportunities exemplify barriers for women endemic to most Research I institutions. A dawning recognition that these barriers can best be addressed by institutional, rather than individual changes became evident from the statement released after the MIT meeting on January 29, 2001 and from the focus of the ADVANCE initiative from NSF.

BARRIERS IDENTIFIES BY POWRE AWARDEES

In order to be most effective, the institutional changes attempted should address institutional barriers identified by women scientists and engineers as most problematic. Data from the almost 400 respondents to an e-mail survey of fiscal year 1997, 1998, 1999, and 2000 NSF Professional Opportunities for Women in Research and Education (POWRE) awardees reveals the barriers that academic women scientists and engineers identify as most challenging for their careers. Since POWRE was the NSF initiative that

ADVANCE replaced in 2001, the quantitative and qualitative data from the entire POWRE awardee cohort should be particularly relevant in exposing the barriers that institutions should change to empower and enable women scientists and engineers.

Established in 1997, the POWRE program stated two main objectives in its attempts to address the need to develop full use of the nation's human resources for science and engineering:

To provide opportunities for further career advancement, professional growth, and increased prominence of women in engineering and in the disciplines of science supported by NSF; and to encourage more women to pursue careers in science and engineering by providing greater visibility for women scientists and engineers in academic institutions and in industry. (NSF 1997, 1)

Women scientists or engineers who were U.S. citizens at any rank in tenured, tenure track, or non-tenure track positions at any four-year college, comprehensive, or research university were eligible to apply to POWRE. Although a few tenured, full professors, faculty from four-year institutions, and/or non-tenure track individuals received awards, the vast majority of POWRE awardees were untenured assistant professors in tenure track positions at research universities. All POWRE new grant awardees for fiscal years 1997, 1998, 1999, and 2000 were sent a questionnaire via e-mail. The questionnaire included the following two questions: First, what are the most significant issues/challenges/opportunities facing women scientists today as they plan their careers? Second, how does the laboratory climate (or its equivalent in your sub-discipline) impact upon the careers of women scientists?

Sixty-seven of the 96 POWRE awardees for fiscal year 1997, 119 of the 173 awardees for fiscal year 1998, 98 of the 159 fiscal year 1999 awardees, and 108 of the 170 fiscal year 2000 awardees to whom the questions were posed by e-mail responded. For each year, no responses came from between 23 percent and 37 percent of the awardees; some failures to respond were the result of invalid e-mail addresses. The sample responding to the e-mail questionnaire in all years appeared to be representative of the population of awardees with regard to discipline, and the non-respondents did not appear to cluster in a particular discipline. The limited data available from the e-mail responses revealed no other respondent or non-respondent bias (Rosser 2001).

The details of the procedure used to develop the 16 basic categories for responses to question have been previously published for 1997 awardees (Rosser and Zieseniss 2000); the same codes and categories were applied to the responses from 1998, 1999, and 2000 awardees. Although most respondents replied with more than one answer, in some years at least one awardee gave no answer to the question (see Table 10.1).

TABLE 10.1 Total Responses to Question 1

Question 1 What are the most significant issues/challenges/opportunities facing women scientists today as they plan their careers?

Categories	1997 % of responses	1998 % of responses	1999 % of responses	2000 % of responses
1 Balancing work with family responsibilities (children, elderly relatives, etc.)	62.7 (42/67)	72.3 (86/119)	77.6 (76/98)	71.3 (77/108)
2 Time management/ balancing committee responsibilities with research and teaching	22.4 (15/67)	10.1 (12/119)	13.3 (13/98)	13.0 (14/108)
3 Low numbers of women, isolation and lack of camaraderie/ mentoring	23.9 (16/67)	18.5 (22/119)	18.4 (18/98)	30.6 (33/108)
4 Gaining credibility/ respectability from peers and administrators	22.4 (15/67)	17.6 (21/119)	19.4 (19/98)	21.3 (23/108)
5 "Two career" problem (balance with spouse's career)	23.9 (16/67)	10.9 (13/119)	20.4 (20/98)	20.4 (22/108)
6 Lack of funding/ inability to get funding	7.5 (5/67)	4.2 (5/119)	10.2 (10/98)	8.3 (9/108)
7 Job restrictions (location, salaries, etc.)	9.0 (6/67)	9.2 (11/119)	7.1 (7/98)	5.6 (6/108)
8 Networking	6.0 (4/67)	<1 (1/119)	0 (0/98)	4.6 (5/108)
9 Affirmative action backlash/ discrimination	6.0 (4/67)	15.1 (18/119)	14.3 (14/98)	12.0 (13/108)
10 Positive: active recruitment of women/more opportunities	6.0 (4/67)	10.1 (12/119)	9.2 (9/98)	14.8 (16/108)
11 Establishing independence	3.0 (2/67)	0 (0/119)	6.1 (6/98)	2.8 (3/108)
12 Negative social images	3.0 (2/67)	3.4 (4/119)	2.0 (2/98)	<1 (1/108)
13 Trouble gaining access to nonacademic positions	1.5 (1/67)	1.7 (2/119)	1.0 (1/98)	1.9 (2/108)
14 Sexual harassment	1.5 (1/67)	<1 (1/119)	2.0 (2/98)	1.9 (2/108)
15 No answer	0 (0/67)	<1 (1/119)	1.0 (1/98)	1.9 (2/108)
16 Cut-throat competition	— —	— —	1.0 (1/98)	1.9 (2/108)

Career Challenges and Opportunities

In response 1, an overwhelming number of respondents for all four years found balancing work with family to be the most significant challenge facing women scientists and engineers. Adding restrictions because of spousal situations based on responses 5 and 7 suggests that category A—pressures women face in balancing career and family—is the most significant barrier identified by women scientists and engineers (Table 10.2). A second grouping (responses 3, 4, 8, 10, and 12) appears to result from the low numbers of women scientists and engineers and consequent stereotypes surrounding expectations about their performance. Isolation and lack of mentoring, as well as gaining credibility and respectability from peers and administrators, typify category B. Category C responses to questions 2, 6, and 16 includes issues faced by both men and women scientists and engineers in the current environment of tight resources that may pose particular difficulties for women, either because of their low numbers or their balancing act between career and family. For example, in response 2, time management/balancing committee responsibilities with research and teaching can be a problem for both male and female faculty. However, because of their low numbers in science and engineering, women faculty are often asked to serve on more committees, even while they are still junior, and to advise more students, either formally or informally (NSF 1997). Cut-throat competition makes it difficult for both men and women to succeed and obtain funding. Gender stereotypes that reinforce women's socialization to be less overtly competitive may make it more difficult for a woman scientist or engineer to succeed in a very competitive environment. In category D, responses 9, 11, 13, and 14 identify barriers of overt harassment and discrimination faced by women scientists and engineers. Sometimes even a positive response, such as active recruitment of women/more opportunities in response 10 leads to backlash and difficulties gaining credibility from peers who assume the woman obtained the position to fill a quota for affirmative action. Example quotations from the respondents from all four years provide the qualitative context for the categories. The women express the specific barriers for their careers.

Category A. Pressures women face in balancing career and family:

- For me, the biggest issue was children—not just the physical act of bearing them. But the emotional act each day of raising them. I'm unusual for a female researcher. I had two children in graduate school and still finished in four years. Now I'm trudging along the way—no one's stopped my clock or bought me out of a course. No institution has ever given me a break. While I've had a couple of wonderful fairy godfathers in my career (which is probably why I'm still in this career at all), the institutions themselves have felt quite cold and unforgiving. I

TABLE 10.2   Categorization of Question 1

Question 1   What are the most significant issues/challenges/opportunities facing women scientists today as they plan their careers?

		Means of responses (%)			
Categories	Response numbers[b]	1997	1998	1999	2000
A Pressures women face in balancing career and family	1, 5, 7	27.1	30.5	35	32.4
B[a] Problems faced by women because of their low numbers and stereotypes gender	3, 4, 8, 10, 12	12.3	10.1	9.8	14.5
C[a] Issues faced by both men and women scientists and engineers in the current environment of tight resources, which may pose particular difficulties for women	2, 6, 16	10.8	4.8	7.9	7.7
D More overt discrimination and harassment	9, 11, 13, 14	3.0	4.4	5.8	4.6

[a] The alphabetic designation for categories B and C have been exchanged, compared with earlier papers (Rosser and Zieseniss, 2000) to present descending response percentages.

[b] Given the responses from all four years, after receiving faculty comments at various presentations of this research, and after working with the data, we exchanged two questions from both category B and D to better reflect the response groupings. Specifically, responses 10 and 12 (considered in category D in Rosser and Zieseniss, 2000) were moved to category B. Similarly, responses 11 and 13 (included in category B in Rosser and Zieseniss, 2000) were placed into category D.

KNOW that a huge amount of my creative energy is siphoned away from my research into their lives and development. I KNOW that if I were a male with a wife at home raising the children, my work would be different. But the institutions have no way of dealing with this inequity (1998 respondent 11).

- At the risk of stereotyping, I think that women generally struggle more with the daily pull of raising a family or caring for elderly parents, and this obviously puts additional demands on their time. This is true for younger women, who may struggle over the timing of having and raising children, particularly in light of a ticking tenure clock, but also for more senior women, who may be called upon to help aging parents (their own or in-laws). Invariably they manage, but not without guilt (2000 respondent 63).

- In contrast to other issues related to women choosing careers in science, the two-body problem has received far too little public as well as governmental attention. Universities are basically tackling the problem individually; some act progressively, others don't. The fates of these capable women depend too much on the individual deans or department chairs involved (1998 respondent 45).

In terms of managing dual career families (particularly dual academic careers, one respondent noted that "Often women take the lesser position in such a situation. Ph.D. women are often married to Ph.D. men. Most Ph.D. men are not married to Ph.D. women" (2000 respondent 16).

Category B. Problems faced by women because of their low numbers and stereotypes held by others regarding gender:

• I think that women have to prove their competence whereas men have to prove their incompetence. For example, I have often heard men question whether a particular woman scientist (say, one who is defending her thesis or is interviewing for a faculty position) actually contributed substantially to the work she presents, whereas, I have never heard a man questioned on this (1997 respondent 6).

• Although possibly less now than before, women scientists still comprise a small proportion of professors in tenure-track positions. Thus, there are few "models" to emulate and few to get advice/mentoring from. Although men could also mentor, there are unique experiences for women that perhaps can only be felt and shared by other women faculty, particularly in other Ph.D. granting institutions. Some examples of this: a different (i.e., more challenging) treatment by undergraduate and graduate students of women faculty than they would of male faculty; difficulties in dealing with agencies outside of the university who are used to dealing with male professors; difficulties related to managing demands of scholarship and grantsmanship with maternity demands. More women in a department would possibly allow a better environment for new women faculty members to thrive in such a department through advice/ mentoring and more awareness of issues facing women faculty members (2000 respondent 26).

• There remains a disconnect between women faculty and the upper administration of Universities, which is male dominated. The natural tendency to pass on information in casual networks can lead to exclusion of women from the inner circles of information, not necessarily maliciously, but just due to human nature (2000 respondent 51).

• The biggest challenge that women face in planning a career in science is not being taken seriously. Often women have to go farther, work harder and accomplish more in order to be recognized (2000 respondent 21).

• In my field (concrete technology), women are so poorly represented that being female certainly creates more notice for you and your work, particularly when presenting at conferences. This can be beneficial, as recognition of your research by your peers is important for gaining tenure; it can also add to the already large amount of pressure on new faculty (2000 respondent 70).

Category C. Issues faced by both men and women scientists and engineers in the current environment of tight resources, which may pose particular difficulties for women:

- I have noticed some problems in particular institutions I have visited (or worked at) where women were scarce. As a single woman, I have sometimes been viewed as "available," rather than as a professional co-worker. That can be really, really irritating. I assume that single men working in a location where male workers are scarce can face similar problems. In physics and astronomy, usually the women are more scarce (1997 respondent 26).

- I still find the strong perception that women should be doing more teaching and service because of the expectation that women are more nurturing. Although research as a priority for women is given a lot of lip service, I've not seen a lot of support for it (2000 respondent 1).

Category D. More overt discrimination and/or harassment:

- There are almost no women in my field, no senior women, and open harassment and discrimination are very well accepted and have never been discouraged in any instance I am aware of (1998 respondent 53).

- I have often buffered the bad behavior of my colleagues—and over the years I have handled a number of sexual harassment or "hostile supervision" cases where a more senior person (all of them male) was behaving inappropriately toward a lower social status woman (or in rarer cases a gay man) (1999 respondent 59).

- The discrimination they continue to face in the workplace. We seem to be making virtually no gains in terms of rates at which women are granted tenure or promotion to full professor. The older I get, the more depressing these statistics become. Women's research is often marginalized. Women's approaches are not recognized. Men scientists want to judge women by "their" standard (i.e. the white male way of doing things!). Most men have no appreciation for the power and privilege of their whiteness and maleness (1999 respondent 70).

- The second challenge that I face being in a male dominated field is that of networking and developing mentor and collaborative type relationships. Attending conferences and professional meetings, especially if I am alone, is extremely difficult. On too many occasions, I've had men initiate conversations about technical matters, and then lead into asking for a date. When a man casually suggests we talk shop over lunch, I am very tentative. Again, too many times, this has led to improper propositions on their part and extreme embarrassment on my part. Just last month, an older man was so persistent in asking me to dine with him that he actually followed me for several blocks around DC, cornered me in a market and continued badgering me. Our conversation ended with him storming away in disgust at my refusals. I am not even very attractive, am married, and at one conference (where I had problems with a particular male) I was obviously pregnant! As a result, I keep to myself at conferences and do not attend any of the social events—not good for building a "network" (1999 respondent 64).

LABORATORY CLIMATE

Question two of the e-mail survey, "How does the laboratory climate (or its equivalent in your sub-discipline) impact upon the careers of women scientists?" attempted to explore women's perceptions of their work environment. Responses to the question also provide insights into particular barriers that need to be removed to improve the daily lives of women scientists and engineers. As Table 10.3 documents, in contrast to question one, the responses given to this question reflects less consensus, though "balancing career and family/time away from home" in response 2 remains a significant issue. Although many women did not mention problems in either their laboratory or work environment related to gender issues, the largest number of responses did suggest that to some degree their gender led to their being perceived as a problem, anomaly, or deviant in the laboratory/work environment. "Hostile or intimidating environment" in response 7, and "establishing respectability/credibility" in response 8, when coupled with "boys club atmosphere" in response 6 provide evidence for a negative laboratory environment for women. The "lack of camaraderie/communications and isolation" in response 5 and "lack of numbers/networking" in response 11 suggest a lonely atmosphere for women in the lab. Again, the quotations from the responses of the women scientists and engineers explain the context and provide specific illustrations of the problems and difficulties that impact their careers:

- There is little recognition of the contradiction that researchers are expected to spend personal time in the lab doing research, when especially women are expected to spend their personal time for family obligations (2000 respondent 1).

- Male scientists dominate the scientific community and laboratory, and they tend to form boy's clubs that provide junior male members with more information, education, opportunity, visibility, and protection. Because female scientists have little chance to get benefits of this kind from such clubs, it is mandatory for female researchers to either spend extra effort to communicate with powerful male researchers, or to make an impeccable career record that highly exceeds that of their male colleagues (1998 respondent 4).

- The laboratory climate in my field negatively impacts the careers of women scientists. Many of my colleagues are foreign males who do not take females seriously and do not collaborate with them (2000 respondent 62).

- We do a lot of work with agencies outside of the university that are predominantly dominated by men (police, courts, correctional agencies, legislators). These agencies have also been used to dealing with male professors. Thus, it is difficult for women to establish links and work with these agencies—I am still working on establishing ties with agencies around my area, working closely with other established women and men faculty members (2000 respondent 26).

TABLE 10.3 Responses to Question 2

Question 2 How does the laboratory climate (or its equivalent in your subdiscipline) impact upon the careers of women scientists?

Categories	1997 % of responses	1998 % of responses	1999 % of responses	2000 % of responses
1 Don't know/question unclear	16.4 (11/67)	4.2 (5/119)	7.1 (7/98)	5.6 (6/108)
2 Balancing career and family/time away from home	13.4 (9/67)	19.3 (23/119)	16.3 (16/98)	13.0 (14/108)
3 Have not experienced problems	11.9 (8/67)	16.8 (20/119)	10.2 (10/98)	9.3 (10/108)
4 Not in lab atmosphere/ can't answer	11.9 (8/67)	5.9 (7/119)	1.0 (1/98)	10.2 (11/108)
5 Lack of camaraderie/ communications and isolation	9.0 (6/67)	11.8 (14/119)	9.2 (9/98)	13.9 (15/108)
6 "Boys club" atmosphere	9.0 (6/67)	9.2 (11/119)	18.4 (18/98)	9.3 (10/108)
7 Hostile environment/ intimidating/lack of authority	9.0 (6/67)	14.3 (17/119)	15.3 (15/98)	9.3 (10/108)
8 Establishing respectability/ credibility	9.0 (6/67)	10.9 (13/119)	10.2 (10/98)	3.7 (4/108)
9 No answer	7.5 (5/67)	6.7 (8/119)	5.1 (5/98)	<1 (1/108)
10 Positive impact	6.0 (4/67)	10.1 (12/119)	6.1 (6/98)	11.1 (12/108)
11 Lack of numbering/ networking	4.5 (3/67)	6.7 (8/119)	12.2 (12/98)	5.6 (6/108)
12 General problem with time management	4.5 (3/67)	1.7 (2/119)	5.1 (5/98)	3.7 (4/108
13 Safety concerns/ presence of toxic substances (health concerns)	3.0 (2/67)	0 (0/119)	4.1 (4/98)	1.9 (2/108)
14 Benefit by working with peers	3.0 (2/67)	2.5 (3/119)	3.1 (3/98)	5.6 (6/108)
15 Problem of wanting research independence	3.0 (2/67)	0 (0/119)	1.0 (1/98)	<1 (1/108)
16 Lack of funding	1.5 (1/67)	<1 (1/119)	5.1 (5/98)	<1 (1/108)
17 Benefit from time flexibility/determine own lab hours	3.0 (2/67)	1.7 (2/119)	3.1 (3/98)	1.9 (2/108)
18 Did not answer	0 (0/68)	0 (0/119)	3.1 (3/98)	0 (0/108)
19 Department doesn't understand basic issues	— —	— —	— —	<1 (1/108)
20 Cultural/national stereotypes for women	— —	— —	— —	6.5 (7/108)
21 Space	— —	— —	1.0 (1/98)	0 (0/108)
22 Better bathroom facilities	— —	— —	— —	<1 (1/108)

DISCUSSION

Data from the almost 400 awardees from 1997, 1998, 1999, and 2000 who responded to an e-mail questionnaire provide insights into the barriers that institutions must seek to remove or at least lower to increase the retention of women scientists and engineers and to attract more women to the disciplines. The most pressing, immediate concern that institutions must alleviate is the difficulty women face in balancing family and career. Family-friendly policies that stop the tenure clock (Cook 2001), provide on-site day care, and facilitate dual career hires should help both men and women faculty (Wenniger 2001; Wilson 2001). Because balancing the tenure clock with the biological clock challenges women scientists and engineers who want to become biological mothers in ways never faced by men, such a policy will help women more. In a similar fashion, since most (62 percent) of female scientists and engineers are also married to male scientists and engineers, who are also often in the same field, such women experience more problems with the two-career issue (Williams 2000) than their male colleagues, most of whom are married, but not to women scientists and engineers (Sonnert and Holton 1995).

Although "balancing career with family" and "dual career" relationships appear at first blush to be the result of the individual choices made by women alone and/or in conjunction with their spouse or partner, the predominance of these responses by awardees from all four years in response to an open-ended question suggests that addressing the problem at the level of the individual proves inadequate. Institutional responses will be needed to resolve these family-centered issues identified by overwhelming numbers of POWRE awardees each year.

The situations where women encounter overt and more subtle harassment must also be dealt with at the institutional level. Institutions and professional societies need to establish policies against sexual harassment and gender discrimination, including against pregnant faculty, in hiring, promotion, and tenure if such policies do not exist (Elliott 2001). They must implement and enforce policies where they do exist. Here senior administrators need to play key roles in terms of allocation of human, financial, physical, and time rewards for those who enforce policies that prevent harassment and discrimination. For example, giving the outstanding research award from the university and/or providing a research sabbatical are not appropriate for a documented harasser as mechanisms to get him out of a problem situation. In many fields, sexual harassment and gender discrimination workshops should include substantial focus on cultural/national differences regarding gender roles and expectations in U.S. universities for appropriate professional behavior, including collaboration with women colleagues.

Problems resulting from low numbers and accompanying gender stereotypes become increasingly complex to address at the institutional level because of the considerable variations among fields. As the numbers of women have increased quite markedly in some disciplines (psychology, sociology) and begun to approach parity in others (life sciences), while remaining relatively small in others (engineering and computer science), it may be important to focus on differences women face in different disciplines. Preliminary results (Rosser and Zieseniss 2000) revealed that both women scientists and engineers found low numbers/lack of mentoring and gaining credibility/respect to be major issues. However, women in fields such as engineering, with particularly low numbers, listed these issues much more frequently.

Continuing low numbers provide particular challenges and some opportunities. Low numbers mean that these women often serve as the first or one of few women in their department and college. They may have no senior women colleagues to act as role models and to serve as mentors to provide them access to networks of necessary professional information. These low numbers also lead to being asked to serve on more committees (even at the junior level), and to advise more students. Although these service activities provide opportunities for women to be visible and experience leadership and administration at an early stage in their career, they may not be valued by the institution for promotion and tenure and may lead to difficulties with time management. Research I institutions need to ensure that junior women faculty either are not given extra teaching and service or that the tenure and promotion committees recognize and validate such work to compensate for lost research time and focus.

Similarly, the low numbers that result in active recruitment of women into many areas may have both positive and negative consequences. Demand may give women engineers starting salaries that are equal to or higher than those of their male counterparts (Vetter 1996). The recruitment can lead to various forms of backlash, ranging from overt discrimination to difficulties gaining credibility from peers and administrators who assume she obtained the position to fill a quota. Small numbers make women very visible; visibility draws attention to successful performance, but it also spotlights errors. The variance in numbers from field to field suggests that institutions may need to establish different priorities and policies for women in different disciplines in science and engineering. For example, a one-size-fits-all policy may not work equally well for women in engineering compared to their counterparts in biology.

Flexibility and acceptance of difference may be crucial for retaining and advancing the numbers of women and careers of individual women in science and engineering. Such tolerance may also serve as the keys for new approaches to collaboration and creative generativity. This chapter has focused on barriers identified by women scientists and engineers that institutions need to overcome. Although barriers carry a connotation of negativity, these data should not be understood completely in a negative light.

The tremendous love for science and technology and extreme dedication to their research and profession strongly characterize the responses of the overwhelming majority of POWRE awardees in all four years. Most seek to have the barriers removed so that they can be productive researchers who take creative approaches to the physical, natural world. As in identifying the barriers, the words of the respondents themselves provide the most convincing evidence for the potential of new ideas and approaches women can contribute to science and engineering:

- The most significant challenge I face is favoring "hacker" experience. In the computer science discipline in which I work, respect is conferred upon those who possess knowledge obtained primarily through countless hours investigating the nuances of hardware and operating systems. To many in my peer group, this is a relaxing hobby and way of life. Though I learn these nuances as I need them for my research outside of my work, I read literature, am deeply interested in social issues and am committed to being involved in my child's life. I see this alternate experience base as an asset to my field. As Rob Pike of C language fame recently said, "Narrowness of experience leads to narrowness of imagination." But for now, the perception is still tilted against me (1999 respondent 68).

- I've built a project and a lab with a group of female scientists. It was a mere coincidence (or was it?) to form an interdisciplinary research visualization group in applied medicine (e.g.virtual surgical training, teaching anatomy via 3D visualization, at [my university's] medical school). Because our group consists of computer scientists, computational linguists, cognitive psychologists, anatomists, we had to establish communication between these disciplines . . . somehow we managed to develop an amazing climate to collaborate and also attract female graduate students to do research with us (1998 respondent 50).

- I find the laboratory climate more liberal than, say, the "office climate." I also feel autonomous, powerful and free in this environment (maybe it's because I get to use power tools?) In the laboratory climate, I am able to create and build. I am also able to ask for help and delegate responsibility. Sometimes my colleagues ask me for help. There is a hierarchical structure at the laboratory in which I work, but it is more fluid, roles switch as projects come through. Sometimes I will take the lead and other times I will follow. In terms of my career, working in a laboratory offers a fantastic opportunity to work alone, work with a large group and manage a project, offer support to a colleague, and to build a small community (1997 respondent 27).

11

The Backlash
against Women's Studies

Bonnie J. Morris

Since their formal emergence in the 1970s, women's studies programs have taught students to re-examine and critique male power structures and epistemologies. Thus, not surprisingly, women's studies as a separate field has never enjoyed an easy relationship with those Ivory Tower institutions that accredit women's studies. The feminist standpoint in most curricula actually encourages students to reconsider those "truths" taught elsewhere in university learning. In response, conservative critics have charged that feminist criticism promotes a subversive, even destructive ideological agenda, distinctive from purely intellectual inquiry. Many women's studies professors might respond that the traditional canon of academic "truths" is hardly bias-free or apolitical, having ignored for so long intellectual contributions by women and non-white males. But many women's studies programs have also shifted quite perceptively from the more grassroots feminist approach of the 1970s to the postmodernist-theoretical style of text reading, regrettably alienating many educationally disadvantaged women whose voices should be central to studies in the global female experience.

Speaking at the 1992 New York Women's Studies Association conference, African-American author and publisher Barbara Smith commented that "the early goals of feminism were naming, breaking silence, making plain our oppression, and not obscuring it with theoretical words." Barbara Christian notes that theory, "as hegemonic as the world it attacks" emerged just as people of color began influencing curricula.

The rush to publish, to establish our legitimacy in the Ivory Tower model, integrated a handful of individual women's studies theorists as scholars valued by their institutions. But despite this progress, despite adaptation to 1990s methods of inquiry and language, the women's studies field itself remains a target for ridicule, revealing the ongoing contempt for woman-centered studies. I would contend that what distinguishes women's studies from other academic fields or teaching professions is that an uninformed public does not feel at liberty to make sweeping denunciations. The miracle is that students enroll in women's studies classes at all when inevitably they must defend their choice to parents who consider it a waste of tuition, to academic advisors who snicker outright, and to anxious boyfriends or sorority sisters who believe that taking a women's studies class is a *de facto* declaration of lesbian separatism.

These conditions have worsened, not improved, in the thirty years since women's studies curricula first took root on American campuses. Indeed, one of the enduring myths is that women's studies is a very recent innovation, a politically correct afterthought with no scholarly canon of its own. Hence, on the first day of my Introduction to Women's Studies class, I always hand around my weathered guidebook *Who's Who in Women's Studies, 1974* which lists in dizzying detail the course offerings, majors, and minors then proliferating at every college in the country. That volume shows that both critic Camille Paglia and Supreme Court Justice Ruth Bader Ginsburg were early women's studies faculty, as were interestingly, dozens and dozens of nuns.

The exacerbated backlash against women's studies in the 1990s was two-fold: institutional cutbacks on the one hand and a very well-funded conservative opposition to women's studies on the other. Although women's studies programs of the 1970s and 1980s succeeded in creating enormous interest in and opportunities for research, producing a generation and a half of Ph.D.s and more scholarly books than can be read in a lifetime, the saturated job market cannot place even half of the best of these scholars—current women's studies programs seldom hire at the non-administrative level. Students in the 1970s and 1980s had a better shot at majoring in women's studies than many of today's undergraduates. Most women's studies departments are now "programs," offering a minor concentration but not a bachelor's degree major. A regular department requires more funding, more space, more full-time hires of tenure-line specialized faculty, whereas a "program" can be assembled internally by inviting other faculty from established departments to teach the entire women's studies lineup, which may include: Women and Economics; Women in China; Women in Literature; and so forth. To establish a program, no money need change hands beyond the appointment of one women's studies director and a part-time secretary; students will still earn credit for a specific minor. This floating or ghettoized nature of women's studies in the 1990s meant that participating women's studies faculty might not know one another on sight or ever attend the same faculty meetings. These are professional concerns created by the best universities' insistence upon treating women's studies as expendable. As a personal example, one state university dean where I was a candidate for a visiting position began our conversation by asking, "Will we still need women's studies five years from now?" One can hardly imagine a male humanities candidate being asked to dismiss his profession as terminal during the hiring procedure.

The conservative attack on women's studies, which encourages uninformed students and faculty to see women's studies as ludicrous or debatable, further hurts the scholarly climate. Egged on by right-wing American groups such as the Heritage Foundation, the National Association of Scholars, Accuracy in Academia, the Independent Women's Forum, and similar organizations, students with no other exposure to women's studies are invited to feel superior to its subject matter, to reject uninvestigated curricula as ideological abomination. Any course addressing the reality of women's lives risks this charge of academic bankruptcy. In any other field, while students may often disagree with professors' methods, there is a basic respect for the knowledge being exchanged; unfortunately, "trashing" women's studies has become acceptable sport for those outside the classroom entirely. This permits male students in particular to take potshots at older female faculty, a questionable by-product of the movement for 'traditional values" such as respect and civility.

As a case in point, in 1996 my program chair at George Washington University gave me the go-ahead to develop a course entitled "Gender and Athletics". This course was intended as a forum for addressing the American culture of sports, socially constructed attitudes about competition and physical fitness, the function of sports heroes in both national and international politics, the impact of Title IX on increasing opportunities for talented girls, and so forth. The course attracted a high percentage of student athletes, many of whom had never before been pushed to research and write critically about ideologies of sport. By all accounts the class was a success, and the Women's Sports Foundation subsequently nominated me to its advisory board. However, I was startled to find an attack on my curriculum in the George Washington *Independent* newspaper—a conservative student periodical funded by *off-campus* sources and thus not officially representing George Washington University. The article alleged that my course was silly and embarrassing, the worst example of political correctness in the university. The author had made no effort to contact me or to visit the class, nor had he read my syllabus. His critique was based entirely upon the cover of one textbook I used, which he stumbled upon in the campus bookstore.

Many sympathetic colleagues advised me to ignore the public slam rather than waste my energy responding. I let it go. A year or two later I was invited to teach Gender and Athletics across town as a guest professor at Georgetown University. There, too, within the first month of my instructing a sold-out class, Georgetown University's conservative student paper, also called the *Independent* and funded by the same off-campus benefactors, ran a column attacking women's studies and specifically naming my course as an example of "made-up crap."

This time I did write a letter of complaint, copies of which I forwarded to the regular student paper and to the vice president for academic affairs because the latter's name appeared on my appointment letter. I pointed out that the writer had not met me, nor had he visited my class or read my syllabus or in any way acquainted himself with the content of my course. Yet this individual was publicly suggesting that a guest professor was teaching crap. I questioned the propriety of a male undergraduate student, who had yet to complete his B.A., critiquing the academic knowledge of a female professor with three degrees whom he had not interviewed. I asked for an apology, particularly as the column was so obviously lacking in research integrity and intellectual reason, although the writer had charged women's studies with these very same deficits. But the official school paper at Georgetown, the *Hoya,* never printed my letter, nor did I receive any response or acknowledgement from the vice president for academic affairs.

This climate of hostility and inaction is a wake-up call to the damage done when university officials refuse to stand by a women's studies program or department. But did we ever believe that we would fit in as equals or be welcomed players in the clubhouse? At what point, for instance, is my own socially conditioned desire for approval connected to my sense of academic etiquette? The unresolved tension concerns whether scholars prepared to live as intellectual "outsiders" may reasonably expect funding and sanction from traditional university institutions. And on this point, feminist scholars are in the same boat as faculty in African-American studies programs, who are similarly marginalized, both off- and on-campus. Critics themselves, who have not lived daily with such marginalization, charge that gender and ethnic "studies" programs are an excuse for self-indulgence, and that such curricula are inevitably too personal or too "angry". But in a society with a female majority in its population and, soon to come, a non-white majority as well, it is perhaps fear of angry truth *and* fear of the proven intellectual capacity of the hitherto marginalized population that continues to fuel the backlash.

Bibliography

Allen, Judith A, and Sally L. Kitch. 1998. "Disciplined By Disciplines?: The Need For an Interdisciplinary Research Mission in Women's Studies." *Feminist Studies* 24 (2): 275–299.

Allen, Paula Gunn. 1992. "Border Studies: The Intersections of Gender and Color." In *Introduction to Scholarship in Modern Languages and Literatures,* 2d ed., ed. Joseph Gibaldi. New York: Modern Language Association of America.

Alper, J. 1993. "The Pipeline is Leaking Women All the Way Along." *Science* 260: 409–411.

Alvesson, Mats. 1993. *Cultural Perspectives on Organizations.* Boston, MA: Cambridge University Press.

Alvesson, Mats, and Yvonne Due Billing. 1997. *Understanding Gender and Organization.* London: Sage Publications.

American Association of University Women. 1992. *How Schools Shortchange Girls: Executive Summary.* Commissioned by the AAUW Education Foundation and researched by Wellesley College Center for Research on Women.

Amey, Marilyn J., and Susan B. Twombly. 1993. "Re-visioning Leadership in Community Colleges." In *Women in Higher Education: A Feminist Perspective,* ed. Judith S. Glazer, Estela M. Bensimon, Barbara K. Townsend. Needham Heights, MA: Ginn Press.

Amos, Emma. 1999. "Untitled Essay." In Contemporary Feminism: Art Practice, Theory, and Activism—An Intergenerational Perspective, ed. Mira Shor. *Art Journal* 58, Winter, 9–11.

Ani, Marimba. 1994. *Yurugu.* Trenton, NJ: Africa World Press.

Anzaldúa, Gloria. 1987. *Borderlands/La Frontera.* San Francisco: Spinsters/Aunt Lute.

Astin, Alexander W., and Helen S. Astin. 2000. *Leadership Reconsidered: Engaging Higher Education in Social Change.* Battle Creek, MI: W. K. Kellogg Foundation.

Astin, Alexander W., and Helen S. Astin. 2001. "Principles of Transformative Leadership." *AAHE Bulletin* 53(5). Washington, DC: American Association of Higher Education.

Astin, Helen S., and Carole Leland. 1993. "In The Spirit of the Times: Three Generations of Women Leaders." In *Women in Higher Education: A Feminist Perspective,* ed. Judith S. Glazer, Estela M. Bensimon, and Barbara K. Townsend. Needham Heights, MA: Ginn Press.

Baker, Edith M. 1996. "Leadership Styles of Women in Higher Education." *Journal of the American Association for Women in Junior Colleges and Community Colleges* 8: 12–15.

Baldwin, James. 1985. *The Price of the Ticket.* New York: St. Martin's/Marek.

Balzer, W., N. Boudreau, P. Hutchinson, A.M. Ryan, T. Thorsteinson, J. Sullivan, R. Yonker, and D. Snavely. 1996. "Critical Modeling Principles When Testing for Gender Equity in Faculty Salary." *Research in Higher Education* 37: 633–658.

Barber, L. A. 1995. "U. S. Women in Science and Engineering, 1960–1990: Progress Toward Equity?" *Journal of Higher Education* 66: 213–234.

Barnett, Rosalind Chait, and Janel Shibley Hyde. 2001. "Women, Men, Work, and Family: An Expansionist Theory." *American Psychologist* 56(10): 781–796.

Barrett, Michele. 1991. *The Politics of Truth: From Marx to Foucault.* Stanford, CA: Stanford University Press.

Barrett, Michele. 1992. "Words and Things: Materialism and Method in Contemporary Feminist Analysis." In *Destabilizing Theory: Contemporary Feminist Debates,* ed. Michele Barrett and Anne Phillips. Stanford, CA: Stanford University Press.

Barrett, Michele, and Anne Phillips, ed. 1992. *Destabilizing Theory: Contemporary Feminist Debates.* Stanford, CA: Stanford University Press.

Bartky, Sandra Lee. 1990. *Femininity and Domination: Studies in the Phenomenology of Oppression.* New York and London: Routledge.

Bensimon, Estella M. 1993. "A Feminist Reinterpretation of President's Definitions of Leadership." In *Women in Higher Education: A Feminist Perspective,* ed. Judith Glazer, Estela M. Bensimon, and Barbara K. Townsend. Needham Heights, MA: Ginn Press.

Blackmore, Jill. 1999. *Troubling Women—Feminism, Leadership and Educational Change.* Buckingham: Open University Press.

Blair, S. N., H. W. Kohl, and C. A. Macera. 1995. "Changes in Physical Fitness and All-cause Mortality: A Prospective Study of Healthy and Unhealthy Men." *Journal of the American Medical Association* 273: 1093–1098.

Blair, S. N., H. W. Kohl, R. S Paffenbarger, D. G. Cooper, K. H. and L. W. Gibbons. 1989. "Physical Fitness and All-Cause Mortality: A Prospective Study of Healthy Men and Women." *Journal of the American Medical Association* 262: 2395–2401.

Bonwell, Charles C., and James A. Eison. 1991. *Active Learning: Creating Excitement in the Classroom.* Washington D.C.: School of Education and Human Development, George Washington University.

Bordo, Susan. 1990. "Feminism, Postmodernism, and Gender-Skepticism." In *Feminism/Postmodernism,* ed. Linda Nicholson. London: Routledge.

Bordo, Susan. 1993. *Unbearable Weight: Feminism, Western Culture and the Body.* Berkeley, CA: University of California Press.

Bordo, Susan. 1999. "Feminist Skepticism and the 'Maleness' of Philosophy." In *Feminist Approaches to Theory and Methodology,* ed. Sharlene Hesse-Biber, Christine Gilmartin, and Robin Lydenberg. New York: Oxford University Press.

Boudreau, N., J. Sullivan, W. Balzer, A. M. Ryan, R. Yonker, T. Thorsteinson, and P. Hutchinson. 1997. "Should Faculty Rank be Included as a Predictor Variable in Studies of Gender Equity in University Faculty Salaries?" *Research in Higher Education* 38: 297–312.

Boyer, Ernest L. 1994. "The New American College." *Perspectives* 24: 6–12.

Broude, Norma, and Mary D. Garrard, eds. 1982. *Feminism and Art History: Questioning the Litany.* New York: Icon Editions.

Broude, Norma, and Mary D. Garrard, eds. 1992. *The Expanding Discourse: Feminism and Art.* New York: Icon Editions.

Broude, Norma, and Mary D. Garrard, eds. 1996. *The Power of Feminist Art: The American Movement of the 1970s, History and Impact.* New York: Abrams.

Campbell, K. 2001. "Leaders of 9 Universities and 25 Women Faculty Meet at MIT, Agree to Equity Reviews". *MIT News Office.* http://web.mit.edu/newsoffice/nr/2001/gender.html.

Campbell, P. B., and J. Sanders. 1997. "Uninformed but Interested: Findings of a National Survey on Gender Equity in Preservice Teacher Education." *Journal of Teacher Education* 48: 69–75.

Carli, Linda L. 1998. "Coping With Adversity." In *Arming Athena: Career Strategies for Women in Academe,* ed. Lynn H. Collins, Joan C. Chrisler, and Kathryn Quina. Thousand Oaks, CA: Sage Publications.

Carli, Linda L., and Alice H. Eagly. 1999. "Gender Effects on Social Influence and Emergent Leadership." In *Handbook of Women and Work,* ed. Gary N. Powell. Thousand Oaks, CA: Sage.

Carroll, B. 2001. "Reflections on '2000 Subversions: Women's Studies and the '21st Century.' " *NWSA Journal* 13(1): 139–149.

Chadwick, Whitney. 1997. *Women, Art, and Society,* 2d ed. New York: Thames and Hudson.

Chamberlain, Miriam K. 1988. *Women in Academe: Progress and Prospects,* ed. New York: Russell Sage Foundation.

Chamberlain, Miriam K. 1993. "Women as Trustees." In *Women in Higher Education: A Feminist Perspective,* ed. Judith S. Glazer, Estela M. Bensimon, and Barbara K. Townsend. Needham Heights, MA: Ginn Press.

Chave, Anna C. 1992. "Who Will Paint New York? The World's New Art Center." In *From the Faraway Nearby: Georgia O'Keeffe as Icon,* ed. Christopher Merrill and Ellen Bradbury. New York: Addison-Wesley Publishing.

Chicago, Judy. 1982. *Through the Flower: My Struggle as a Woman Artist,* revised and updated. New York: Doubleday.

Chin, J. L., N. F. Russo, J. Bloom, D. Felicio, M. Madden, C.Z. Enns, E. Stiglitz, P. Rozee, and N. Simi. 1997. In *Shaping the Future of Feminist Psychology: Education, Research and Practice,* ed. Judith Worell and Norine G. Johnson. Washington, DC: American Psychological Association.

Chrisler, Joan C., Linda Herr, and Nelly K. Murstein. 1998. "Women as Faculty Leaders." In *Arming Athena: Career Strategies for Women in Academe,* ed. Lynn H. Collins, Joan C. Chrisler and Kathryn Quina. Thousand Oaks, CA: Sage Publications.

Clarke, Edward H. 1873. *Sex in Education; Or, A Fair Chance for Girls.* Boston: James R. Osgood & Co.

Collins, Patricia Hill. 1999. "Learning from the Outsider Within: The Sociological Significance of Black Feminist Thought." In Feminist Approaches to Theory and Methodology, ed. Sharlene Hesse-Biber, Christine Gilmartin, and Robin Lydenberg. New York: Oxford University Press.

Commission on Professionals in Science and Technology. 2000. *Professional Women & Minorities: A Total Resources Data Compendium.* Washington, D.C.: CPST, Table 5–10.

Connell, R. W. 1995. *Masculinities.* Cambridge, MA: Polity Press.

Cook, S.G. 2001. "Negotiating Family Accommodation Practices on Your Campus." *Women in Higher Education* 10(4): 25–26.

Coyner, Sandra. 1991. "Women's Studies." *NWSA Journal* 3: 349–54.

Crain, W. 1992. *Theories of Development Concepts and Applications,* 3d ed. Englewood Cliffs, NJ: Prentice Hall.

Crosby, Faye. 1993. *Juggling: The Unexpected Advantages of Balancing Career and Home for Women and Their Families.* New York: Free Press.

Crumpacker, Laurie, Linda McMillin, and Francine Navakas. 1998. "Transforming the University: Feminist Musings on Pragmatic Liberal Education." *Liberal Education* (Fall): 32–39.

Curry, D. 2001. "Prime Numbers." *The Chronicle of Higher Education* July 6, A9.

Daniel, Elnor D. 1997. "African American Nursing Administrators in the Academy." In *Black Women in the Academic: Promises and Perils,* ed. Lois Benjamin. Gainesville, FL: University Press of Florida.

Daniel, Jessica Henderson. 2001. August. "Next Generation—Mentoring Women of Color Scholars in Psychology." Symposium presented at the American Psychological Association, San Francisco.

Dawber, T. R. 1980. *The Framingham Study: The Epidemiology of Atherosclerotic Disease.* Cambridge, MA: Harvard University Press.

Danza, R. 1983. "Menarche: Its Effects on Mother-Daughter and Father-Daughter Interaction." In *Menarche,* S. Golub ed. New York: Lexington Books.

Dawson, Martha E. 1997. "Climbing the Administrative Ladder in the Academy. In *Black Women in the Academic: Promises and Perils,* ed. Lois Benjamin. Gainesville, FL: University Press of Florida.

De Beauvoir, Simone. 1963. *The Second Sex.* New York : Bantam Books.

de Lauretis, Teresa. 1988. "Displacing Hegemonic Discourses: Reflections on Feminist Theory in the 1980s." *Inscriptions* 3(4): 127–145.

DeGroot, J., and Maynard, M. 1993. *Women's Studies in the 1990's: Doing Things Differently?* New York: St. Martin's Press.

Deveaux, Monique. 1999. "Feminism and Empowerment: A Critical Reading of Foucault." In *Feminist Approaches to Theory and Methodology,* ed. Sharlene Hesse-Biber, Christine Gilmartin, and Robin Lydenberg. New York: Oxford University Press.

Drucker, Johanna. 1999. "Untitled Essay." In *Contemporary Feminism: Art Practice, Theory, and Activism—An Intergenerational Perspective,* ed. Mira Shor. *Art Journal* 58, Winter, 13–15.

Dueli-Klein, Renate. 1983. *Theories About Women's Studies.* London: Routledge and Kegan.

Duerst-Lahti, Georgia. Forthcoming 2002. *Women Transforming Congress: Gender Analyses of Institutional Life,* ed. Cindy Simon Rosenthal. Norman, OK: University of Oklahoma Press.

Duerst-Lahti, Georgia, and Rita Mae Kelly. 1995. *Gender Power, Leadership, and Governance.* Ann Arbor: University of Michigan Press.

Dziech, B. W., and L. Weiner. 1990. *The Lecherous Professor: Sexual Harassment on Campus,* 2d ed. Chicago, IL: University of Illinois Press.

Eagly, A.H., and B.T. Johnson. 1990. "Gender and Leadership Style: A Meta-analysis." *Psychological Bulletin* 108: 233–256.

Eaker, E. D., J. Pinsky, and W. P. Castelli. 1992. "Myocardial Infarction and Coronary Death Among Women: Psychosocial Predictors for a 20–year Follow-up of Women in the Framingham Study." *American Journal of Epidemiology* 135: 854–864.

Eisenberg, A. 2000. "Computer Science Not Drawing Women." *New York Times,* July 2, G10.

Elliott, S. T. 2001. "Does Your School Discriminate Against Pregnant Faculty?" *Women in Higher Education* 10(7): 23–24.

Engel, G. L. 1980. "The Clinical Application of the Biopsychosocial Model." *American Journal of Psychiatry* 137: 535–544.

Enney, Sally J. 1996. "Field Essay: New Research on Gendered Political Institutions." *Political Research Quarterly* 49: 445–466.

Eyerman, Ron, and Andrew Jamison. 1991. *Social Movements: A Cognitive Approach.* Cambridge, MA: Polity Press.

Faludi, Susan. 1991. *Backlash: The Undeclared War Against American Women.* New York: Doubleday.

Fink, L. Dee. 1998. "Typology of Higher Level Learning." Norman: Instructional Development Program, University of Oklahoma. Manuscript.

Fitzgerald, L. F. 1996. "The Prevalence of Sexual Harassment." In *Combating Sexual Harassment in Higher Education,* ed. B. Lott and M. E. Reilly. Washington, DC: National Education Association.

Foucault, Michel. 1979. *Discipline and Punish: The Birth of the Prison,* trans. Alan Sheridan. New York: Vintage.

Foucault, Michel. 1981. *The History of Sexuality, vol. l, An Introduction.* Harmondsworth, England: Penguin.

Fox, Richard L., and Shirley A. Ronkowski. 1997. "Learning Styles of Political Science Students." *PS: Political Science* 30 (4): 732–737.

Fox-Genovese, Elizabeth. 1996. *Feminism is Not the Story of My Life.* New York: Nan A. Talese Doubleday.

Freeman, B. C. 1977. "Faculty Women in the American University: Up the Down Staircase." *Higher Education* 6: 165–188.

Freire, Paolo. 1976. *Pedagogy of the Oppressed.* Myra A. B. Ramos, trans. Continuum International Publishing Group.

Fuchs, C. S., J. J. Stampfer, G. A. Colditz, E. L. Giovanucci, J. E. Manson, I. Kawachi, D. J. Hunter, S. E. Hennekens, B. Rosner, F. E., Speizer, and W. C. Willett. 1995. "Alcohol Consumption and Mortality Among Women." *New England Journal of Medicine* 332: 1245–1250.

Gherardi, Silvia. 1995. *Gender, Symbolism and Organizational Cultures.* London: Sage Publications.

Gibson, Ruth-Elaine. 1996. "Deaf Women Academics in Higher Education." In *Breaking Boundaries: Women in Higher Education,* ed. Louise Morley and Val Walsh. London: Taylor & Francis.

Glazer, P., and Slater, M. 1987. *Unequal Colleagues.* New Brunswick, NJ: Rutgers University Press.

Glazer-Raymo, Judith. 1999. *Shattering the Myths: Women in Academe.* Baltimore, MD: The Johns Hopkins University Press.

Goodwin, Stephanie A., and Susan T. Fiske. 2001. In *Handbook of the Psychology of Women and Gender,* ed. Rhonda T. Unger. New York: Wiley.

Gouma-Peterson, Thelma, and Patricia Mathews. 1987. "The Feminist Critique of Art History." *Art Bulletin* 69 (September): 326–357.

Graham, Tiffany, and William Ickes. 1997. "When Women's Intuition Isn't Greater Than Men's. In *Empathic Apathy,* ed. William John Ickes. New York: Guilford Press.

Grahn, J. 1993. *Blood, Bread and Roses: How Menstruation Created the World.* Boston, MA: Beacon Press.

Grant, Rebecca, and Kathleen Newland. ed. 1991. *Gender and International Relations.* Buckingham: Open University Press.

Green, Phyllis. 1997. "Strong Rites of Passage and Rights of Way." In *Black Women in the Academic: Promises and Peril,* ed. Lois Benjamin. Gainesville, FL: University Press of Florida.

Grogan, Margaret. 2000. "Laying the Groundwork for a Reconception of the Superintendency From Feminist Postmodern Perspectives." *Educational Administration Quarterly* 36 (1): 117–142.

Grumet, Madeleine, and Kate McCoy. 1997. "Education: Discipline Analysis." Baltimore, MD: Towson State University National Center for Curriculum Transformation Resources on Women.

Haug, Frigga. 1992. *Beyond Female Masochism-Memory-work and Politics.* London: Verso.

Heckman, D. 1997. "On the Eve of Title IX's 25th Anniversary: Sex Discrimination in the Gym and Classroom." *Nova Law Review* 21 (Winter): 545–661.

Hensel, Nancy. 1997. "The Contemporary Challenge: Family and Work Issues for Women in Higher Education." In *The Minority Voice in Educational Reform: An Analysis by Minority Women College of Education Deans,* ed. Louis A. Castenell and Jill M. Tarule. Greenwich, CT: Ablex Publishing.

Heward, Christine. 1996. "Women and Careers in Higher Education: What is the Problem?" In *Breaking Boundaries: Women in Higher Education,* ed. Louise Morley and Val Walsh. London: Taylor & Francis.

Higonnet, Margaret R. 1994. "Introduction." In *Borderwork: Feminist Engagements with Comparative Literature,* ed. Margaret R. Higonnet. Ithaca, NY: Cornell University Press.

Hine, Darlene Clark. 1997. "The Future of Black Women in the Academy: Reflections on Struggle." In *Black Women in the Academic: Promises and Peril,* ed. Lois Benjamin. Gainesville, FL: University Press of Florida.

Hirsch, Marianne, and Evelyn Fox Keller. 1990. "Practicing Conflict in Feminist Theory." In *Conflicts in Feminism,* ed. Marianne Hirsch and Evelyn Fox Keller. New York: Routledge.

Hirschman, Albert. 1970. *Exit, Voice and Loyalty: Responses to Decline in Firms, Organizations and States.* Cambridge, MA: Harvard University Press.

Homer, William Innes. 1999. *The Language of Contemporary Criticism Clarified.* Madison, CT: Sound View Press.

hooks, bell. 1984. *Feminist Theory: From Margin to Center.* Boston: South End Press.

hooks, bell. 1990. *Yearning: Race, Gender and Cultural Politics.* Boston: South End Press.

hooks, bell. 2000. *Feminism is for Everybody.* Cambridge, MA: South End Press.

Hornby, Pat, and Sue Shaw. 1996. "Women in Management Education: The Token Topic?" In *Breaking Boundaries: Women in Higher Education,* ed. Louise Morley and Val Walsh. London: Taylor & Francis.

Horton, Myles, Herbert Kohl, and Judith Kohl. 1998. *The Long Haul: An Autobiography.* New York: Columbia University Press.

Humm, Maggie. 1996. "Equal Opportunities and Higher Education." In *Breaking Boundaries: Women in Higher Education,* ed. Louise Morley and Val Walsh. London: Taylor & Francis.

Janis, Irving. 1982. *Groupthink: Psychological Studies of Policy Decisions and Fiascoes,* 2d ed. Boston, MA: Houghton Mifflin.

Johnson, Fern L. 1993. "Women's Leadership in Higher Education: Is the Agenda Feminist?" *CUPA Journal* (Summer): 9–14.

Jones, Amelia. 1999. "Untitled Essay." In Contemporary Feminism: Art Practice, Theory, and Activism—An Intergenerational Perspective, ed. Mira Shor. *Art Journal* 58, Winter, 17–20.

Jones, M. Colleen. 1997. "Does Leadership Transcend Gender and Race?" In *Black Women in the Academic: Promises and Perils,* ed. Lois Benjamin. Gainesville, FL: University Press of Florida.

Kahle, J. B. 1988. "Recruitment and Retention of Women in College Science Majors." *Journal of College Science Teaching* 382–384.

Kandiyoti, Deniz. 1999. "Islam and Patriarchy: A Comparative Perspective." In *Feminist Approaches to Theory and Methodology,* ed. Sharlene Hesse-Biber, Christine Gilmartin, and Robin Lydenberg. New York: Oxford University Press.

Kanter, Rosabeth M. 1977. *Men and Women in the Organization.* New York: Basic Books.

Kathlene, Lyn, and Judd Choate. 1998. "Running for Elected Office: A Ten-Week Political Campaign Simulation for Upper-Division Courses." *PS: Political Science and Politics* 31 (March): 69–76.

Katzenstein, Mary Fainsod. 1998. *Faithful and Fearless: Moving Feminist Protest inside the Church and Military.* Princeton, NJ: Princeton University Press.

Kettle, Jane. 1996. "Good Practices, Bad Attitudes: An Examination of the Factors Influencing Women's Academic Careers. In *Breaking Boundaries: Women in Higher Education,* ed. Louise Morley and Val Walsh. London: Taylor & Francis.

Kiecolt-Glaser, J. K., J. R. Dura, C. E. Speicher, O. J. Trask, and R. Glaser. 1991. "Spousal Caregivers of Dimentia Victims: Longitudinal Changes in Immunity and Health." *Psychosomatic Medicine* 53: 345–362.

Kiecolt-Glaser, J. K., C. S. Dyer, and E. C. Shuttleworth. 1988. "Upsetting Social Interactions and Distress Among Alzhemer's Disease Family Caregivers: A Replication and Extension." *American Journal of Community Psychology* 16: 825–837.

Klein, Julie Thompson. 1990. *Interdisciplinarity: History, Theory, and Practice.* Detroit, MI: Wayne State University Press.

Klein, Julie Thompson. 1996. *Crossing Boundaries: Knowledge, Disciplinarities, and Interdisciplinarities.* Charlottsville, VA: University Press of Virginia.

Klein, J., and I. F. Litt. 1983. "Menarche and Dysmenorrhea." In *Girls at Puberty,* ed. J. Brooks-Gunn and A. Petersen. New York: Plenum Press.

Kolb, D.A. 1984. *Experiential Learning: Experience as the Source of Learning and Development.* Englewood Cliffs, NJ: Prentice-Hall.

Kolodny, Annette. 1998. *Failing the Future: A Dean Looks at Higher Education in the Twenty-First Century.* Durham, NC: Duke University Press.

Koss, M. P., and M. R. Harvey. 1994. "Rape is Widespread." In *Violence Against Women,* ed. B. Leone. San Diego, CA: Greenhaven Press.

Kronsell, Annica. 1990–1997. Notes taken during post-graduate studies.

Kronsell, Annica. 2001. "Feminist Standpoint Theory and IR Research." Paper presented at the International Studies Association Conference in Chicago, February.

Kronsell, Annica, and Erika Svedberg. 2001. "The Duty to Protect: Gender in the Swedish Practice of Conscription." *Cooperation and Conflict* 36 (2): 153–176.

Lal, Jayati. 1999. "Situating Locations: The Politics of Self, Identity, and 'Other' in Living and Writing the Text." In *Feminist Approaches to Theory and Methodology,* ed. Sharlene Hesse-Biber, Christine Gilmartin, and Robin Lydenberg. New York: Oxford University Press.

Lamport, M. A. 1993. "Student–Faculty Informal Interaction and the Effect on College Student Outcomes: A Review of the Literature." *Adolescence* 28: 971–990.

La Porte, Todd R., and David Hadwiger. 1991. "Teaching Public Administration Through Field Research: California Agency Reconnaissance Project." *PS: Political Science and Politics* 24 (December): 707–12.

Leder, G. C.. 1986. "Mathematics: Stereotyped as a Male Domain?" *Psychological Reports* 59: 955–958.

Lee, V. E., C. Mackie-Lewis, and H. M. Marks. 1993. "Persistence to the Baccalaureate Degree for Students Who Transfer From Community College." *American Journal of Education* 102: 80–114.

Lewis, Judith A., and Judith Bernstein. 1996. *The Health of Women: A Relational Perspective Across the Life Cycle.* Sudbury, MA: Jones & Bartlett Publishers.

Lindsay, Beverly. 1997. "Surviving the Middle Passage: The Absent Legacy of African American Women Education Deans." *The Minority Voice in Educational Reform: An Analysis by Minority Women College of Education Deans,* ed. Louise A. Castenell and Jill M. Tarule. Greenwich, CT: Ablex Publishing.

Lin, Y., and W. P. Vogt. 1996. "Occupational Outcomes for Students Earning Two-Year College Degrees." *Journal of Higher Education* 67(4): 446–475.

Lippard, Lucy. 1989. "Both Sides Now (A Reprise)." *Heresies* 6: 29–34.

Locke, Mamie E. 1997. "Striking the Delicate Balance." In *Black Women in the Academic: Promises and Perils,* ed. Lois Benjamin. Gainesville, FL: University Press of Florida.

Logan, D., J. Calder, and B. Cohen. 1980. "Menarche and Dysmenorrhea." In *Girls at Puberty,* J. Brooks-Gunn and A. Petersen, ed. New York: Plenum Press.

Looker, E. D. 1993. "Gender Issues in University: The University as Employer of Academic and Nonacademic Women and Men." *The Canadian Journal of Higher Education* XXIII 19–43.

Lott, Bernice, and Lisa M. Rocchio. 1998. "Standing Up, Talking Back, and Taking Charge: Strategies and Outcomes in Collective Action Against Sexual Harassment." In *Arming Athena: Career Strategies for Women in Academe,* ed. Lynn H. Collins, Joan C. Chrisler and Kathryn Quina. Thousand Oaks, CA: Sage Publications.

Lundeberg, Mary Anna, and Susan Diemert Moch. 1995. "Influence of Social Interaction on Cognition: Connected Learning in Science." *Journal of Higher Education* 66 (May-June): 312–35.

Lynes, Barbara Buhler. 1992. "The Language of Criticism: Its Effects on Georgia O'Keeffe's Art in the 1920s." In *From the Faraway Nearby: Georgia O'Keeffe as Icon,* ed. Christopher Merrill and Ellen Bradbury. New York: Addison-Wesley Publishing.

Lyon, Arabella. 1992. "Interdisciplinarity: Giving Up Territory." *College English* 54: 681–694.

Madden, Margaret E., and Nancy Felipe Russo. 1997. "Psychology: Discipline Analysis." Baltimore, MD: Towson State University National Center for Curriculum Transformation Resources on Women.

Madden, Margaret E., and Janet Shibley Hyde. 1998. "Integrating Gender and Ethnicity Into Psychology Courses." *Psychology of Women Quarterly* 22: 1–12.

Maddock, Sue. 1999. *Challenging Women, Gender, Culture and Organization.* London: Sage Publications.

Maguire, Meg. 1996. "In the Prime of Their Lives? Older Women in Higher Education." In *Breaking Boundaries: Women in Higher Education,* ed. Louise Morley and Val Walsh. London: Taylor & Francis.

Mann, Patricia S. 1994. *Micro-Politics—Agency in a Postfeminist Era.* Minneapolis: MN: University of Minnesota Press.

Marcus, Jane. 1989. "Alibis and Legends: The Ethics of Elsewhereness, Gender, and Estrangement." In *Women's Writing in Exile,* ed. Mary Lynn Broe and Angela Ingram. Chapel Hill, NC: University of North Carolina Press.

Martin, Emily. 1999. "The Egg and the Sperm: How Science Has Constructed a Romance Based on Stereotypical Male-Female Roles." In *Feminist Approaches to Theory and Methodology,* ed. Sharlene Hesse-Biber, Christine Gilmartin, and Robin Lydenberg. New York: Oxford University Press.

Martin, Jane Roland. 2000. *Coming of Age in Academe: Rekindling Women's Hopes and Reforming the Academy.* New York and London: Routledge.

Maslow, A. H. 1954; 2001. In *Notable Selections in Human Development,* 2d ed.,
    ed. R. Diessner and J. Tiegs. Guilford, CT: McGraw-Hill/Dushkin.

Maynard, C. et al. 1996. "Influence of Sex on the Use of Cardiac Procedures in
    Patients Presenting to the Emergency Department: A Prospective Multicenter
    Study." *Circulation* (November) 94: 93–98.

McClish, Glen. 1995. "Virginia Woolf: Androgyny and the Discipline of
    Communication." *Furman Studies* (June): 55–65.

McKay, Nellie Y. 1997. "A troubled peace." In *Black Women in the Academic:
    Promises and Perils,* ed. Lois Benjamin. Gainesville, FL: University Press of
    Florida.

Merrill, Christopher, and Ellen Bradbury, ed. 1992. *From the Faraway and Nearby:
    Georgia O'Keeffe as Icon.* New York: Addison-Wesley Publishing Co.

Miller, Julia R., and Gladys Gary Vaughn. 1997. "African American Women
    Executives." In *Black Women in the Academic: Promises and Perils,* ed. Lois
    Benjamin. Gainesville, FL: University Press of Florida.

Miller, Penny M. 1996. "Teaching Women in the News: Exposing the 'Invisible
    Majority." *PS: Political Science and Politics* 29 (September): 513–17.

Millet, Kate. 1969. *Sexual Politics.* New York: Avon Books.

Minh-ha, Trinh. 1991. *Framer Framed.* New York: Routledge.

Mohanty, Chandra Talpade Mohanty. 1988. "Under Western Eyes: Feminist
    Scholarship and Colonial Discourses." *Feminist Review* 30: 61–88.

Mohanty, Chandra Talpade Mohanty. 1992. "Feminist Encounters: Locating the
    Politics of Experience." In *Destabilizing Theory: Contemporary Feminist Debates,*
    ed. Michele Barrett and Anne Phillips. Stanford, CA: Stanford University Press,.

Mohanty, Chandra Talpade Mohanty. 1999. "Women Workers and Capitalist
    Scripts: Ideologies of Domination, Common Interests, and the Politics of
    Solidarity." In *Feminist Approaches to Theory and Methodology,* ed. Sharlene
    Hesse-Biber, Christine Gilmartin, and Robin Lydenberg. New York: Oxford
    University Press.

Molesworth, Helen. 1999. "Untitled Essay." In Contemporary Feminism: Art
    Practice, Theory, and Activism—An Intergenerational Perspective, ed. Mira
    Shor. *Art Journal* 58, Winter, 20–21.

Morgan, Gareth. 1986. *Images of Organization.* London: Sage Publications.

Morley, Louise. 1999. *Organising Feminisms—the Micropolitics of the Academy.*
    New York: St. Martin's Press.

Moses, M. S. 2001. "Affirmative Action and the Creation of More Favorable
    Contexts of Choice." *American Educational Research Journal* 38: 3–36.

Moses, Yolanda T. 1997. "Black Women in Academe." In *Black Women in the
    Academic: Promises and Perils,* ed. Lois Benjamin. Gainesville, FL: University
    Press of Florida.

National Center for Education Statistics. 1992. *Students at Less-Than-4-Year-
    Institutions* (Statistical Analysis Report NCES 92–206). Washington, DC: U. S.
    Government Printing Office.

National Center for Education Statistics. 1994. *Digest of Education Statistics*
    (Report NCES 94–115). Washington, DC: U. S. Government Printing Office.

*National Research Council's Women in Science and Engineering: Increasing Their
    Numbers in the 1990s.* 1991. Washington, D.C.: National Academy Press.

National Science Foundation. 1997. *Professional opportunities for women in research and education.* Program announcement. Washington, D.C.: Author.

National Science Foundation. 2001. *Women, Minorities, and Persons with Disabilities in Science and Engineering."* Arlington, VA (NSF 00–327).

National Science Foundation. 2001. *ADVANCE. Program Solicitation.* Arlington, VA: Author.

National Science Foundation. 2002. *Women, Minorities, and Persons with Disabilities in Science and Engineering.* Arlington, VA.

Nochlin, Linda. 1971. "Why Have There Been No Great Women Artists?" *Artnews* 69 (January): 22–39, 67–71.

Nora, A., A. Cabrera, L. S. Hagedorn, and E. Pascarella. 1996. "Differential Impacts of Academic and Social Experiences on College Related Behavioral Outcomes Across Different Ethnic and Gender Groups at Four-Year Institutions." *Research in Higher Education* 37: 427–451.

Norrell, J. E., and T. H. Norrell. 1996. "Faculty and Family Policies in Higher Education." *Journal of Family Issues* 17 (2): 204–226.

Nussbaum, Martha C. 1997. *Cultivating Humanity: A Classical Defense of Reform in Liberal Education.* Cambridge, MA: Harvard University Press.

Oakes, Janna L. 1999. "Women as Capable Leaders in Higher Education Administration: A Historical Journey With Implications for Professional Mentoring." *A Leadership Journal: Women in Leadership—Sharing the Vision* 3(2): 57–62.

Paffenbarger, R. S., Jr., R. T. Hyde, A. L. Wing, and C. C. Hsieh. 1986. "Physical Activity, All-Cause Mortality and Longevity of College Alumni." *New England Journal of Medicine* 315: 605–613.

Paffenbarger, R. S., Jr., M. E. Laughlin, A. S. Gima, and R. A. Black. 1970. "Work Activity of Longshoremen as Related to Death From Coronary Heart Disease and Stroke." *New England Journal of Medicine* 282: 1109–1114.

Patai, Daphne, and Noretta Koertge. 1994. *Professing Feminism: Cautionary Tales from the Strange World of Women's Studies.* New York: Basic Books.

Peters, Sarah Whitaker. 1991. *Becoming O'Keeffe.* New York: Abbeville Press.

Pollack, Barbara. 2001. "The New Look of Feminism." *Artnews* 100 (September): 132–36.

Pollock, Griselda. 1988. *Vision and Difference: Femininity, Feminism and the Histories of Art.* London and New York: Routledge.

Pollock, Griselda. 1996. "Theory, Ideology, Politics: Art History and Its Myths." *Art Bulletin* 78 (March): 16–22.

Pollock, Griselda, and Rozsika Parker. 1981. *Old Mistresses: Women, Art and Ideology.* New York: Pantheon Books.

Price, Liz, and Judy Priest. 1996. "Activists as Change Agents: Achievements and Limitations." In *Breaking Boundaries: Women in Higher Education,* ed. Louise Morley and Val Walsh. London: Taylor & Francis.

Pryse, M., Chair, and Members of the Task Force on Faculty Roles and Rewards of the National Women's Studies Association. 1999. "Defining Women's Studies Scholarship." A Statement of the National Women's Studies Association Task Force on Faculty Roles and Rewards. College Park, MD: National Women's Studies Association.

Quina, Kathryn, Maureen Cotter, and Kim Romenesko. 1998. "Breaking the (plexi-) Glass Ceiling in Higher Education." In *Arming Athena: Career Strategies for Women in Academe,* ed. Lynn H. Collins, Joan C. Chrisler, and Kathryn Quina. Thousand Oaks, CA: Sage Publications.

Ransom, M. R. 1990. "Gender Segregation by Field in Higher Education." *Research in Higher Education* 31(5): 477–491.

Regan, Helen B., and Gwen H. Brooks. 1995. *Out of Women's Experience: Creating Relational Leadership.* Thousand Oaks, CA: Corwin Press.

Rosenthal, Cindy Simon. 1998. "One Experience is Worth a Thousand Words: Engaging Undergraduates in Field Research on Gender." *PS: Political Science and Politics* 31 (March): 63–68.

Rosenthal, Cindy Simon, James A. Rosenthal, and Jocelyn Jones. 2001. "Preparing for Elite Political Participation: Simulations and the Political Socialization of Adolescents." *Social Science Quarterly* 82 (September): 633–646.

Ross, Catharine. 1996. "Struggling for Inclusion: Black Women in Professional and Management Education." In *Breaking Boundaries: Women in Higher Education,* ed. Louise Morley and Val Walsh. London: Taylor & Francis.

Rosser, S. A., ed. 1995. *Teaching the Majority: Breaking the Gender Barrier in Science, Mathematics, and Engineering.* New York: Teachers College Press.

Rosser, S. A. 2001. "Balancing: Survey of Fiscal Year 1997, 1998,and 1999 POWRE Awardees." *Journal of Women and Minorities in Science and Engineering* 7(1): 1–11.

Rosser, S. A., and M. Zieseniss. 2000. "Career Issues and Laboratory Climates: Different Challenges and Opportunities for Women Engineers and Scientists: Survey of fiscal year 1997 POWRE Awardees." *Journal of Women and Minorities in Science and Engineering* 6(2): 1–20.

Rowley, Daniel James, and Herbert Sherman. 2001. *From Strategy to Change: Implementing the Plan in Higher Education.* San Francisco, CA: Jossey-Bass.

Rush, R. R. 1993. "A Systematic Commitment to Women in the Academy." *Journalism Education* 71–79.

Sadker, M., and D. Sadker. 1994. *Failing at Fairness: How Schools Cheat Girls.* New York, NY: Touchstone.

Sagaria, Mary Ann D. 1993. "Administrative Mobility and Gender: Patterns and Processes in Higher Education." In *Women in Higher Education: A Feminist Perspective,* ed, Judith S. Glazer, Estela M. Bensimon, and Barbara K. Townsend. Needham Heights, MA: Ginn Press.

Sandler, B. 1997a. "Too Strong for a Woman: The Five Words that Created Title IX." *About Women on Campus* 5(2) (Spring): 5.

Sandler, B. R. 1997b. "The Chilly Climate—A Guide to Improve the Education of Women." In *1997 WISE Best Practices Guidebook: The Classroom.* [On-line]. Available: http://www.cic.uiuc.edu/wise/Best1Guidebook/chilly_climate.htm

Sandler, B. R., and R. J. Shoop. 1997. "What is Sexual Harassment?" In *Sexual Harassment on Campus,* ed. B. R. Sandler and R. J. Shoop. Needham Heights, MA: Allyn and Bacon.

Sattler, Cheryl L. 1997. *Talking About a Revolution—The Politics and Practice of Feminist Teaching.* Cresskill, NJ: Hampton Press.

Sax, L. J., A. W. Astin, M. Arredondo, and W. S. Korn. 1996. *The American College Teacher: National Norms for the 1995–96 HERI Faculty Survey.* Los Angeles, CA: Higher Education Research Institute, UCLA.

Schmitz, B., and A. S. Williams. 1983. "Seeking Women's Equity Through Curricular Reform: Family Perceptions of an Experimental Project." *Journal of Higher Education* 54: 556–565.

Schneider, A. 2000. "Female Scientists Turn Their Backs on Jobs at Research Universities." *The Chronicle of Higher Education* (August 18) A12–A14.

Schor, Mira, ed. 1999. "Contemporary Feminism: Art Practice, Theory, and Activism—An Intergenerational Perspective." *Art Journal* 58 (Winter): 8–28.

Schuster, Marilyn, and Susan Van Dyne. 1985. *Women's Place in the Academy.* Lanham, MD: Rowman and Littlefield.

Schwarz, E. E. 1982. "Testing the Biopsychosocial Model: The Ultimate Challenge Facing Behavioral Medicine?" *Journal of Consulting and Clinical Psychology* 50: 1040–1053.

Scott, Joan. 1999. "The Evidence of Experience." In *Feminist Approaches to Theory and Methodology*, ed. Sharlene Hesse-Biber, Christine Gilmartin, and Robin Lydenberg. New York: Oxford University Press.

SDS April 25 2001, Sydsvenskan, http://sydsvenskan.se/pub/hpsart 5590303.html.

SDS July 7, 2001, "Kön anger lönen för professorer", Sydsvenskan.

Seals, B. 1997. "Faculty-to-Faculty Sexual Harassment". In *Sexual Harassment on Campus*, ed. B. R. Sandler and R. J. Shoop. Needham Heights, MA: Allyn and Bacon.

Seymour, E. 1992a. " 'The Problem Iceberg' in Science, Mathematics and Engineering Education: Student Explanations for High Attrition Rates." *Journal of College Science Teaching* 230–238.

Seymour, E. 1992b. "Undergraduate Problems with Teaching and Advising in SME Majors: Explaining Gender Differences in Attrition Rates." *Journal of College Science Teaching* 284–292.

Shields, Portia. 1997. "Deaning at a Historically Black Institution: Challenges, Opportunities, Promise." In *The Minority Voice in Educational Reform: An Analysis by Minority Women College of Education Deans*, ed. Louis Castenell and Jill M. Tarule. Greenwich, CT: Ablex Publishing.

Shor, Ira. 1992. *Empowering Education: Critical Teachings for Social Change.* Chicago: University of Chicago Press.

Shor, Ira, and Paulo Freire. 1986. *A Pedagogy for Liberation: Dialogues on Transforming Education.* Greenwood Publishing Group, Inc.

Silverberg, Helene. 1994. "Organizing a Course That is Attentive to Issues of Racial and Sexual Difference." *PS: Political Science and Politics* 27 (December): 718–19.

Sjolander, Sverre. 1985. "Long-Term and Short-Term Interdisciplinary Work: Difficulties, Pitfalls, and Built-In Failures." In *Inter-disciplinarity Revisited*, ed. Lennart Levin and Ingeman Lind. Linkoping, Sweden: Linkoping University.

Solomon, B. M. 1985. *In the Company of Educated Women.* New Haven, CN: Yale University Press.

Solomon, Deborah. 2001. "Portrait of the Artists: The Women Behind Photography's New Golden Age." *New York Times Magazine* 9 September, 39–40.

Sonnert, G., and J. Holton. 1995. *Who Succeeds in Science? The Gender Dimension.* New Brunswick, NJ: Rutgers University Press.

Spalter-Roth, Roberta, and Heidi Hartmann. 1999. In *Feminist Approaches to Theory and Methodology*, ed. Sharlene Hesse-Biber, Christine Gilmartin, and Robin Lydenberg. New York: Oxford University Press.

Spivak, Gayatri Chakravorty. 1990. *The Postcolonial Critic: Interviews, Strategies, Dialogue.* New York: Routledge

Stake, J. E., and F. L. Hoffman. 2001. "Changes in Student Social Attitudes, Activism, and Personal Confidence in Higher Education: The Role of Women's Studies." *American Educational Research Journal* 38: 411–436.

Stallings, Jane. 1997. "Recharting the Paths of Women and Minority Leaders: A Journey of Consequence." In *The Minority Vote in Educational Reform: An Analysis by Minority Women College of Education Deans,* ed. Louis Castenell and Jill M. Tarule. Greenwich, CT: Ablex Publishing.

Stanley, Liz. 1997. "Introduction: On Academic Borders, Territories, Tribes, and Knowledges." In *Knowing Feminisms: On Academic Borders, Territories and Tribes,* ed. Liz Stanley. London: Sage Publications.

Stanton, Donna C., and Abigail J. Stewart. 1995. "Remodeling Relations: Women's Studies and the Disciplines." In *Feminisms in Academy,* ed. Donna C. Stanton and Abigail J. Stewart. Ann Arbor, MI: University of Michigan Press.

Statsvetenskaplig Tidskrift. 1997. Special Issue: A World in Transition: Feminist Perspectives on International Relations 100 (1).

Steinberg, Deborah Lynn. 1997. "All Roads Lead to Problems with Discipline." In *A Question of Discipline: Pedagogy, Power and the Teaching of Cultural Studies,* ed. Joyce and Debbie Epstein. Boulder, CO: Westview Press.

Stevens, P. E. 1992. "Lesbian Health Care Research: A Review of the Literature from 1970–1990." *Health Care for Women International* 13(2): 91–120.

Stimpson, Catherine R. 1978. "Women's Studies: an Overview." *University of Michigan Papers in Women's Studies* (May): 14–26.

Svinicki, Marilla D., and Nancy M. Dixon. 1987. "The Kolb Model Modified for Classroom Activities." *College Teaching* 35 (December): 141–46.

Sylvester, Christine. 1994. *Feminist Theory and International Relations in a Postmodern Era.* Cambridge, MA: Cambridge University Press.

Tannen, Deborah. 1998. *The Argument Culture.* New York: Random House.

Task Force on Women in Academe. 2000. "Women in Academe: Two Steps Forward, One Step Back." Washington, DC: American Psychological Association.

Taylor, Andrew J. 1994. "Teaching Politics Panoramically: American Government and the Case Method." *PS: Political Science and Politics* 27 (September): 535–37.

Terenzini, P. T., and E. T. Pascarela. 1980. "Student/faculty Relationships and Freshman Year Educational Outcomes: A Further Investigation." *Journal of College Student Personnel* 521–528.

Thompson, M. 2001. "Informal Student-Faculty Interaction: Its Relationship to Educational Gains in Science and Mathematics Among Community College Students." *Community College Review.* (Summer) [On-line]. Available: http://www.findarticles.com/cf_0/m0HCZ/1_29/77481462/print.jhtml

Titus, J. J. 1993. "Gender Messages in Education Foundations Textbooks." *Journal of Teacher Education* 44: 38–43.

Toutkoushian, R. K. 1999. "The Status of Academic Women in the 1990s: No Longer Outsiders, But Not Yet Equals." *The Quarterly Review of Economics and Finance* 39: 679–698.

Townsend, Barbara K., and Susan B. Twombly. 1998. "A Feminist Critique of Organizational Change in the Community College." In *New Directions for Community Colleges: Organizational Change in the Community Colleges: A Ripple or a Sea Change,* ed. John S. Levin. San Francisco, CA: Jossey-Bass.

Truax, A. T. 1996. "Sexual Harassment in Higher Education: What We've Learned." In *Combating Sexual Harassment in Higher Education,* ed. B. Lott and M. E. Reilly. Washington, DC: National Education Association.

Varnedoe, Kirk. 1999. *Women Artists: The Other Side of the Picture.* Princeton, NJ: Films for the Humanities and Sciences. Videocassette.

Vetter, B. 1996. "Myths and Realities of Women's Progress in the Sciences, Mathematics, and Engineering." In *The Equity Equation: Fostering the Advancement of Women in the Sciences, Mathematics, and Engineering,* ed. C.S. Davis, A.B. Ginorio, C. S. Hollenshead, B.B. Lazarus, P.M. Rayman, and Associates. San Francisco, CA: Jossey-Bass.

Ware, N. C., N. A. Steckler, and J. Leserman. 1985. "Undergraduate Women: Who Chooses a Science Major?" *Journal of Higher Education* 73–84.

Waugh, P., ed. 1992. *Postmodernism—A Reader.* New York: Edward Arnold/Hodder & Stoughton.

Weiler, Kathleen. 1987. *Women Teaching for Change: Gender, Class and Power.* Greenwood Publishing Group, Inc.

Wenniger, M.D. 2001. "Partner Hires: A Fact of Life on Most Campuses." *Women in Higher Education* 10(4): 5.

Widerberg, Karin. 1995. *Kunskapens kön: Minnen, Reflektioner och Teor.* Stockholm: Nordstedts.

Widerberg, Karin. 1998. "Teaching Gender Through Writing Experience Stories." *Women's Studies International Forum* 21(2): 193–198.

Wilding, Faith. 1999. "Untitled Essay." In *Contemporary Feminism: Art Practice, Theory, and Activism—An Intergenerational Perspective,* ed. Mira Shor. *Art Journal* 58, Winter, 27–29.

Williams, Joan. 2000. October. "How the Tenure Track Discriminates Against Women." *The Chronicle of Higher Education.* Career Network website. http://chronicle.com/jobs/2000/10/2000102703c.htm.

Williams, J. 2000. "What Stymies Women's Academic Careers? It's Hiring Couples." *The Chronicle of Higher Education.* December 15, B10.

Wilson, R. 2001. "The Backlash Against Hiring Couples." *The Chronicle of Higher Education.* April 13, A16.

Winterson, Jeanette. 1994. *Written on the Body.* New York: Vintage Books.

Wolfman, Brunette Reid. 1997. "Light as From a Beacon." In *Black Women in the Academic: Promises and Perils,* ed. Lois Benjamin. Gainesville, FL: University Press of Florida.

Women Artists: The Other Side of the Picture. 1999. Princeton, NJ: Films for the Humanities and Sciences. Videocassette.

Women's Studies. 1990. In *Liberal Learning and the Arts and Sciences Major. V.II. Reports from the Fields.*

Wood, Julia T. 1994. *Gendered Lives: Communication, Gender and Culture.* Belmont, CA: Wadsworth Co.

Woolf, Virginia. 1957. *A Room of One's Own.* New York: Harcourt Brace.

Woolf, Virginia. 1981. *Mrs. Dalloway.* New York: Harcourt Brace.

Worell, Judith, and Johnson, Norine G. 1997. *Shaping the Future of Feminist Psychology: Education, Research and Practice.* Washington, DC: American Psychological Association.

Yoder, Janice D. 2001a. "Needed: Effective Women Leaders." *Psychology of Women: Newsletter of the Society for the Psychology of Women* (Division 35, American Psychological Association) 28(1): 1–2.

Yoder, Janice D. 2001b. "Making Leadership Work More Effectively for Women." *Journal of Social Issues* 57(4): 815–828.

Zalk, Sue Rosenberg. 1997. "From Activist to Advocate to Administrator: Changing Roles and Identities." Paper presented at the American Psychological Association, Chicago.

Zimmerman, B. 2000. Building NWSA. *NWSA Journal* 12(1): 165–168.

Index

About the Contributors

JoANN DiGEORGIO-LUTZ is an Assistant Professor of Political Science and University Honors Director at Texas A&M University—Commerce in Commerce, Texas.

PEGGY DOUGLAS has a Ph.D. in Environmental Economics and Rural Sociology. She has previously taught at Chattanooga State Technical Community College.

SHARLENE HESSE-BIBER is a Professor of Sociology in the Department of Sociology at Boston College in Chestnut Hill, Massachusetts.

J. SUSAN ISAACS is an Associate Professor and Art Historian at Towson University in Wilmington, Delaware.

JUSTYNA KOSTKOWSKA is an Assistant Professor in the Department of English at Middle Tennessee State University in Murfreesboro, Tennessee.

ANNICA KRONSELL teaches in the Department of Political Science at Lund University, Sweden.

MARGARET MADDEN is Dean of Academic Affairs at Southampton College of Long Island University in Southampton, New York.

KENNETH L. MILLER is an Assistant Professor in the Department of Counseling at Youngstown State University in Youngstown, Ohio.

SUSAN M. MILLER is a faculty member in Educational/Psychology Studies at Temple University in Philadelphia, Pennsylvania.

BONNIE J. MORRIS is an Assistant Professor in the Women's Studies Program at George Washington University in Washington, D.C.

CINDY SIMON ROSENTHAL is an Assistant Professor of Political Science at the University of Oklahoma and Assistant Director of the Carl Albert Congressional Research and Studies Center.

SUE V. ROSSER is Dean of Ivan Allen College at Georgia Institute of Technology in Atlanta, Georgia.

MARGARET KONZ SNOOKS is a Lecturer in the School of Human Sciences and Humanities at the University of Houston—Clear Lake in Houston, Texas.